THE FATHERS
OF THE CHURCH

A NEW TRANSLATION

VOLUME 13

THE FATHERS OF THE CHURCH

A NEW TRANSLATION

EDITORIAL BOARD

Hermigild Dressler, O.F.M.
Quincy College
Editorial Director

Robert P. Russell, O.S.A.
Villanova University

Thomas P. Halton
The Catholic University of America

Robert Sider
Dickinson College

Sister M. Josephine Brennan, I.H.M.
Marywood College

Richard Talaska
Editorial Assistant

FORMER EDITORIAL DIRECTORS

Ludwig Schopp, Roy J. Deferrari, Bernard M. Peebles

SAINT BASIL

LETTERS

VOLUME 1 (1-185)

Translated by
SISTER AGNES CLARE WAY, C.D.P.
with notes by
ROY J. DEFERRARI

THE CATHOLIC UNIVERSITY OF AMERICA PRESS
Washington, D.C.

NIHIL OBSTAT

JOHN M. A. FEARNS, S.T.D.
Censor Librorum

IMPRIMATUR:

✠ FRANCIS CARDINAL SPELLMAN
Archbishop of New York

November 24, 1951

The Nihil obstat and Imprimatur are official declarations that a book or pamphlet is free of doctrinal or moral error. No implication is contained therein that those who have granted the Nihil obstat and Imprimatur agree with the contents, opinions or statements expressed.

Library of Congress Catalog Card No.: 65-18318

ISBN-13: 978-0-8132-1557-0 (pbk)

Copyright © 1951 by

THE CATHOLIC UNIVERSITY OF AMERICA PRESS, INC.

All rights reserved

Second Printing 1965
Third Printing 1981
First paperback reprint 2008

CONTENTS

*Letters**   *Page*

1 (*165*). To Eustathius, the Philosopher 3
2   (*1*). To Gregory 5
3 (*173*). To Candidianus 12
4 (*169*). To Olympius 13
5 (*188*). A Letter of Condolence to Nectarius 14
6 (*189*). A Letter of Condolence to the Wife of Nectarius 17
7   (*2*). To His Companion, Gregory 20
8 (*141*). An Apology to the Caesareans for His Withdrawal, and a Defense of the Faith . . . 21
9 (*41*). To the Philosopher Maximus 40
10 (*175*). To a Widow 44
11 (*239*). Without Address, through Friendship 44
12 (*171*). To Olympius 45
13 (*172*). To Olympius 45
14 (*19*). To Gregory, His Companion 46
15 (*415*). To Arcadius, Imperial Administrator . . . 48
16 (*168*). Against Eunomius, the Heretic 49
17 (*384*). To Origen 50
18 (*211*). To Macarius and John 51
19   (*3*). To Gregory, a Companion 52

---

* Italicized numbers indicate the older order of the Letters, as distinguished from the Benedictine order which has been followed.

Letters			Page
20	(83).	To Leontius, the Sophist	52
21	(375).	To Leontius, the Sophist	54
22	(411).	Concerning the Perfection of the Monastic Life	55
23	(283).	Admonition to a Monk	61
24	(54).	To Athanasius, Father of Athanasius, Bishop of Ancyra	62
25	(53).	To Athanasius, Bishop of Ancrya	64
26	(362).	To Caesarius, Brother of Gregory	66
27	(6).	To Eusebius, Bishop of Samosata	68
28	(62).	A Letter of Condolence to the Church of Neo-Caesarea	68
29	(67).	A Letter of Condolence to the Church of Ancrya	73
30	(7).	To Eusebius, Bishop of Samosata	74
31	(267).	To Eusebius, Bishop of Samosata	75
32	(84).	To the Master Sophronius	76
33	(358).	To Aburgius	79
34	(5).	To Eusebius, Bishop of Samosata	79
35	(236).	Without an Address, in Behalf of Leontius	81
36	(228).	Without an Address, for Assistance	82
37	(248).	Without an Address, for a Foster Brother	82
38	(43).	To His Brother Gregory, concerning the Difference between Substance and Person	84
39	(206).	Julian to Basil	96
40	(207).	Julian to Basil	98
41	(208-9)	To Julian, in Answer	100
42	(1).	To Chilo, His Pupil	102
43	(2).	Admonition to the Young	111
44	(3).	To a Fallen Monk	112
45	(4).	To a Fallen Monk	115
46	(5).	To a Fallen Virgin	118

Letters	Page
47 (4). To Gregory, His Companion	128
48 (254). To Eusebius, Bishop of Samosata	130
49 (408). To Arcadius, the Bishop	131
50 (409). To Bishop Innocent	132
51 (86). To Bishop Bosporius	133
52 (300). To the Canonesses	135
53 (76). To the Suffragan Bishops	140
54 (181). To the Suffragan Bishops	142
55 (198). To Paregorius, a Presbyter	144
56 (354). To Pergamius	145
57 (56). To Meletius, Bishop of Antioch	147
58 (44). To Gregory, His Brother	148
59 (46). To Gregory, His Uncle	150
60 (45). To Gregory, His Uncle	153
61 (47). To Athanasius, Bishop of Alexandria	154
62 (185). A Letter of Consolation to the Church of Parnassus	155
63 (371). To the Governor of Neo-Caesarea	156
64 (350). To Hesychius	157
65 (363). To Atarbius	158
66 (48). To Athanasius, Bishop of Alexandria	159
67 (50). To Athanasius, Bishop of Alexandria	162
68 (57). To Meletius, Bishop of Antioch	163
69 (52). To Athanasius, Bishop of Alexandria	164
70 (220). Without Address, concerning a Synod	168
71 (33). To Gregory	170
72 (351). To Hesychius	173
73 (388). To Callisthenes	174
74 (379). To Martinianus	176
75 (361). To Aburgius	181

| Letters | Page |

76 (*331*). To the Master Sophronius 182
77 (*226*). Without an Address, concerning Therasius . . 183
78 (*215*). Without an Addresss, in Behalf of Elpidius . 184
79 (*308*). To Eustathius, Bishop of Sebaste 184
80 (*49*). To Athanasius, Bishop of Alexandria . . . 185
81 (*319*). To Bishop Innocent 186
82 (*51*). To Athanasius, Bishop of Alexandria . . . 188
83 (*427*). To an Assessor 189
84 (*389*). To an Official 191
85 (*305*). Concerning the Fact That It Is Unnecessary
          to Take an Oath 193
86 (*179*). To an Official 194
87 (*390*). Without Address, concerning the Same Subject 195
88 (*243*). Without Address, for a Tax-Collector . . . 196
89 (*273*). To Meletius, Bishop of Antioch 197
90 (*61*). To the Most Holy Brothers and Bishops of
          the West 198
91 (*324*). To Valerian, Bishop of the Illyrians . . . 201
92 (*69*). To the Bishops of Italy and Gaul 202
93 (*289*). To the Patrician Caesaria, about Communion 208
94 (*372*). To Elias, Governor of the Province . . . 209
95 (*261*). To Eusebius, Bishop of Samosata 212
96 (*332*). To the Master Sophronius 213
97 (*68*). To the Senate of Tyana 214
98 (*259*). To Eusebius, Bishop of Samosata 216
99 (*187*). To Count Terentius 218
100 (*256*). To Eusebius, Bishop of Samosata 223
101 (*202*). A Letter of Consolation 224
102 (*183*). To the Citizens of Satala 226
103 (*296*). To the People of Satala 227

Letters	Page
104 (*279*). To the Prefect Modestus	228
105 (*301*). To the Deaconesses, the Daughters of Count Terentius	229
106 (*407*). To a Soldier	231
107 (*287*). To the Widow Julitta	231
108 (*288*). To the Guardian of the Heirs of Julitta	232
109 (*422*). To Count Helladius	233
110 (*277*). To the Prefect Modestus	234
111 (*276*). To the Perfect Modestus	235
112 (*464*). To the Leader Andronicus	236
113 (*203*). To the Presbyters at Tarsus	239
114 (*204*). To Cyriacus and His Followers in Tarsus	241
115 (*87*). To the Heretic Simplicia	242
116 (*174*). To Firminus	244
117 (*234*). Without Address, on the Practice of Asceticism	245
118 (*318*). To Jovinus, Bishop of Perrha	247
119 (*307*). To Eustathius, Bishop of Sebaste	247
120 (*58*). To Meletius, Bishop of Antioch	249
121 (*195*). To Theodotus, Bishop of Nicopolis	251
122 (*313*). To Poemenius, Bishop of Satala	252
123 (*343*). To the Monk Urbicius	253
124 (*328*). To Theodorus	254
125 (*78*). A Transcript of Faith Dictated by the Most Holy Basil, Which Eustathius, Bishop of Sebaste, Signed	255
126 (*364*). To Atarbius	261
127 (*253*). To Eusebius, Bishop of Samosata	262
128 (*265*). To Eusebius, Bishop of Samosata	263
129 (*59*). To Meletius, Bishop of Antioch	266
130 (*196*). To Theodotus, Bishop of Nicopolis	269

Letters	Page
31 (*382*). To Olympius	271
32 (*315*). To Abramius, Bishop of Batnae	273
33 (*320*). To Peter, Bishop of Alexandria	274
34 (*341*). To the Presbyter Paeonius	275
35 (*167*). To Diodorus, Presbyter of Antioch	276
36 (*257*). To Eusebius, Bishop of Samosata	278
37 (*366*). To Antipater	280
38 (*8*). To Eusebius, Bishop of Samosata	281
39 (*71*). To the Alexandrians	284
40 (*60*). To the Church at Antioch	286
41 (*262*). To Eusebius, Bishop of Samosata	289
42 (*418*). To the Accountant of the Prefects	291
43 (*419*). To the Second Accountant	292
44 (*420*). To the Prefects' Administrator	293
45 (*255*). To Eusebius, Bishop of Samosata	293
46 (*268*). To Antiochus	294
47 (*356*). To Aburgius	295
48 (*376*). To Trajan	296
49 (*377*). To Trajan	297
50 (*392*). To Amphilochius, in the Name of Heracleidas	298
51 (*81*). To Eustathius, the Physician	302
52 (*374*). To Victor, a Commander	304
53 (*428*). To Victor, the Ex-Consul	304
54 (*337*). To Ascholius, Bishop of Thessalonica	305
55 (*241*). Without Address, in the Case of a Trainer	307
56 (*342*). To Evagrius, a Presbyter	308
57 (*270*). To Antiochus	311
58 (*271*). To Antiochus	311
59 (*387*). To Eupaterius and His Daughter	312
60 (*197*). To Diodorus	314

Letters	Page

161 (*393*). To Amphilochius, on His Consecration as
        Bishop 319
162 (*258*). To Eusebius, Bishop of Samosata 321
163 (*378*). To Count Jovinus 322
164 (*338*). To Ascholius, Bishop of Thessalonica . . . 323
165 (*339*). To Ascholius, Bishop of Thessalonica . . . 326
166 (*251*). To Eusebius, Bishop of Samosata 327
167 (*252*). To Eusebius, Bishop of Samosata 329
168 (*269*). To Antiochus the Presbyter, a Nephew of
        Eusebius, Who Was Living with His Uncle
        in Exile 329
169 (*412*). To Gregory 330
170 (*414*). To Glycerius 332
171 (*413*). To Gregory 333
172 (*335*). To Bishop Sophronius 333
173 (*302*). To the Canoness Theodora 335
174 (*283*). To a Widow 336
175 (*410*). To Count Magnenianus 337
176 (*394*). To Amphilochius, Bishop of Iconium . . . 338
177 (*334*). To the Master Sophronius 339
178 (*360*). To Aburgius 340
179 (*380*). To Arinthaeus 341
180 (*333*). To the Master Sophronius, in Behalf of
        Eumathius 342
181 (*316*). To Otreius of Meletine 342
182 (*266*). To the Presbyters of Samosata 343
183 (*294*). To the Senate of Samosata 343
184 (*306*). To Eustathius, Bishop of Himmeria 344
185 (*310*). To Theodotus, Bishop of Berrhoea 345

INTRODUCTION

THE LETTERS OF St. Basil, three hundred and sixty-eight in number, which comprise the most vivid and most personal portion of his works, give us, perhaps, the clearest insight into the wealth of his rich and varied genius.[1] They were written within the years from 357, shortly before his retreat to the Pontus, until his death in 378, a period of great unrest and of persecution of the orthodox Catholic Church in the East. Their variety is striking, ranging from simple friendly greetings to profound explanations of doctrine, from playful reproaches to severe denunciations of transgressions, from kindly recommendations to earnest petitions for justice, from gentle messages of sympathy to bitter lamentations over the evils inflicted upon or existent in the churches.

As may be expected, the style in these letters is as varied as their subject matter. Those written in his official capacity as pastor of the Church, as well as the letters of recommendation and the canonical letters, are naturally more formal in tone, while the friendly letters, and those of appeal, admonition, and encouragement, and, more especially, those of consolation, show St. Basil's sophistic training, although even in these he uses restraint. He had the technique of ancient rhetoric at his finger tips, but he also had a serious purpose and a sense

---

[1] Cf. Eugene Fialon, *Etude historique et littéraire sur Saint Basile* (Paris 1869) 178.

of fitness of things. To St. Basil's letters can be ascribed the qualities he attributed to the heartily approved book written by Diodorus,[2] which qualities may be summed up as fullness of thought, clearness, simplicity, and naturalness of style. He himself disapproved of a too ornate style and carefully avoided it. His early education, however, had trained him for the use of rich diction and varied and charming figures, and when the occasion warranted it he proved himself a master in their use.[3]

Whether we look at them from an historical, an ecclesiastical, or a theological point of view, the letters are an important contribution. They acquaint us intimately with St. Basil himself, the tireless scholar following his master from country to country;[4] the ascetic, withdrawn from the world, with his mind and heart fixed firmly on God, disregarding wealth, pleasures, and companionship of the world;[5] the kindly advocate and friend of all in need, always ready to plead for justice and mercy, or for assistance and support;[6] the stern spiritual father, tempering his denunciations of vice with loving appeals for repentance;[7] and the inflexible ruler of the Church and champion of orthodoxy, voicing his opposition even to emperors in his ardent defense of true doctrine. In the letters, too, we come to know his nobility of character, enhanced by the humility and sufferings of the man, who attributed to his sins the afflictions he endured in body and soul, for he was a sickly man,[8] continually beseiged by illness-

---

[2] Cf. Letter 135.
[3] Cf. Sister Agnes Clare Way, *The Language and Style of the Letters of St. Basil* (Washington, D.C. 1927) 176-204.
[4] Cf. Letter 1.
[5] Cf. Letter 2.
[6] Cf. Letter 32, *et passim*.
[7] Cf. Letter 44.
[8] Cf. Letters 136 and 138.

es which brought him to the brink of the grave. Besides, he was beset by suspicions of heresy roused up against him, and by misunderstandings and deliberate opposition to his labors for the Church. The Scriptural quotations throughout the letters testify to St. Basil's intimate knowledge of the Bible and the exact application of that knowledge to every situation in life. He depended entirely on the Holy Scriptures for the guidance of his conduct and that of his monks.

He gives us a glimpse of Cappadocia and its people in several letters telling of the famine gripping the region and of the winters during which the country was buried in snow and people were forced to remain hidden in their houses for months at a time. A description of the peculiar customs of the Magusaeans, who had settled in Cappadocia, coming from Babylon years before and never intermingling with the people of the country, is an interesting revelation of the depravity in which a pagan people lived even when surrounded by Christian influence.[9] Enlightening pictures of social customs, such as that depicted in the story of Glycerius, are contained in Letters 169, 170, and 171. Ramsey[10] regards this episode as an example of the practice in the early Church of substituting a Christian festival for a pagan one, with Christian hymns taking the place of pagan songs, and with modest singing and dancing replacing the license of pagan festivals.

St. Basil's letters are used by ecclesiastical historians such as Tillemont, Fleury, and de Broglie,[11] as a sure source for the period from about 357 to 378. In fact, Tillemont has devoted almost half of the ninth volume of his *Ecclesiastical*

---

9 Cf. Letter 258.
10 W. M. Ramsey, *The Church in the Roman Empire* (New York 1893) 448-462.
11 Cf. Fialon, *op. cit.* 180.

History to St. Basil, on almost every page of which he refers to the letters as his source of information. A casual reading of the letters will reveal the reason for this. They reflect the conditions existing in the whole Church of the East at the time: the rise and spread of heresy, the attacks of the heretics, the artifices used by them, the exiling of orthodox prelates, the seizure of orthodox sees by Arian bishops, the suspicions and consequent accusations and abuses among the prelates within the fold of the Church, and the relations between Eastern and Western Church.

The letters make very apparent the difference in this age in the conditions existent in the East and West. St. Basil made frequent appeals to the Western bishops for assistance and support in the struggles of the Eastern Church. He insisted that, because of unity of belief, they should be near to each other despite the long distance separating them, and that, moreover, as the head had need of the feet, so the West had need of the East.[12] His appeals must have been answered, for in Letter 263, to the Westerners, he thanks them for the happiness which the Eastern Church has received from their letter and from the sympathy they had extended.

To the student of theology St. Basil's letters offer some interesting moments. Many of his letters are really treatises explaining difficult passages of Scriptures, as Letter 260, concerning the much debated quotation, 'Whoever shall kill Cain shall discharge seven times the things to be expiated.' St. Basil gives a briefer and then a more elaborate explanation of this passage, pointing out that the guilt of Cain's sin was sevenfold, and consequently that seven expiations would be effected by the death of Cain. In some instances he expounds the doctrine of the Church. Letter 38, in which he

---
12 Cf. Letter 243.

discusses the doctrine of the Blessed Trinity, and Letter 125, which contains a transcript of faith dictated by St. Basil and subscribed by Eustathius, Bishop of Sebaste, are examples of this type. Other letters give us the laws and regulations of the Church. Several of these, called Canonical Letters, 188, 199, and 217, were placed by the Council of Chalcedon among the Canons of the Church.[13]

Other English translations of St. Basil's Letters are those of Dr. Roy J. Deferrari in the Loeb Classical Library, and of B. Jackson in the *Nicene and Post-Nicene Fathers*. The present translation has been based on the Garnier and Maran edition and the modern critical edition by Roy J. Deferrari. The chronology of the letters and their order and arrangement into three classes according to the Benedictine editors have been retained. In the arrangement the first class includes all the letters adjudged by them to have been written before St. Basil's episcopate, in the years from 357 until 370, Letters numbered 1 to 46; the second, those written during his episcopate, from 370 until 378, Letters 47 to 291; and the third, letters of uncertain date, doubtful letters, and those clearly spurious, numbered Letters 292 to 365. Three more, Letter 366, included by Mai and also by Migne in their editions, and Letters 367 and 368, lately discovered by Mercati, have been added in the translation.

---

13 Cf. Fialon, *op. cit.* 180.

SELECT BIBLIOGRAPHY

Texts and Translations:

Garnier and Maran, *Basilii Caesareae Cappadociae Archiepiscopi Opera Omnia* (Paris 1839).

J. P. Migne, *S. P. N. Basilii Opera Omnia* (*Patrologia Graeca* 32, Paris 1886).

B. Jackson, *The Letters of St. Basil the Great* (*Select Library of Nicene and Post-Nicene Fathers* 8, New York 1895).

R. J. Deferrari, *St. Basil. The Letters* (*Loeb Classical Library*, 4 vols., London 1926-1934).

Secondary Works:

J. Bessières, 'La Tradition manuscrite de la correspondance de Saint Basile,' *Journal of Theological Studies* 21 (1919); also separately published (Oxford 1923).

E. Fialon, *Etude historique et littéraire sur Saint Basile* (Paris 1861).

F. Loofs, *Eustathius von Sebaste und die Chronologie der Basiliusbriefe* (Halle 1898).

Pr. Maran, *Vita S. Basilii M.* (*Patrologia Graeca* 29, Paris 1886).

W. M. Ramsey, 'Basil of Caesarea,' *The Expositor* 3 (1896).

J. Schäfer, *Basilius des Grossen Beziehungen zum Abendlande* (Munster 1909).

M. Tillemont, *Mémoires pour servir à l'histoire ecclésiastique des six premiers siècles* 9 (Paris 1693-1712).

LETTERS

1-185

Translated
by

SISTER AGNES CLARE WAY, C.D.P. Ph.D.
Our Lady of the Lake College

with notes by
ROY J. DEFERRARI, Ph.D.
The Catholic University of America

1. To Eustathius, the Philosopher[1]

THOUGH I had for some time been disheartened by the malice of what men call Fortune, which has always put some obstacle in the way of our meeting, you cheered and consoled me mightily by your letter. As it chanced, I was already pondering the question of whether or not there is any truth in the popular saying that a certain Necessity or Fate controls our affairs, both great and small; that we in ourselves are masters of nothing; or, at any rate, that a sort of chance directs the lives of men. You will readily pardon these reflections when you learn the causes which provoked them.

Disdaining all things there, I left Athens, drawn by the renown of your philosophy. The city on the Hellespont[2] I passed by as no Odysseus ever avoided the songs of the Sirens.[3] And admiring Asia, I hurried on toward the mother-city,[4] set in the midst of her splendors. Many varied and unexpected obstacles beset my path from the moment I reached the fatherland, where I sought but did not find you, the object of my search. For, I seemed fated either to be ill and for this reason to miss you or to be prevented from setting out with you for the East. And when at length, after innumerable

---
1 From St. Basil's own letter we may infer that this Eustathius was an itinerant pagan philosopher. As St. Basil left Athens in 356, but on reaching Caesarea missed Eustathius, whom he was eager to hear, the date of this letter is evidently 357.
2 Constantinople.
3 Cf. *Odyssey* 12.158.
4 Probably Caesarea.

troubles, I did reach Syria, I was not able to join my philosopher because he had departed for Egypt. Therefore, I, in turn, had to 'go to Egypt, a long and weary way,'[5] not even there attaining the object of my pursuit. But I was so drawn by love that either I had to continue my journey toward Persia and then accompany you to the uttermost limits of the land of the barbarians—whither you steadfastly proceeded, so persistently was chance keeping us apart—or else I had to take up my abode at Alexandria. This latter course I adopted. For, if I had not grown weary of following you as a lamb follows the green bough held out before it, I think that you would have been driven on even beyond the Indian Nyssa,[6] or, if there is an uttermost region of our world, you would have wandered there.

But, why go to such lengths? To conclude, then, though you are now tarrying in the fatherland, it has not been in my power, because of long illnesses, to meet you. And if these illnesses do not finally become more moderate, we shall not meet your Eloquence[7] this winter. Is not this the work of Fate, as you yourself would say? Is it not the work of Necessity? Have not these happenings almost surpassed even the poets' myths of Tantalus? But, as I said, I have been much encouraged by your letter and no longer entertain the same fanciful notions. And I now say that I ought to feel grateful to God for the benefits He gives, and not be dissatisfied with what He bestows. If, then, He should allow us to join you, we shall consider it at once best and most pleasing; but, if He should defer the meeting, we shall endure the privation without complaint. At all events, He manages our affairs better than should we ourselves were we given the choice.

---

5 *Odyssey* 4.483.
6 In the Punjab. Cf. Sophocles, *Ajax* 700.
7 *Logiótēti*—a Byzantine title of address used by St. Basil for laymen only.

2. Basil to Gregory[1]

I recognized your letter just as men recognize the children of friends from their unmistakable resemblance to their parents. For, you say that the environment is not important in implanting in your soul a desire to live with us until you learn something of our customs and our manner of life. This disposition of mind was characteristically yours and worthy of your soul, which regards all things here below as nothing in comparison with the promised happiness reserved for us hereafter. But, I hestitate to write what I myself do in this solitude, night and day, seeing that, although I have left the distractions of the city, which are to me the occasion of innumerable evils, I have not yet succeeded in forsaking myself. I am like the inexperienced seafarers, distressed and ill because of their lack of skill in sailing. They ascribe their discomfort to the size of the boat and its consequent tossing upon the sea; even upon changing to a dinghy or a light boat, they still complain of their distress, not recognizing that they take the nausea and the bile along with them. Such is our situation. Since we carry around with us our innate passions, we are everywhere subject to the same disturbances. Therefore, we have not profited much from this solitude. This is what we should do and it would have enabled us to follow more closely in the footsteps of Him who showed the way to salvation (for He says, 'If anyone wishes to come after me, let him deny himself, and take up his cross, and follow me').[2]

We should try to keep the mind in tranquillity. For, as the eye which is continually gazing about, at one time darting to

---
[1] St. Basil is attempting to induce St. Gregory of Nazianzus to join him by explaining the practices of the monastic life. The letter was written about 358, shortly after St. Basil's retirement to the Pontus.
[2] Matt. 16.24.

one side and again to the other, frequently casting glances hither and yon, is not able to see clearly what is lying before it, but must fix its gaze firmly on that object, if a clear image of it is to be obtained—so, too, the mind of man is incapable of perceiving the truth clearly, if it is distracted by innumerable worldly cares. Wild desires, unruly impulses, and passionate yearnings greatly disturb him who is not yet united in the bonds of wedlock; and a tumultuous throng of different cares awaits him who already has taken a wife: the longing for children, if he is childless; the solicitude for their training, if he has children; the watchfulness over his wife, the care of his home, the protection of his servants, the losses on contracts, the contentions with his neighbors, the lawsuits, the business risks, the farm work. Each day, as it comes, brings its own shadow for the soul, and the nights, taking over the troubles of the day, beguile the mind with the same phantasies.

There is but one escape from these distractions, a complete separation from the world. Withdrawing from the world, however, does not mean mere bodily absence, but implies a disengagement of spirit from sympathy with the body, a renunciation of city, home, personal possessions, love of friends, property, means of livelihood, business, social relations, and learning acquired by human teachings; also, a readiness to receive in one's heart the impressions produced there by divine instruction. And this disposition follows the unlearning of worldly teachings which previously held possession of the heart. Just as it is not possible to write in wax without first smoothing down the letters already engraved upon it, so it is impossible to impart the divine teachings to the soul without first removing from it the conceptions arising from worldly experiences.

Now, solitude provides us with the greatest help toward this achievement, quieting our passions, and giving leisure to our reason to uproot them completely from the soul. Just as animals, if they are stroked, are more easily subdued, so desires, wraths, fears, and griefs, the venomous evils of the soul, if they have been lulled to sleep by silence and have not been kept aflame by constant provocation, are more easily overcome by reason. Therefore, choose a place such as ours, removed from association with men, so that nothing from the outside will interrupt the constant practices of the ascetic life.

A life of piety nourishes the soul with divine thoughts. What, then, is more blessed than to imitate on earth the choirs of angels; hastening at break of day to pray, to glorify the Creator with hymns and songs, and, when the sun is brightly shining and we turn to our tasks, to accompany them everywhere with prayer, seasoning the daily work with hymns, as food with salt? For, the inspirations of the sacred songs give rise to a joyousness that is without grief. Silence, then, is the beginning of purification in the soul, since the tongue is not busied with the affairs of men, nor the eyes looking around at fair complexions and graceful forms, nor the ears lessening the harmony of the soul by listening to melodies made for fleeting pleasure or to the sayings of wits and jesters, a course of action which tends especially to weaken the spiritual timbre of the soul. When the mind is not engaged by external affairs, nor diffused through the senses over the whole world, it retires within itself. Then, it ascends spontaneously to the consideration of God. Illumined by that splendor, it becomes forgetful of its own nature. Since, then, it does not drag the soul down either to the thought of sustenance or to a solicitude for bodily apparel, but enjoys freedom from earthly cares, it turns all its zeal to the acquisition of eternal goods—pondering how to attain temperance and fortitude, justice and prudence, and all other consequent virtues, all of which prompt the earnest man to fulfill properly each separate duty.

Meditation on the divinely inspired Scriptures is also a most important means for the discovery of duty. The Scriptures not only propose to us counsels for the conduct of life, but also open before us the lives of the blessed handed down in writing as living images for our imitation of life spent in quest of God.

Accordingly, by a continual practice of that virtue in which he perceives himself deficient, each one finds, just as he would in some public apothecary shop, a suitable remedy for his infirmity. One who aspires to a perfect chastity reads constantly the story of Joseph and from him learns the beauty of chaste habits, finding Joseph not only self-controlled in regard to sensual pleasures, but also a habitual lover of all virtue. Fortitude he learns from Job, who, in spite of having suffered great reverses in life, being changed in an instant from a rich man into a poor one, and from the father of beautiful children into a childless man, remained the same, always preserving untarnished his nobility of soul. And not even when his friends, coming to console and taking advantage of his unfortunate condition, aggravated his sufferings was he provoked to anger. In turn, if one considers how he may be meek and at the same time high-spirited, so as to use wrath against sin but gentleness toward men, he will find David noble in the brave deeds of war but gentle and dispassionate in the punishment of enemies. Such, also, was Moses, who rose up in great wrath against those offending God, but endured with a meek spirit the slanders against himself. And in general, just as artists, when they are using models, strive by looking at the original to transfer its distinctive features to their own canvas, so he who is striving to reach perfection in all the virtues in turn, by looking steadfastly at the lives of the saints, as if at living models, must endeavor to make their good qualities his own through imitation.

Prayers, too, following reading, take hold upon a fresher and more vigorous soul already stirred to a longing for God. And prayer which imprints in the soul a clear conception of God is an excellent thing. This abiding of God in our memory is the indwelling of God. Thus we become in a special manner the temples of God when earthly thoughts cease to interrupt our continual remembrance of Him, and unforeseen passions to agitate the mind, and when the lover of God, fleeing all these, withdraws with Him and, driving out the passions which tempt him to incontinence, spends himself in the practices which lead to virtue.

And, indeed, as a point of primary importance, one should be careful not to be boorish in conversation, but to question simply and to answer without self-display, not interrupting the speaker when he makes an apt statement nor wishing to interpose his own words ostentatiously, but speaking and listening moderately. One should receive instruction modestly and teach graciously. If he has learned anything from another, he should not conceal the fact after the manner of degraded wives who palm off as belonging to their husbands their baseborn children, but he should candidly declare the father of his idea.

A moderate tone of voice is to be preferred, not so soft as not to be heard nor of such volume as to sound vulgar. One should speak in public only after having considered what one is to say. He should be courteous in his social contacts, refreshing in his conversations, not seeking satisfaction in a display of wit, but maintaining the refinement of gracious speech. He must at all times avoid harshness, even when there is need of censure. For, if you yourself have evinced true humility, your ministrations will be pleasing to him who requires them. We frequently find useful the method of rebuke employed by the Prophet[3] who, when David sinned, did not of himself impose a definite sentence, but, setting forth the sin as being that of another, constituted David the judge of his own crime, so that, having already pronounced judgment against himself, David no longer blamed the accuser.

The humble and abject spirit often manifests itself by a gloomy countenance and a downcast eye, a careless appearance, unkempt hair, and soiled clothes,[4] so that we by mere chance portray in ourselves these characteristics that mourners adopt designedly. The tunic should be drawn close to the body by a belt which is not to be placed above the flanks in an effeminate manner nor left loose, so that the tunic slips around slovenly under it. The gait must not be overleisurely, lest it indicate a laxity of the soul, nor, on the other hand, should it be hasty and swaggering, intimating instability of character. Clothing should be used for one purpose only—to cover the body fittingly for winter and summer. Brilliancy of color should not be sought, nor delicacy and softness in material. In fact, the looking to splendor of color in clothing for self-adornment resembles the practice common among women who tint their cheeks and hair with dyes from other lands. Then, too, the tunic ought to be so thick that no additional garment is needed to keep the wearer warm. Sandals should be inexpensive but sufficiently fulfill their purpose.

As, in general, one should consider utility in a garment,

---

3 Cf. 2 Sam. 11-12. The prophet Nathan, by presenting for judgment a feigned crime of adultery and murder, induced David, who had committed adultery with Bethsabee and then had Urias, her husband, slain, to pronounce sentence against himself.

4 The mark of the old pagan philosophers. Cf. Aristophanes, *Birds* 1282; they were dirty, they were like Socrates.'

so nourishment in the matter of food. Bread will satisfy the actual need; water will relieve the thirst of a healthy person; and the products of the land can preserve the strength of the body for necessary duties. One should not eat with an exhibition of avid gluttony, but should maintain everywhere calmness, mildness, and restraint in satisfying the palate. Not even at meal time should the mind neglect the consideration of God, but should make the very nature of the food and the condition of the body receiving them an occasion of divine praise, marvelling how He who governs all things contrived the varied forms of food adapted to the particular need of the human body. Prayers which are due for the gifts of God, both those He is now giving and those stored up for the future, should be said before meals, as also after, including a thanksgiving for the gifts received and a petition for those promised. One regular hour is to be assigned for meals, so that of the twenty-four hours of the day and night just this one is devoted to the body, the remaining hours to be wholly occupied by the ascetic in the activities of the mind.

Sleep should be light and easily broken, a natural consequence of the meagreness of the diet, and it should be deliberately interrupted for meditations on lofty subjects. For, to be overcome by a deep torpor, with the limbs relaxed, and opportunity provided for absurd imaginations, places those who so sleep daily in danger of death. What dawn is to others, this, midnight, is to the men who practice piety, especially since the quiet at dead of night gives leisure to the soul and neither eyes nor ears convey hurtful sounds or sights to the heart, but the mind alone with itself communes with God, amends itself by the recollection of its sins, makes its rules for the avoidance of evil, and seeks the co-operation of God for the accomplishment of its earnest endeavors.

3. To Candidianus[1]

When your letter came into my hands, it aroused a feeling worthy of your hearing. I was in awe of it, thinking it was bringing some official announcement; while I was breaking the seal, I dreaded to look at it as any Spartan prisoner ever dreaded to see the Laconian Dispatch.[2] But, upon opening and examining it in every detail, I was moved to laughter, partly indeed from the pleasure of hearing no bad news, and partly because of the comparison I made of your actions with those of Demosthenes. He, when he defrayed the cost of bringing out a chorus with some few dancers and flute players, demanded that no longer should he be called Demosthenes, but chorus leader.[3] You, on the contrary, are the same whether acting as leader or not, though truly you are defraying the expenses of myriads more of soldiers than is the number of individuals whose expenditures he provided. Moreover, you do not write to us with a show of rank, but in your usual style; and you give up not at all your love for eloquence. But, as Plato[4] says, 'in the storm and stress' of affairs you, 'withdrawing,' as it were, 'under some strong wall,' remain untroubled amid the tumult; nay more, you do not, according to your power, even allow others to be disturbed. And indeed, such conduct on your part seems great and admirable even to casual observers, though it is not astonishing to one who judges it in comparison with the whole policy of your life. But, hear in turn our troubles, which, although they are

---

1 Candidianus, governor of Cappadocia, was a close friend of St. Basil. This letter, a plea for protection, may also be dated 358.
2 For messages of state the Spartans used a staff or baton around which was rolled spirally a strip of leather with a message written lengthwise. When the strip was unrolled, the message was unintelligible. The recipient was supposed to have a staff of similar thickness on which he rolled the strip so as to read the message.

incredible, nevertheless have occurred according to our deserts.

A certain country fellow living among us here at Annesi, on the death of a servant of my household, without saying that he had any bond against him or bringing any charge against him, or presenting his case to me, without asking for payment, though I would willingly have given it, and without threatening violence if I should not pay, suddenly attacked our house with other desperate men like himself. He beat up our women servants who were guarding it, broke open the doors, carried off everything, taking some of the things himself, and setting out the rest as plunder for any who wanted it.

Therefore, in order that I may not be considered an example of the extremity of weakness and seem to everyone a fit subject for attack, let me beg of you to employ now that interest which you have always shown in my affairs. Only by placing myself under your protection could I remain free from public disturbances. If the culprit should be arrested by the magistrate of the district and shut up in prison for a short time, I would consider this a sufficient punishment. For, not only do I feel vexed because of what I have suffered, but I also need assurance of safety for the future.

4. To Olympius[1]

What are you doing, O wondrous man,[2] driving my loved Poverty, the guardian of philosophy, out of my solitude? You would likely have to flee prosecution for ejecting her, if she

---

3 Plutarch, *Mor.* 817C (*Prae. Ger. Reipub.*).
4 *Rep.* 6.10.

---

1 Olympius was a wealthy citizen of Neo-Caesarea and a friend of St. Basil. This letter was written in 358.
2 *Thaumásie*—a title of distinction which St. Basil used for both clergy and laymen.

should perchance receive the gift of speech. She would probably say: 'I chose to dwell with this man, because now he praises Zeno, who, having lost everything in a shipwreck, uttered no complaining words, but said, "Well done, O Fortune, you are helping to reduce me to one threadbare cloak."' Again, he praises Cleanthes,³ who hired himself out to draw water from a well to earn money for his living and for his teachers' fees. And never did he cease admiring Diogenes, who, aspiring to be content with the gifts of nature alone, threw away even his drinking cup as soon as he had learned from a boy how to bend over and drink from his hollowed hands. In these and similar words would you be censured by my companion Poverty, driven out with your magnificent gifts. And she might also add some such threat as this: 'If I catch you here again, I will show you that your previous experiences were of Sicilian or Italian fastidiousness, so severely will I punish you with all the resources at my command.'

But, enough of this jesting. I am delighted to hear that you have already begun your course of treatment, which I pray may help you. Bodily activity free from pain would be worthy of your holy soul.

5. *A Letter of Condolence to Nectarius*¹

On the third or fourth day after I had received the dazing report of your crushing misfortune, while I was still be-

---

3 Cleanthes was also called Phreantlus, 'one who draws from a well.' Cf. Val. Max. III. 7: Sen., *Ep.* 44.

1 This Nectarius, according to Tillemont, was the future bishop of Constantinople (381-397), the successor of St. Gregory of Nazianzus and predecessor of St. John Chrysostom. He appears as St. Nectarius in the Orthodox Menaion for October 11. This letter was written in 358, in the early part of St. Basil's retirement.

wildered because of the meagerness of detail given by the messenger who brought the distressing news, and, moreover, while I was still skeptical of the current report because of my earnest wish that it might not be true, a letter came from the bishop giving in full the pitiable tidings. I need not say how grieved I was nor how many tears I shed. For, who is so stony-hearted or so entirely devoid of human sympathy as to hear unfeelingly of such a sorrowful event or to give his soul to only moderate grief?

The heir of an illustrious house, the pillar of his family, the hope of his father, the offspring of pious parents, reared in an atmosphere of prayer, in the very flower of his youth has been snatched from the hands of his parents and is gone from our midst. What human heart, even though it were adamant, would these sorrows not melt into deepest compassion? It is not surprising, therefore, that the misfortune most profoundly touched us, also, since from the beginning we have been whole-heartedly attached to you and have made your joys and griefs our own. And, although it seemed, until the present time, that your sorrows were few and that, for the most part, your affairs flowed smoothly with the stream, yet, suddenly, by the malice of the Devil,[2] all that domestic felicity and spiritual joy vanished, and, in consequence, life has become a dreary tale. A lifetime will not suffice us fittingly to weep and deplore this misfortune. Although all the world should mourn with us, not even then can the expression of grief equal our suffering. Nay, more, should all the waters of the rivers become tears,[3] they would not suffice to fill up the measure of our grief over this sad occurrence.

If, however, we are now willing to bring forward the gift which God has placed in our hearts—I mean sound reason-

---
2 Cf. Luke 13.16; 2 Cor. 12.7.
3 Cf. Lam. 2.18.

ing—and if we permit it to repeat continually to us its advice, we shall quickly find some measurable relief from suffering. For, indeed, sound reasoning is able in prosperity to keep our soul within moderate bounds, and in the darker circumstances of life to remind us of the lot of mortal man. It suggests to us what we have already seen and heard, that life is full of such sufferings and examples of human miseries, and, besides, that God has commanded the followers of Christ not to grieve for the dead, because of the hope of resurrection and because the Judge has reserved great crowns of glory for patient endurance. Therefore, I exhort you, as a noble combatant, to withstand the blow, great though it is, and not to fall under the weight of your grief, nor to permit your soul to be overwhelmed, being persuaded that, even if the reasons for God's manner of dispensing His graces elude us, what is dispensed to us by a wise and loving God, although it may be painful, nevertheless is assuredly acceptable. God Himself knows how He apportions advantages to each and why He sets unequal terms of life for all. Doubtless, there is some cause incomprehensible to men for which some are taken sooner out of this world, while others are left to endure for a longer time this life of suffering.

Consequently, we ought in all things to reverence His loving kindness and not to be inordinately grieved, calling to mind that great and famous saying of Job, the mighty champion of God. He, when he saw his ten children crushed in one brief instant while they were sitting together at table, said: 'The Lord gave, and the Lord hath taken away; as is hath pleased the Lord, so is it done.'[4] Let us make these admirable words our own. There is an equal recompense from the just Judge for those showing equally noble deeds. We have not been deprived of a child, but we have given

---
4 Job 1.21.

him back to the One who lent him; his life has not been destroyed, but has been changed for the better. The earth has not concealed our loved one, but heaven has received him. Let us wait a little and we shall be with him whose loss we now mourn. The time of separation is not long, since we in this life, as travellers on a road, are all hastening to the same place of rest, where one is already abiding, another has just arrived, and still another is hastening; yet, the one goal will welcome us all.[5]

Now, even if your son has finished his course more quickly, we still shall all go the same way. Only, may God grant that through virtue we become like him in purity, so that by guilelessness of character we may obtain the same repose as those who are children in Christ.

6. *A Letter of Condolence to the Wife of Nectarius*[1]

I had thought to maintain silence toward your Modesty,[2] considering that, just as the most delicate of remedies causes pain to an inflamed eye, so also condolence offered in a moment of excessive pain, even though it brings much consolation, seems in some way to be distressing to a soul afflicted with deep anguish. But, when it occurred to me that my words would be addressed to a Christian who had long since been taught to recognize the ways of Divine Providence and who was prepared for the vicissitudes of life, I concluded it was not right for me to omit my duty. I know how deep are

---

[5] Cf. ps.-Plutarch, *Mor.* 113C (*Consol. ad Apollon.*), where the same figure of life as a journey is used.

[1] Accompanies Letter 5.
[2] *Kosmiótēta*—a title of address used frequently by St. Basil for both clergy and laymen.

the affections of mothers,³ and, when I ponder the kindliness and gentleness which you in particular show toward all, I realize how great must be your grief in the present circumstances. You have lost a son whom, while he lived, all mothers blessed and prayed that their own sons might resemble, and, when he died, all bewailed as if each one had buried her own. His death was a blow to two countries, our own and that of the Cilicians.⁴ With him a great and illustrious family has reached its end—shattered, as it were, when its support was snatched away. O plague of an evil spirit, how much harm has he been able to inflict! O earth, forced to endure such a calamity! Well might the sun, had it possessed a sense of feeling, have shuddered at that sad spectacle.

However, God's providence orders all circumstances of our life, for we have learned from the Gospel that not even a sparrow falls without the will of the Father.⁵ Consequently, whatever has come to pass has happened by the will of Him who created us. And who has withstood the will of God? Let us accept what has befallen us; for we do not improve our lot by bearing it unwillingly, but, rather, destroy ourselves. Let us not question the just decisions of God. We are too ignorant to examine His hidden judgments. The Lord is making a trial of your love for Him. Yours is the opportunity of receiving through patient endurance the portion allotted to martyrs. The mother of the Maccabees⁶ beheld the death of seven sons, and she neither lamented nor shed an ignoble tear, but she thanked God that she saw them released from

---
3 St. Basil's own mother Emmelia, who numbered three saints among her ten children, was a model of Christian womanhood.
4 The native lands of St. Basil and Nectarius. This helps to identify Nectarius as future bishop of Constantinople, since that bishop was from Tarsus in Cilicia.
5 Cf. Matt. 10.29.
6 Cf. Macc. 7.

the bonds of the flesh, although it was by fire and sword and most cruel tortures. Accordingly, she was adjudged glorious in the sight of God and worthy of renown among men. Great is the suffering, I do admit, but great also are the rewards reserved by the Lord for those who endure.

When you became a mother, and seeing your son gave thanks to God, you realized fully that you, a mortal mother, had given birth to a mortal child. What wonder, then, if this mortal son, subject to death, has died? But the untimeliness of his death grieves us. Yet, that this is not a timely death is not certain, since we ourselves do not know how to choose most advantageously for our souls nor how to determine the limits appointed for the life of men. Consider the whole universe in which you live, where all things visible are mortal, and all are subject to annihilation. Look up toward the heavens which also will some day be destroyed. At the sun—not even it will remain. The stars, each and every one; living creatures on land and in the sea; the beauties of earth; the earth itself—all are perishable, all in a short time will have ceased to exist. Let this thought be a consolation in your misfortune. Do not measure your suffering in itself alone, for in this way it will appear unbearable to you, but compare it with all human happenings, and therein you will find consolation. Above all, I have this to say most forcibly: 'Have consideration for your husband; be a comfort one to the other; do not make the affliction harder for him to bear by wearing yourself out with grief.' On the whole, I do not think that words alone suffice for consolation, but I believe that there is need of prayer under the present circumstances. Therefore, I pray the Lord Himself, by touching your heart with His ineffable power, to enlighten your soul through the good use of reason, so that you may have from within yourself the sources of consolation.

7. To His Companion, Gregory[1]

Even when I was writing to your Eloquence, I knew well that every theological expression is less than the thought in the mind of the speaker and less than the interpretation desired by him who seeks, because speech is in some way too weak to serve perfectly our thoughts.[2] If, therefore, our thought is deficient, and the tongue more so than the thought, what ought we to have expected in regard to our utterances except criticism for poverty of words? For this reason it really was not possible to pass over your question in silence. For, there is danger of disloyalty to Him in not really answering those who love the Lord when they ask questions concerning God. My former explanation, then, whether it seems to be adequate or to be in need of more accurate elaboration, requires an appropriate occasion for revision.

For the present, however, we urge you, as we already have done, to employ yourself whole-heartedly in the support of truth and in the intensifying of desires engendered in your mind by God for the strengthening of the good, being satisfied with this and seeking nothing more from us. For, since we are much inferior to what anyone suspects, we obscure the meaning on account of our weakness rather than add any strength to the truth through our support.

---
1 Written in 358, in the early days of St. Basil's retirement.
2 For an elaboration of this statement, cf. the homily, *On the Holy Birth of Christ*.

8. An Apology to the Caesareans for His Withdrawal, and a Defense of the Faith[1]

I have frequently wondered at your affection toward us, and your marks of deference to our insignificance, petty and weak as we are, and possessed, probably, of so few lovable qualities. For, you encourage us with your words, mentioning our friendship and our fatherland as though trying, by an appeal to my patriotism, to induce a fugitive to return to you once more. I indeed admit that I have become a fugitive, nor would I deny it; but now, since you desire, you may learn the cause.

First of all, then, bewildered at the time by the unforeseen event,[2] as men are who are suddenly terrified by unexpected confusions, I could not control my reason, but I fled the

---

[1] The authenticity of this letter has been questioned at various times. J. Schäfer, *Basilius des Grossen Bezukungen zum Abendlande* (Munster, i. W. 1909) 4, considers it unauthentic; M. Bessières, 'La Tradition de la Correspondence de St. Basile,' *Journal of Theological Studies* 23 (1922) 344, since he finds it among the letters in only one manuscript (Parisinus 1020 S), does not consider it as belonging to the tradition of the letters. Moreover, Robert Melcher in an article entitled 'Der 8 Brief des hl. Basilius, ein Werk des Evagrius Pontikus' (*Münsterische Beitrage zur Theologie*, Heft 1, 1923) shows very convincingly that the letter does not belong to St. Basil but, most probably, to Evagrius, and that its date is toward the end of the fourth century. This and several letters of St. Basil, in great measure, determined the orthodox Greek terminology of the doctrine of the Blessed Trinity. The most important terms as defined by St. Basil are:
  anómoios, dissimilis: unlike.
  ousia, substantia (although the Latin rendering is etymologically the same as *hypóstasis*): substance.
  homooúsios, consubstantialis: consubstantial.
  homoioúsios, similis quoad substantiam: of similar substance.
  hómois, similis: like.
  hypóstasis, persona: person.

[2] An unforeseen event which dismayed St. Basil was the action of Dianius of Caesarea in subscribing to the Creed of Ariminum. St. Basil immediately broke off all relations with him and hastened to St. Gregory of Nazianzus for support.

situation afar off, and have spent a considerable time away from you. Moreover, a longing came upon me for the divine teaching and its inherent philosophy. How would I be able, I said, to overcome the evil dwelling within me? Who could be to me a Laban, freeing me from Esau and guiding me to the heavenly philosophy? But, since with God's grace we have attained our object in proportion to our power, and have found a chosen instrument[3] and a deep reservoir—I mean, of course, Gregory, the mouthpiece of Christ—grant us a little time; just a little, I entreat. We ask this, not because we desire a sojourn in the cities,[4] for we are aware that the Evil Spirit deceives men by such means, but because we judge that association with holy men is in the highest degree helpful. For, by discussing the divine teachings and by hearing them more frequently expounded, we form a habit of contemplation which is not easily lost. This is truly our present position.

But you, holy and dearest of all friends to me, be on your guard against the shepherds of the Philistines, lest someone subtly obstruct your wells and defile the clear knowledge of your faith. Their object is always this: not through divine Scriptures to instruct the more guileless souls, but through false wisdom to obscure the truth. For, he who is introducing into our faith 'unbegotten' and 'begotten,' and declaring that He who has always existed at one time did not exist,[5] and that He, who by nature and from all eternity was Father, was made a father, and that the Holy Spirit is not eternal, is he not clearly a Philistine? Is he not one who bewitches the sheep of our patriarch, that they may not drink from the pure water which springs up unto life everlasting,[6] but may

---
3 Cf. Acts 9.15.
4 The city in which St. Basil stayed was probably Nazianzus, the home of his friend Gregory, or more exactly the suburb Carbala or Caprales (modern Gelvere), where Gregory's estate was situated.
5 The Arian formula is: 'There was a time when he was not.'
6 Cf. John 4.14.

draw down upon themselves the saying of the Prophet:[7] 'They have forsaken me, the fountain of living water, and have digged to themselves cisterns, broken cisterns, that can hold no water'? For, they should confess that the Father is God, the Son is God, and the Holy Spirit is God, as the divine Word teaches, and as they who have pondered it more deeply have taught.

To those who insolently charge us with the doctrine of three gods, let this be said: that we confess one God, not in number, but in nature. Now, everything which is said to be one in number is not one in reality and simple in nature. But, God is universally confessed to be simple and uncompounded. Therefore, God is not one in number. What I mean is this. We say that the universe is one in number, but not one in nature, nor is it something simple. For we divide it into the elements out of which it was formed, into fire, water, air, and earth.[8] Again, man is called one in number. For we frequently say man. But he is not something simple, since he is formed of body and soul. We likewise say the angel is one in number, but not one in nature or simple, for we consider the person of the angel as composed of substance with sanctity. Therefore, if everything which is one in number is not one in nature, and what is one in nature and simple is not one in number, and we say that God is one in nature, how do they bring into our idea, number, which we banish entirely from that blessed and spiritual nature? For, number pertains to quantity, and quantity is added as an attribute of corporeal nature. Doubtless, then, number is an attribute of corporeal nature. Further, we have believed that our Lord is the Creator of bodies. Therefore, also, all number indicates those things which are assigned to have a material and cir-

---

7 Jer. 2.13 (almost verbatim from the Septuagint).
8 Cf. Aristotle, *Met.* 1.3 for the elements of the Greek philosophers.

cumscribed nature, but 'aloneness' and 'oneness' are indicative of the simple and uncircumscribed substance. Accordingly, he who confesses the Son of God or the Holy Spirit as number or creature unconsciously introduces a material and circumscribed nature. And by a circumscribed nature I mean one not only encompassed by space, but also included in the foreknowledge of Him who is to lead it from non-existence into existence, and consequently one capable of comprehension by the understanding. Now, everything holy which has its nature circumscribed and its holiness acquired is not unsusceptible to evil. But the Son and the Holy Spirit are the fountains of holiness from which every rational creature in proportion to its virtue is made holy.

Yet we, according to the true doctrine, do not say that the Son is either like[9] or unlike[10] the Father. Each of these expressions is equally impossible, since 'likeness' and 'unlikeness' are used in speaking of qualities, and the Divinity is not restricted by quality.[11] However, admitting the identity of nature, we also accept the identity of substance, and we reject compositeness, since He who in substance is God and Father has begotten Him who in substance is God and Son. From this fact identity in substance is proved. For, He who in substance is God is consubstantial with Him who is God in substance.

But, when man also is called god, as in the words: 'I have said, you are gods,'[12] and when the Evil Spirit is called

---

9 So declared at Seleucia and Ariminum.
10 Cf. St. Basil, *On the Holy Spirit*, where he deals at length with the heretic Aetius' sophism that things naturally unlike are expressed in unlike terms, and, conversely, that things expressed in unlike terms are naturally unlike.
11 By reason of the simplicity of His nature, God's attributes and His nature are one and the same. The attributes of God are not really, but only virtually, distinct from one another and from His nature.
12 Ps. 81.6.

god, as in the saying: 'The gods of the gentiles are devils,'[13] well, the first are so called because of grace, but the latter are so called falsely. And God alone is God in substance. Moreover, whenever I say 'alone' I affirm that the substance of God is holy and uncreated. The word 'alone' is also used in reference to a particular man as well as to human nature in general. It is used for a particular man, as, let us say, for Paul, where it is written that 'he alone was caught up into the third heaven, and heard secret words, that man may not repeat';[14] and for human nature in general,[15] as when David says: 'Man's days are as grass.'[16] For in this case he does not mean some particular man, but human nature in general. Now, every man is short-lived and mortal. And so we consider that the following statements were made concerning the divine nature: 'Who alone has immortality,'[17] and 'To the only wise God,'[18] and, 'No one is good but God only,'[19]—for the word 'one' [*heis*] there signifies the same thing as 'only' [*mónos*]—and 'who alone spreadeth out the heavens,'[20] and again, 'Thou shalt adore the Lord thy God, and shalt serve him only,'[21] and 'There is no other God besides me.'[22] Now, 'one' and 'alone' are used in the Scripture when referring to God, not in distinction from the Son or the Holy Spirit, but in contrast to those who, although they

---

13 Ps. 95.5.
14 Cf. 2 Cor. 12.4: 'That he was caught up into paradise and heard secret words that man may not repeat.' The first part of St. Basil's quotation differs markedly from our version of the New Testament. He adds 'alone' and substitutes 'into the third heaven' for 'into paradise.'
15 I.e., by metonymy.
16 Ps. 102.15.
17 Tim. 6.16.
18 Rom. 16.27.
19 Luke 18.19.
20 Job 9.8.
21 Cf. Deut. 6.13. St. Basil has substituted *proskunéseis* (adore) for *phobēthésēi* (fear), as found in the Septuagint version.
22 Deut. 32.39.

are not gods, are falsely so called. The following are examples: 'The Lord alone was their leader, and there was no strange god with them,'[23] and 'The children of Israel put away Baalim and Astaroth, and served the Lord only,'[24] and again, the words of Paul:[25] 'For indeed there are many gods, and many lords, yet for us there is only one God, the Father from whom are all things, and one Lord, Jesus Christ, through whom are all things.'[26]

But, we ask here how it was that, when he had said, 'one God,' he was not satisfied with the words—for we have said that 'alone' and 'one' used in regard to God refer to the nature—but that he added also 'Father' and made mention of Christ. Well, I suspect that Paul, the chosen instrument, did not think that it was sufficiently explicit in this place to proclaim only the Son God and the Holy Spirit God, which indeed was made clear by the expression 'one God,' unless he should also, by adding 'the Father,' signify Him from whom are all things; and by mentioning 'the Lord,' indicate the 'Word' through whom are all things; and again, by bringing in 'Jesus Christ,' recall the Incarnation, renew in thought the Passion, and present anew the Resurrection. For, the words 'Jesus Christ' place such thoughts as these before our minds. Therefore, before His Passion, the Lord sought not to be made known as Jesus Christ, and 'He strictly charged his disciples to tell no one that he was Jesus the Christ';[27] for it was His intention, after the fulfillment of His mission, and after His resurrection from the dead and ascension

---

23 Deut. 32.12 (Septuagint).
24 1 Kings 7.4 (almost verbatim from the Septuagint).
25 Cf. 1 Cor. 8.5-6. St. Basil quotes accurately, with apparently purposeful omission of irrelevant material.
26 In this passage St. Basil has been defending his contention that 'one' cannot be predicated of God.
27 Matt. 16.20.

into heaven, to permit them to announce that He was Jesus the Christ. Similar in meaning are these passages, also: 'That they may know thee, the only true God, and him whom thou hast sent, Jesus Christ';[28] and 'You believe in God, believe also in me.'[29] Consequently, the Holy Spirit is everywhere safeguarding our judgment, lest in attaining one truth we fall away from another, and being intent on theology we disregard the divine dispensation,[30] and in thus falling short we engender impiety within our souls.

But, as our opponents seize upon the words of the Sacred Scripture, twist them to fit their own views, and then cite them for us in order to take away the glory of the Only-begotten, let us likewise scrutinize them and lay open their meaning as far as we are able. Let us first propose these words: 'I live because of the Father,'[31] since this is one of the darts launched against heaven by those using it sacrilegiously. In this place the expression, as I believe, does not refer to His life before time[32]—for nothing which has life because of something else can be self-existent; just as nothing that is heated by something else can be heat itself; and our Christ and God has said: 'I am the life.'[33] But the life which He lived because of the Father is this life which He has had in the flesh and here in time. Now, of His own will He began to live the life of man; and He did not say: 'I lived because of the Father,' but: 'I live because of the Father,' clearly indicating the present time. And it is possible to say the 'life'

---

28 John 17.3.
29 John 14.1.
30 The distinction here made is between *theologia,* (theology) or what pertains to the divinity and eternity of Christ, and *oikonomia* (divine dispensation) or whatever belongs to the Incarnation and all that resulted therefrom.
31 John 6.58.
32 I.e., before the creation of the world.
33 Cf. John 11.25.

which Christ lives, He having in Himself the Word of God. That this is the meaning we shall see from the following. 'And he who eats me,'[34] He says, 'he also shall live because of me.' Now, we eat His flesh and we drink His blood, being made sharers, through the Incarnation and through His corporeal life, of the Word and His wisdom. For, He spoke of His whole mystical sojourn as His flesh and His blood, and He revealed His doctrine composed of the principles relating to the real,[35] the natural, and the theological, through which doctrines the soul is nourished and is, in the meantime, prepared for the contemplation of realities. And this is probably the meaning of the expression.

And again, consider the words: 'My Father is greater than I.'[36] Those most ungrateful creatures, the offspring of the Evil One, make use of this saying, also. Yet, I am convinced that by this expression the Son of God is proved to be consubstantial with the Father, since I know that comparisons hold good only in the case of things of the same nature. For, we say that an angel is greater than another angel, and a man is more just than another man, and a bird is swifter than another bird. If, therefore, comparisons are made of objects of the same species, and the Father, by comparison, is said to be greater than the Son, the Son is consubstantial with the Father. But, there is also another thought contained in this saying. Nay, what wonder is it, if He confessed that the Father was greater than He Himself, since, being the Word and having been made flesh,[37] He seemed less than the angels in glory and less than man in appearance. For, 'Thou hast made him,' it is said, 'a little

---

34 Cf. John 6.58.
35 *Praktikós* probably means 'real' as opposed to 'speculative' or 'logical.' St. Basil uses *pragma* frequently to denote 'reality.'
36 Cf. John 14.28.
37 Cf. John 1.14.

less than the angels';[38] and again, 'him who was made a little lower than the angels';[39] and, 'We have seen him, and there was no sightliness nor beauty, but his appearance was the most abject of all men.'[40] And He endured all these things because of His great love for His creatures, that He might rescue the lost sheep and, having saved it, bring it back; that He might lead back in sound health to his own fatherland him who had gone down from Jerusalem to Jericho and thus fallen among robbers.[41]

And will the heretic indeed make the manger a subject of reproach to Him, the manger in which, while a helpless infant, He was nurtured by the Word? And will he taunt Him for His poverty, because He, the son of a carpenter, was not provided with a cradle? For this further reason the Son is less than the Father, because for your sake He died in order that He might free you from death and cause you to share in the heavenly life. So it would be if one would censure a physician because, in bending over the bed of pain in order to treat the patient, some of the foul odor should cling to him.

For your sake, also, He does not know the hour or the day of judgment; yet nothing is unknown to true Wisdom, for through It[42] are all things made. Moreover, among men no one is ever ignorant of what he has made. But He so provides because of your weakness, lest sinners, by reason of the brief time allotted them, fall into despair, believing that no time is left for repentance; and again, lest those fighting a long battle against the opposing force, because of its protracted duration, should desert their posts. Therefore, He

---

38 Ps. 8.6.
39 Heb. 2.9.
40 Cf. Isa. 53.2-3.
41 Cf. Luke 10.30.
42 Cf. John 1.3.

provides for both by assuming ignorance; for the latter, indeed, He cuts short the time because of the glorious contest; for the other, He metes times for repentance because of his sins. Yet, in the Gospels, He numbered himself with the ignorant because, as I said, of the weakness of the many. In the Acts of the Apostles, as if separately addressing the perfect, and making an exception of Himself, He says: 'It is not for you to know the times or dates, which the Father has fixed by his own authority.'[43] Let these things in a rather rough way suffice for our original design. I now must scrutinize more deeply the meaning of the expression, and I must knock at the door of the understanding, to see if in some way I may be able to arouse the Master of the house who gives spiritual bread to those who ask for it, since they to whom we wish to give a feast are friends and brothers.

The holy disciples of our Saviour, having reached the highest degree of contemplation possible for men, and having been purified by the Word,[44] seek the end, desiring to know the ultimate beatitude, and this our Lord declared neither His angels nor He knew. For, by 'day' He meant the complete and accurate perception of the designs of God, and by 'hour' the contemplation of the 'oneness' and 'aloneness.' The knowledge of these He assigned to the Father alone. I surmise, therefore, that God is said to know concerning Himself that which is, and not to know that which is not. In fact, God is said to know justice and wisdom, being Himself Justice and Wisdom; but to be ignorant of injustice and wickedness for the God who created us is not injustice or wickedness. If, therefore, God is said to know concerning Himself that which is, and not to know that which is not,

---
43 Acts 1.7.
44 Cf. John 15.3.

and if our Lord is not, according to the purpose of the Incarnation and to empirical knowledge,[45] the ultimate end desired, then our Saviour does not know, as it seems, the end and final beatitude. But not even the angels know this, He says;[46] that is, not even the contemplation which is in them nor the principles of their services are the ultimate end desired. For, their knowledge is dim in comparison with that which the beatific vision gives.[47]

Only the Father, He says, knows, since He Himself is the end and final beatitude. For, when we learn to know God no longer in a mirror, nor through an alien medium, but we approach Him as the Only and the One, then we also shall know the final beatitude. For, it is said that the kingdom of Christ is all our material knowledge, but that of God the Father, the immaterial and, as one might say, the contemplation of the Divinity Itself. But, our Lord is also the end itself and final beatitude, according to the design of the Lord. For, what does He say in the Gospel?[48] 'And I will raise him up on the last day'; meaning by the word 'raising up' the change from material knowledge to immaterial contemplation, and using the 'last day' to signify this knowledge, beyond which there is no other. For, then our mind is arisen and awakened to blessed heights whenever it contemplates the 'oneness' and 'aloneness' of the Word.

But our dulled intellect is bound up with earthy material and mixed with clay, and so is unable to be intent on pure contemplation. It apprehends the activities of the Creator

---

45 By *pachutéran* (denser), St. Basil seems to mean acquired or empirical knowledge; cf. beginning of second paragraph below. Cf. Isa. 6.10; Matt. 13.15; Acts 28.27.
46 Cf. Mark 13.32.
47 Cf. edition of Garnier-Maran, *ad loc.*
48 John 6.40.

only by being led through the beauties[49] akin to its own body, and meanwhile it learns to know these things from their effects, so that, strengthened little by little, it may at some time be able to approach the unveiled Divinity Itself. It is with this meaning, I think, that the following words were spoken: 'My Father is greater than I,'[50] and 'That is not mine to give you, but it belongs to those for whom it has been prepared by my Father.'[51] For, this is also the meaning of Christ handing over the kingdom to God and the Father,[52] since He is the first-fruits[53] and not the end according, as I have said, to the empirical knowledge, which looks to us and not to the Son Himself. That these things are so is evident from His reply in the Acts of the Apostles, when the disciples asked a second time: 'Wilt thou at this time restore the kingdom to Israel?'[54] and He answered: 'It is not for you to know the times and dates which the Father has fixed by his own authority.'[55] That is, the knowledge concerning such a kingdom is not for those still imprisoned in flesh and blood.

In fact, the Father has fixed the acquiring of this knowledge by His own authority; by 'authority' He implies those under His power, and by 'His own' He implies those whom ignorance of things below does not hold back from Him. But do not think, I beg you, that the times and dates are those of the senses; they are certain differences of knowl-

---

49 St. Basil speaks in a similar way of 'the beauties of the earth' in Letter 6, and, in his commentary on Isaias, the Church is spoken of as 'adorned with ornaments which become it.' Cf., also, Gregory of Nazianzus, Letter 107.
50 John 14.28.
51 Matt. 20.23.
52 Cf. 1 Cor. 15.24.
53 Cf. 1 Cor. 15.20,23.
54 Acts 1.6.
55 Cf. Acts 1.7.

edge due to the mental sun.⁵⁶ For, it is needful that that prayer of our Master be brought to fulfillment, since Jesus is the One offering the prayer: 'Grant to them, that they may be one in us, even as thou, Father, and I are one.'⁵⁷ Since, then, God is one, if He is in each individual, all are one; and number ceases to exist, because of the presence of 'oneness.'

And this meaning I arrived at in my second attempt. If anyone should interpret it better or should with reverence revise our efforts, let him both interpret and revise, and the Lord will reward him for us. For, no envy abides in us, because we did not undertake the examination of these words through rivalry or vanity, but for the benefit of our brothers, lest the earthen vessels⁵⁸ holding the treasure of God should seem to be led astray by these stony-hearted and uncircumcised men who have armed themselves with a foolish wisdom.

Again, according to the words of the wise Solomon in the Proverbs,⁵⁹ He was created. 'For the Lord,' he says, 'created me.' And He is called 'the beginning of the evangelical ways' which lead us to the kingdom of heaven, since He is not a creature in substance, but was made the 'way' in the divine dispensation. For, 'being made' and 'being created' have the same meaning. In fact, as He was made a way, so also was He made a door, a shepherd, a messenger, a sheep, and, in turn, a high priest and apostle,⁶⁰ different names being given according to the different conceptions. Again, what would the heretic say concerning the unsubjected God and One who was made sin⁶¹ for our sakes? For, it is written: 'And

---

56 I.e., the days and hours of inner experience marked by a timekeeper within us.
57 Cf. John 17.20-22.
58 Cf. 2 Cor. 4.6.7.
59 Prov. 8.22 (Septuagint).
60 Cf. Heb. 3.1.
61 Cf. 2 Cor. 5.21.

when all things are made subject to him, then the Son himself will also be made subject to him who subjected all things to him.'[62] Do you not fear, O man, the God who is called unsubjected? For He makes your subjection His own, and, because of your struggle against virtue, He calls Himself unsubjected. Thus, He even said at one time that He Himself was the One persecuted; for He says:[63] 'Saul, Saul, why dost thou persecute me?' when Saul was hastening to Damascus, desiring to put in bonds the disciples of Christ. Again, He calls Himself naked, if anyone of His brethren is naked. 'I was naked,' He says, 'and you covered me.'[64] And still again, when another was in prison, He said that He Himself was the One imprisoned. For He Himself took up our infirmities and bore the burden of our ills.[65] And one of our infirmities is insubordination, and this He bore. Therefore, even the adversities which happen to us the Lord makes His own, taking upon Himself our sufferings because of His fellowship with us.

But the enemies of God, for the undoing of those who listen to them, even seize upon this text: 'The Son can do nothing of himself.'[66] Yet, to me, this saying also proclaims emphatically that the Son is of identical nature with the Father. For, if it is possible for every rational creature to do anything of itself, having in its own power the decision for better or for worse, and the Son is not able to do anything of Himself, then the Son is not a creature. And, if He is not a creature, He is consubstantial with the Father. Again, no creature is able to do everything it wishes. But, the Son did all things whatsoever He wished, both in heaven and upon

---
62 I Cor. 15.28.
63 Acts 9.4.
64 Cf. Matt. 25.36.
65 Cf. Isa. 53.4; also, Matt. 8.17.
66 John 5.19.

earth. Therefore, the Son is not a creature. Again, all creatures are either made up of contrary inclinations or are capable of them.[67] But, the Son is Justice itself and immaterial. Therefore, the Son is not a creature. And if He is not a creature, He is consubstantial with the Father. And this examination of the passage proposed, being made to the best of our ability, is sufficient for us.

Let us now direct our words against those who are opposed to the Holy Spirit, and let us bring low all their haughtiness of spirit which 'exalts itself against the knowledge of God.'[68] You say that the Holy Spirit is a creature. But, every creature is subject to its creator. 'For all things,' it is said, 'serve thee.'[69] If He is subject, He also has a holiness that is acquired. But, everything which has its holiness acquired is capable of evil. The Holy Spirit, however, being holy in substance, is called the 'fount of sanctification.'[70] Therefore, the Holy Spirit is not a creature. If He is not a creature, He is consubstantial with God. But, how will you call Him subject, tell me, who frees you through baptism from servitude? 'For the law,' St. Paul says, 'of the Spirit of life has delivered me from the law of sin.'[71] Moreover, you will never dare to say that His substance is liable to change, as compared with the nature of the adverse Power who, as a flash of lightning, fell from the heavens[72] and was banished from true life, because the holiness he had was acquired, and change followed upon his evil design. For that very reason, also, having fallen from 'oneness' and having thrown away the angelic dignity, he

---

67 St. Basil doubtless has in mind the famous passage of St. Paul, Rom. 7.15-25.
68 2 Cor. 10.5.
69 Ps. 119.91.
70 Cf. Rom. 1.4.
71 Cf. Rom. 8.2.
72 Cf. Luke 10.18.

was called from his character 'Devil,'[73] since he had lost his previous state of bliss, and this adverse power had been fastened upon him.

If, then, the heretic calls the Holy Spirit a creature, he represents His nature as limited. How, therefore, will the sayings stand: 'The spirit of the Lord hath filled the whole world,'[74] and 'Whither shall I go from thy spirit?'[75] But, as it seems, he does not even confess Him as simple in nature, for he calls Him one in number. And whatever is one in number, as I said, is not simple. But, if the Holy Spirit is not simple, He is composed of substance and sanctity, and as such is composite. And who is so foolish as to say that the Holy Spirit is composite, and not simple and—according to the meaning of 'simplicity'—consubstantial with the Father and the Son?

But, if we must go on with our discussion and make a deeper study, let us, from this point, contemplate especially the divine power of the Holy Spirit. We find three creations mentioned in the Scripture; the first, the eduction from non-existence into existence; the second, the change from worse to better; and the third, the resurrection of the dead. In these you will find the Holy Spirit co-operating with the Father and the Son. Take, for instance, the calling into existence of the heavens. And what does David say? 'By the word of the Lord the heavens were established, and all the power of them by the spirit of his mouth.'[76] Now, man is created a second time through baptism, 'for if any man is in Christ, he is a new creature.'[77] And what does the Saviour

---
73 *Diábolos* alone is used in the Bible several times with the meaning of 'slanderer,' but *ho diábolos* is applied always to 'the Slanderer' as the prince of devils and the author of evil.
74 Wisd. 1.7.
75 Ps. 138.7.
76 Ps. 32.6.
77 2 Cor. 5.17.

say to the disciples? 'Go, make disciples of all nations, baptizing them in the name of the Father, and of the Son, and of the Holy Spirit.'[78] You see here, also, the Holy Spirit present with the Father and the Son. But, what would you say concerning the resurrection of the dead, when we shall have departed and returned into our dust, 'for we are dust and unto dust we shall return'?[79] 'And He will send forth the Holy Spirit, and He will create us, and He shall renew the face of the earth.'[80] For, what St. Paul spoke of as the resurrection David called renewal.

Let us hear again from him who was snatched up to the third heaven. What does he say? 'That you are the temple of the Holy Spirit who is in you.'[81] But, every temple is a temple of God. If, then, we are the temple of the Holy Spirit, the Holy Spirit is God. We also speak of the temple of Solomon, but meaning his who built it. Even if we are in this sense the temple of the Holy Spirit, the Holy Spirit is God, for 'He who created all things is God.'[82] But, if it means the temple is His who is worshipped and who dwells in us, let us confess that He is God. 'For the Lord thy God shalt thou worship, and him only shalt thou serve.'[83] And if they avoid the use of the word 'God,' let them learn what this name signifies. Without doubt He is named 'God' [*Theós*] because of His having established [*tetheikénai*] all things, or of His seeing [*theâsthai*] all things.[84] If, therefore, He is called God because of His having established or of His seeing all things, and if the Holy Spirit knows all the things which are of

---

78 Cf. Matt. 28.19.
79 Cf. Gen. 3.19.
80 Cf. Ps. 103.30.
81 Cf. 1 Cor. 6.19.
82 Heb. 3.4.
83 Matt. 4.10.
84 A false etymology, of course; *theos* is properly connected with *thúo* (I sacrifice).

God,[85] just as the spirit in us knows the things pertaining to us, then the Holy Spirit is God.

Again, if 'the sword of the spirit is the word of God,'[86] the Holy Spirit is God. For, the sword is His whose Word it is called. And if He is also called the right hand of the Father (for, 'the right hand of the Lord hath wrought strength,'[87] and 'Thy right hand, O Lord, hath slain the enemy';[88] but the Holy Spirit is the finger of God, according to the text: 'If I cast out devils by the finger of God,'[89] which in another Gospel is written: 'If I cast out devils by the Spirit of God'[90]), then the Holy Spirit is of the same nature as the Father and the Son.

Concerning, then, the adorable and holy Trinity, let this much suffice for the present. In fact, it is not now possible to go more into detail concerning it. But you, having received from our Lowliness[91] the seeds, produce full ears in season, because, as you know, we also demand interest from such things. But, I trust in God that, because of the purity of your lives, you will bear fruit thirty, sixty, and a hundredfold. For, 'Blessed,' He says, 'are the pure of heart, for they shall see God.'[92] And consider, brethren, that the kingdom of heaven is nothing else than the true contemplation of the realities, which the Holy Scriptures also call beatitude. 'For the kingdom of heaven is within you.'[93] And as regards the inner man, it consists of nothing but contemplation. The kingdom of heaven, then, must be contemplation.

---

85 Cf. 1 Cor. 2.10-11.
86 Cf. Eph. 6.17.
87 Ps. 117.16.
88 Cf. Exod. 15.6.
89 Luke 11.20.
90 Matt. 12.28.
91 *Tapeinōseos*—a Byzantine title used by St. Basil in speaking of himself.
92 Matt. 5.8.
93 Cf. Luke 17.21.

For, of these things of which we now behold the shadows, as in a mirror, later, when we have been freed from this earthy body and have put on an incorruptible and immortal one, we shall see distinctly the archetypes. But, we shall see them provided we guide our lives toward that which is right and take thought for the right faith, for without these things no one will see the Lord. 'For wisdom will not enter,' it is said, 'into a malicious soul, nor dwell in a body subject to sins.'[94] And let no one find fault with me, saying: 'You ignorant of everyday matters, philosophize to us about incorporeal and entirely immaterial substance.' I think that it is absurd to allow the senses to be filled without hindrance with their own material food, and to let the mind alone be excluded from its proper activity. For, as the senses apply themselves to sensible objects, so the mind applies itself to mental perceptions.

And at the same time we must also say this, that God who created us made the natural sense faculties independent of instruction. For, no one teaches how to perceive the sight of colors or figures, nor the hearing of noises and sounds, nor the smell of fragrant and foul odors, nor the taste of flavors and savors, nor the touch of objects soft and hard, hot and cold. Nor would anyone teach the mind how to grasp mental perceptions. Just as the senses, if they should suffer somewhat, need only additional care to enable them to fulfill easily their proper function, so also the mind, being united with the flesh and filled with the phantasies arising therefrom, needs faith and upright conduct of life, which 'make its feet like the feet of harts and set it upon high places.'[95] And this very recommendation the wise Solomon

---
94 Wisd. 1.4.
95 Cf. Ps. 17.34.

makes. At one time,[96] indeed, he brings forward the ant as an example of the worker who has no reason for shame, and through it he suggests a practical road for us. At another time[97] he brings forward the wise bee's wax-moulding implement,[98] and through it he suggests contemplation of nature, in which is blended also the doctrine of the Holy Trinity, if, indeed, the Creator is seen by analogy through the beauty of the things created.

But, now, giving thanks to the Father and to the Son and to the Holy Spirit, let us bring our letter to an end, since, as the proverb says,[99] everything is best in due measure.

9. To the Philosopher Maximus[1]

Words are truly the pictures of the soul. Therefore, we have come to know you through your letter, just as, according to the proverb, we know the lion by his claws.[2] And we are delighted in the discovery that you are not negligent in regard to the principal and greatest of virtues—love both for God and for your neighbor. We consider your kindness toward us a proof of the latter; your zeal for learning, of the former.

---

96 Cf. Prov. 6.6.
97 Cf. Eccli. 11.3. According to Rufinus, the Latin Church ascribes this book to Solomon, but in the Greek Church it is known as 'the Wisdom of Jesus son of Sirach' (translation of Origen's *Homily on Numbers* 17).
98 Cf. Sophocles, frag. 366.5 (Nauck): 'The very gaudy wax-moulding implement of the yellow bee.' The actual words used by St. Basil belong to Sophocles and not to Ecclesiasticus.
99 This saying was attributed to Cleobulus, one of the Seven Sages, who lived in Lindus in Rhodes at about 580 B.C.; cf. Diog. Laert. 89-93.

---

1 The date of this letter is about 361.
2 The origin of the proverb is found in Lucian, *Hermatimus* 34: 'They say indeed that one of the sculptors, Pheidias, I believe, after looking at a lion's claw, calculated the size of the whole lion when fashioned in proportion to the claw.'

It is well known to every disciple of Christ that all virtues are contained in these two.

The writings of Dionysius[3] for which you ask we indeed received, and they were very numerous; but, as the books are not now at hand, we have not sent them. Our judgment of them is this. We do not admire all the opinions of the man, and there are some we disagree with altogether. In fact, as regards this present impiety which is being spread abroad, I mean that of the doctrine of unlikeness,[4] this man is, as far as we know, the one who first furnished its seeds. Still, I think the cause is not perversity of judgment, but the excessive desire of opposing Sabellius.[5] At all events, I like to compare Dionysius with a gardener, who, in endeavoring to correct the distortion of a bent young tree, misses the mean entirely by excessive counterpull, drawing the plant over to the opposite extreme. We find something similar has happened in the case of this man. For, while vehemently opposing the impiety of the Libyan, he has by his excessive love of display been unconsciously carried over to the opposite evil. At any rate, although it was sufficient for him to show that the Father and the Son are not the same in substance[6] [*hypokeiménoi*] and to have the victory over the blasphemer, yet, in order that he might win a brilliant and overwhelming triumph, he establishes not only a difference of persons [*hypostáseis*] but also a different of substance [*ousía*], a subordination of power, and a variation of glory. As a result, he has exchanged evil itself for evil, deviating from correctness of doctrine. Moreover, he

---

3 Dionysius of Alexandria, a most eminent bishop of the third century, a pupil of Origen and his second successor as head of the Alexandrian School.
4 I.e., the doctrine supported by Actius and Valens and their followers, the Anomoeans, that there is no likeness in substance of the Father and Son.
5 Sabellius, second and third century.
6 Aristotle, *Met.* VI.3.1, says: 'Substance seems most of all to be that which first exists.' He has reference here to matter in the metaphysical sense.

is inconsistent in his writings, at one time denying the doctrine of identity of substance [*homooúsion*] because his opponent misused it for the rejection of the three persons, and at another time admitting it in the defense which he sent to his namesake.[7] Besides, he has also made use of utterly unbefitting expressions concerning the Spirit, banishing Him from the Divinity we worship and ranking Him lower, somewhere in the created and ministering order. Such, then, is the man.

But, if I express my personal opinion, I accept the term 'like in substance' if 'invariably' is added to it, for then it conveys the same meaning as consubstantial, according, assuredly, to the sound conception of the word 'consubstantial.' And the Fathers in Nicea, because they also held this view, consistently introduced the word 'consubstantial' when they addressed the Only-begotten as Light from Light and True God from True God, and so on. Now, it is impossible to conceive of any variation of light in relation to light, or of truth in relation to truth, or of the substance of the Only-begotten in relation to that of the Father. Therefore, if anyone accepts this interpretation as I have given it, I approve. But, if the qualification 'invariably' is omitted, as was done by those at Constantinople,[8] I hold the expression in suspicion on the grounds that it lessens the glory of the Only-begotten. In

---

7 Dionysius of Rome, a Greek by birth, consecrated July 22, A.D. 259, on the death of Xystus, in the persecution of Valerian. Upon the receipt of a satisfactory explanation, he declared Dionysius of Alexandria free from suspicion of holding doctrines similar to those of Sabellius. Cf. Athan. *Ep. de Senectute Dionysii* 1.252. However, Dionysius of Alexandria had clearly been incorrect in thought and word, as St. Basil declared.
8 At the Acacian Council of Constantinople (360), fifty bishops accepted the creed of Ariminum as revised at Nica (at or near modern Hofsa, just to the south of Adrianople), proscribing 'substance' and 'person' and declared the Son 'like the Father, as say the Holy Scriptures.' Cf. Theod. 2.16 and Soc. 2.40.

fact, we are frequently accustomed to think of 'likeness' meaning resemblance as faint and for the most part inferior to the archetype. Therefore, because I believe the word 'consubstantial' is less liable to misinterpretation, I myself adopt it.

But, why do you not visit us, my noble Friend,[9] so that we may speak with each other personally and not entrust subjects of so much importance to lifeless letters, especially since we have quite determined not to make our own opinion public? Now, see that you do not give us the answer that Diogenes gave to Alexander: 'It is as near from you to this place as from here to you.' For, because of ill health, we are held fast almost like the plants, always in the same place. At the same time we consider it among the greatest of blessings to live a life of retirement. But you, so the report is, are in good health, and, since you have also made yourself a citizen of the world, it would be right for you to come even here, to a part of your own country, as it were, to visit us. For, although the districts and the cities in which you display your excellent achievements are suited to your active personality, yet, for contemplation and for the activity of the mind through which we are linked to God, the best helpmate is solitude. And this quietude, profound and abundant, we cultivate here on the outskirts of the world, so that we may speak with God Himself, who provided it for us. But, if you must by all means honor the powerful and despise us, the lowly, at all events write on other matters to us, and thereby make us happier.

---

9 *Ariste*—A title of distinction used by St. Basil for laymen.

10. To a Widow[1]

There is a certain method used for hunting doves, such as this. When the fowlers have caught a bird, they tame it so that it will eat in their presence. Then, rubbing its wings with perfume, they allow it to join the flock outside. The sweet odor of that perfume wins for the owner the rest of the wild birds, which follow the fragrance and the tame dove into the cote. But why am I beginning my letter thus? Because after taking your son Dionysius, formerly called Diomedes[2] and anointing the wings of his soul with the divine perfume, I have sent him out to your gracious Ladyship,[3] so that you yourself may fly up with him and reach the nest which he has made at our side. If, then, I should in my lifetime see this and behold your gracious Ladyship brought over to our lofty way of life, I shall need to fill many roles worthy in God's sight in order to pay in full the honor due to Him.

11. Without Address, through Friendship[1]

We spent the holy day, by the grace of God, with our children,[2] who, because of their extraordinary love of God, really made it a perfect feast day with the Lord. Now we

---

[1] St. Basil writes during his retreat to an unknown widow.
[2] A second name given at baptism. For the sake of personal safety, names not Christian were frequently given at baptism during the first three centuries. This practice was later discarded.
[3] *Semnoprépeian*—a title of address applied to both clergy and laity. St. Basil alone is cited as using it.

---

[1] A greeting sent to a friend, probably Olympius, to whom St. Basil frequently writes. Cf. Letters 4,12,13,211. Letters 10-13 are all of the same date.
[2] I.e., his friend's children.

have sent them on in good health to your Nobility[3] with a prayer to the loving God that they may be given an angel of peace as a support and companion on the way, and that they may find you in good health and in perfect tranquillity, that, wherever you may be, serving the Lord and giving thanks to Him, you may continue, as long as we are in this life, to gladden us with good news of yourself. But, if the holy God grants you the grace to be more quickly freed from your present cares, we urge you to choose life with us in preference to anything else. For, I think that you have not found any others who love you so much and esteem your friendship so highly as we. As long, therefore, as the Holy One imposes this separation, deign, on every possible pretext, to console us with a letter.

12. To Olympius

Formerly you wrote us, but briefly; now, not even a few words. Since your brevity keeps increasing with time, it is likely to become complete silence. Return, therefore, to your first practice; we shall no longer find fault with you for the laconic terseness of your letters. On the contrary, we shall highly esteem even your brief messages as tokens of your great love. Only, write us.

13. To Olympius

Just as everything else which is seasonal appears in its own proper time—flowers in spring, ears of corn in summer, and apples in autumn—so intellectual discussions are the fruit of winter.

---
3 *Eugéneian*—a title of address used by St. Basil for laymen only.

14. To Gregory, His Companion[1]

Although my brother Gregory wrote that for a long time he had been wanting to visit with us, and added that you also had the same desire, I am unable to remain here because, having been frequently deceived, I am reluctant to rely upon your coming, and also because I am drawn away by business. I must immediately depart for the Pontus, where perhaps some day, if God wills, we shall cease from our wandering. For, after giving up with difficulty the vain hopes which I once entertained regarding you, or rather, to speak more truly, the dreams (for I agree with the man who said that hopes are the dreams we have when fully awake), I went to the Pontus in search of a place of habitation. There, at length, God showed me a spot exactly according with my frame of mind, so that I beheld in truth a place such as I have been accustomed frequently to fashion in my imagination when idly amusing myself.

There is a lofty, densely wooded mountain, watered on the north by cold, transparent streams. At its foot is spread out a flat plain, constantly enriched by the moisture from the mountain. A forest of trees of every color and variety, a spontaneous growth around this plain, has become almost an enclosing wall, so that even Calypso's isle which Homer seems to have admired more than all others for its beauty is insignificant in comparison. In fact, it falls little short of being an island, since it is encompassed on all sides by defenses. Deep ravines have broken it off on two sides, and along the third side the river, descending from the overhanging cliff, forms an unbroken and inaccessible barrier. Because the mountain extends along the other side and is joined to the ravines by crescent-shaped spurs, the approaches at its

---

[1] This letter was written after 360, but before St. Basil became a presbyter.

base are walled off. There is one entrance to it, of which we are the master. Adjacent to my dwelling is a sort of narrow neck of land which supports a high ridge at its extremity, below which the plain lies spread out beneath. our eyes, and from which eminence the encircling river can be seen. This affords me no less pleasure, I think, than the Strymon affords those viewing it from Amphipolis.² The latter, spreading out its rather leisurely stream to form a lake, almost ceases in its stillness to be a river; while the former, flowing the most swiftly of all rivers I have ever seen, is suddenly roughened in its course by a rocky margin, and the rebounding water is whirled around in a deep eddy, providing a most pleasant sight for me and for everyone who sees it, and giving to the inhabitants of the place self-supporting employment, since numberless fish breed therein.

And what need to mention the land fragrances or the river breezes? Someone else might admire the abundant flowers or the multitudinous songbirds, but to these I do not have leisure to turn my mind. The greatest praise we can give of this place is that, besides being suited, because of its singularly apt location, for the production of every kind of fruits, it nourishes the sweetest of all fruits to me—solitude; not only because it is free from the uproar of the city, but also because it is removed from the encroachment of travelers, except for those who come to us for the purpose of hunting. In addition to all else, it is productive of game; not the bears or wolves of your country, may God forbid, but it feeds herds of deer and wild goats, hares, and other similar animals.

---

2 The Strymon, or Struma, is a river of Macedonia which flows through Lake Presias, and a little below Amphipolis, which it almost encircles; it empties into a bay of the Aegean Sea, called Strymonicus Sinus. Cf. Hes. *Th.* 339; Aesch. *Ag.* 192; Hdt. 7.75; Thuc. 2.96, 4.108, 5.7; and Strabo, p. 323.

Do you not realize, then, how great a risk I was foolishly taking in my eagerness to exchange such a place for the Tiberina,³ the pit of the world? You must pardon me for hurrying on now to such a place. For, not even Alcmaeon could longer endure his wandering after he had discovered the Echinades.⁴

15. To Arcadius, Imperial Administrator¹

The citizens of our capital conferred a greater favor than they received when they provided me with an opportunity of writing to your Honor.² For truly, because of your usual innate gentleness toward all, the privilege they sought to obtain through a letter from us was theirs even before the letter was written.

In fact, we regarded it an exceptional advantage to have the opportunity of addressing your peerless Honor,³ and we prayed to the holy God that we might continue to take delight in your growing favor with Him and in your increasing earthly renown, and also that we might rejoice with those favored by your patronage. We also prayed that you might receive and look kindly upon those presenting our letter to

---

3 The Tiberina was a district near Gregory's home at Nazianzus; cf. Greg. Naz. *Epp.* 6 and 7.
4 Alcmaeon, because he had slain his mother, was relentlessly pursued by the Erinnys, the avenger of matricide, and was allowed rest in no place until he reached the Echinades. These islands, formed in the mouth of the river Achelous by its muddy stream, had not been in existence at the time of the murder and so could offer him relief.

---

1 The imperial administrator managed the enormous revenues of the treasury and kept an account of the privileges granted by the emperor. This letter was written during St. Basil's retirement in the Pontus.
2 *Timiótēta*—a title of address used by St. Basil for both clergymen and laymen.
3 *Kalokagathían*—a title of address used by St. Basil for laymen only.

you and send them back completely gratified, proclaiming your courtesy and realizing that our intercession with your unsurpassed Honor was not unavailing.

16. Against Eunomius, the Heretic[1]

He who says that it is possible to attain to a knowledge of things really existing has, no doubt, directed his process of thought by some method and orderly procedure having its inception in his actual knowledge of existing things, and, after he has trained himself by the comprehension of objects rather insignificant and easily understood, he has simply advanced his perceptive faculty to the apprehension of that which is beyond all understanding.

Let him, therefore, who boasts that he has arrived at a knowledge of things actually existing explain the nature of the most trifling of visible objects. Let him expound the nature of the ant. Is its life sustained by breath and respiration? Is its body provided with bones? Is its framework braced with sinews and ligaments? Is the position of the sinews held secure by the covering of muscles and glands? Is the marrow stretched along the spinal vertebrae from the front of the head to the tail? Does it give the stimulating force to the members which have motion by its covering of sinewy membrane? Does it have a liver and a gall bladder near the liver; also kidneys, a heart, arteries and veins, membranes

---

1 Eunomius was the bishop of Cyzicus against whose *Liber Apologeticus* St. Basil wrote his *Adversus Eunomium*. However, this letter is similar almost word for word to a passage in the tenth book of St. Gregory of Nyssa's treatise against Eunomius written in 380 or 381. F. Diekamp, 'Ein angeblicher Brief des hl. Basilius gegen Eunomius,' *Theologische Quartalschrift* 77 (1895) 277-285, considers it the work of St. Gregory. Bessières, *op. cit.* 349, also thinks that it is not by St. Basil

and cartilage? Is it hairless or covered with hair? Has it an uncloven hoof, or feet divided into toes? How long does it live? What is its manner of reproduction? How long is the period of gestation? And how is it that all ants are not merely crawling insects, nor all winged, but some belong to those which travel on the ground and others fly through the air? To begin with, therefore, let him who boasts of the knowledge of things actually existing explain the nature of the ant. Then let him investigate in the same manner the nature of the power which surpasses every intellect. But, if you have not yet, by your investigation, understood the nature of the smallest ant, how can you boast that the incomprehensible power of God is clear to your mind?

17. To Origen[1]

Listening to you delights us, but reading your expositions gives us even more pleasure. And great is our gratitude to the good God, who did not permit the truth to be brought to naught because of its betrayal by would-be erudites, but, on the contrary, supplied through you a defense for the word of true religion. Certainly, those men, like hemlock or leopard's bane, or any other deadly herb, after flourishing for a short time, will quickly wither away. But on you, for your defense of His name, will the Lord bestow His reward fresh and ever new. May the Lord, therefore, grant you all prosperity in your home and may He also hand on the blessing to your children's children. It was indeed with joy that I

---

1 A Christian apologist, evidently a layman, about whom there is no further information than that contained in this letter, which was written during the reign of Julian.

saw and embraced your most noble sons, striking images of your Excellency;[2] in my prayers I ask for them all that a father himself would ask.

18. To Macarius and John[1]

The work of the farm does not surprise the farmer, nor the storm at sea astonish the sailor, nor the sweat of summer dismay the hireling; so, in truth, afflictions of the present life do not find unprepared those who choose to live holily. Each of these occupations is accompanied by its proper labor, well known to those pursuing it—a labor not chosen for its own sake but for the enjoyment of the anticipated good. Hopes, encompassing and welding together the whole life of man, mitigate these hardships.

Now, some who toil for the fruits of the earth or for mundane gains have been altogether disappointed in their hopes and have enjoyed their expectations only in imagination. Others, for whom the result has by chance accorded with their wish, soon have need of a second hope, the first, realized, having quickly spent itself and wasted away. Those alone who labor for holiness are not deceived in their hopes; the end has justified the struggle which gives them the firm and enduring kingdom of heaven.

As long, therefore, as truth is on our side, let no deceitful slander trouble you, no threat of the powerful frighten you, nor the laughter and the insult of your acquaintances grieve you, nor even the condemnation of those pretending con-

---

2 *Chrēstótēta*—a title of address used by St. Basil for laymen.

1 This letter was probably written during the reign of Julian.

cern for you, holding out the powerful enticement of delusive advice. Oppose all of these with right reason, invoking as its ally and guide our Lord Jesus Christ, the teacher of true religion, for whom to suffer evil is sweet, 'to die is gain.'[2]

19. To Gregory, a Companion[1]

We have just received your letter; yours in the strict sense of the word, not so much in the distinctiveness of the handwriting as in the characteristic style of the letter itself. The words were few but thought-filled. We did not answer immediately, since we ourselves were away from home when the carrier delivered the letter to one of our friends and immediately departed. But now we salute you through Peter, paying a debt of friendly greeting and at the same time furnishing you an opportunity for a second letter. Assuredly, there is no labor involved in writing a laconic letter such as are all those which we receive from you.

20. To Leontius, the Sophist[1]

Our letters to you are, it is true, infrequent, but not more so than yours to us, although people have been continually coming from your country to visit us. Now, if you were dispatching letters by all of these, one after another, we could easily imagine ourselves with you and enjoy you just as if

---
2 Phil. 1.21.

---
1 This brief answer to a letter of St. Gregory of Nazianzus was probably written from Caesarea shortly after St. Basil became a presbyter.

---
1 A Leontius is referred to in Letter 35. This letter was written in 364.

we were actually in your company, so continuous has been the stream of arrivals here.

But, why do you not write? Certainly, a sophist has no other work except to write. And if you are lazy of hand, you have no need to write, for another will perform that service for you. Only a tongue is necessary. Although it may not converse with us, it assuredly will talk to one of your companions; even if no one is present, it will still talk. Since it is both sophistic and Attic, it will certainly not keep silent any more than the nightingales when stirred to song by spring. Now, in our case, the many duties presently engaging us should, perchance, justify the scarcity of our letters. Furthermore, the fact that we are slovenly in expression, as it were, because of a deep-rooted habit of colloquial speech, reasonably causes us to hesitate in addressing you sophists, who will be displeased and impatient with anything not consonant with your own wisdom. But for you, surely it is reasonable for you to make public all your utterances on every occasion, since of all the Greeks that I myself know you are the most fit to speak. And I think I know the most famous among you. Therefore, there is no excuse for your being silent. So much, then, for these matters.

I have also sent you my work against Eunomius,[2] and whether it should be called child's play or something a little more serious than child's play I leave you to decide. You are no longer, I think, in need of it for your own self, but I hope it will be no mean weapon for you against chance perverse acquaintances. We do not rely so much on the force of the treatise, but we know definitely that you are exceedingly

---

2 A dogmatic work in three books, 'Refutation of the Apologetic of the Impious Eunomius,' composed in 363 or 364. In the year 360, Eunomius had been deprived of his episcopate in Cyzicus because of his Arian views.

ingenious even with slight resources. And if any statement appears to you to be insufficiently strong, do not hesitate to criticize. For, in this point especially the friend differs from the flatterer, in that the latter talks to please, but the former does not refrain even from words that pain.[3]

21. *To Leontius, the Sophist*[1]

The good Julian seems to be deriving some personal advantage from the general state of affairs. For, at present, when all the world is full of men demanding payment and bringing charges, he also is clamoring for payment and vehemently making accusations. Only, in his case, it is not arrears in taxes but in letters. Yet, I fail to understand how it is possible that anything has been left unpaid to him. For whenever he gave a letter he received one in return. Unless you have a preference, too, for that well-known 'fourfold';[2] for even the Pythagoreans esteemed the *'tetractys'*[3] less than the present tax collectors do the 'fourfold.' Yet, the reasonable view would rather be that, since you are a sophist and so abound in words, you should yourself be liable to us for the payment

---

3 For the maxim, see Plutarch: 'How one should distinguish a flatterer from a friend.'

---

1 Leontius himself must be the 'good Julian' whom St. Basil playfully chides for claiming that answers to his letters are due to him. Otherwise, this letter is unintelligible. It was written in 364.

2 The Benedictine editors explain this 'fourfold' as a penalty of four times the regular amount, which was demanded for unpaid taxes. Cf. Ammianus Marcellinus, 26.6.

3 The term applied by the Pythagoreans to the sum of the first four numbers, one, two, three, and four—the numbers applied respectively to the point, the line, the surface, and the solid, and considered by them to be the root of all creation.

of the 'fourfold.' Pray do not think that we are writing this because we are annoyed. I take pleasure even in your censures, since it is said that all things done by the beautiful take on an increase of beauty. Therefore, even grief and anger are becoming to them. At all events, one would more gladly see his beloved friend angry than another flattering. So, never cease to bring such accusations. Without doubt, the charges themselves will be letters, than which nothing is dearer to me or gives me more pleasure.

22. Concerning the Perfection of the Monastic Life[1]

There are many things set forth in the divinely inspired Scriptures which must be observed by those who are earnestly endeavoring to please God. But at this time I wish to explain, necessarily briefly, as I understand them from the divinely inspired Scripture itself, only those points which have been questioned among you at present. I am therefore leaving behind me the easily comprehended evidence on each such point, so that those may take note who are engaged in reading and who also will be capable of informing others.

The Christian ought to think thoughts befitting his heavenly calling[2] and to live a life worthy of the Gospel of Christ.[3] The Christian should not exalt himself,[4] nor be drawn away by anything from the remembrance of God and His will and judgments. The Christian, transcending in all things

---

1 This letter shows how completely St. Basil follows the Holy Scriptures in his ideal of the religious life. He here identified the monastic with the ideal Christian life. The date of the letter is probably 364.
2 Cf. Heb. 3.1.
3 Cf. Phil. 1.27.
4 Cf. Luke 12.29.

righteousness merely according to law,[5] ought neither to swear nor to lie. He must not speak evil,[6] act despitefully, nor quarrel,[7] nor avenge himself,[8] nor render evil for evil,[9] nor give way to anger.[10] He should be patient,[11] enduring anything whatsoever, and should rebuke[12] the evil-doer at an opportune moment, not indeed in a passion of personal vengeance, but with a desire of a brother's correction,[13] according to the command of the Lord. He should say nothing against an absent brother with the intention of slandering him,[14] since, indeed, it is slander even if the remarks are true. He must turn away from the slanderer of his brother.[15]

The Christian should not engage in repartee,[16] nor laugh, nor tolerate jesters.[17] He must not indulge in idle conversations, talking of things which are neither for the benefit of those listening nor for any purpose that is necessary and permitted to us by God.[18] Consequently, the laborers will strive to work as much as possible in silence, and they who have been entrusted, after due trial, with directing others for the upbuilding of their faith will stimulate the workers with good discourses in order that the Holy Spirit of God may

---

5 Cf. Matt. 5.20.
6 Cf. Titus 3.2.
7 Cf. 2 Tim. 2.24.
8 Cf. Rom. 12.19.
9 Cf. Rom. 12.17.
10 Cf. Matt. 5.22.
11 Cf. James 5.8.
12 Cf. Titus 2.15.
13 Cf. Matt. 18.15.
14 Cf. 1 Peter 2.1.
15 Cf. James 4.11.
16 Cf. Eph. 5.4.
17 'This charge is probably founded on Luke 6.21 and 25, and James 4.9. Yet our Lord's promise that they who hunger and weep "shall laugh" admits of fulfillment in the kingdom of God on earth. Cheerfulness is a note of the Church, whose members, if sorrowful, are yet always rejoicing. (2 Cor. 6.10)'—Jackson.
18 Cf. Eph. 5.4.

not be grieved. Visitors should not freely approach or talk with any of the brothers before those who have been entrusted with the care of the general discipline have examined what before God is best for the common good. He ought not to be a slave to wine, nor passionately fond of meat,[19] nor in general a lover of any food or drink, for everyone in a contest abstains from all things.[20]

No one should keep or reserve as his own anything that has been given to him for his use,[21] but, devoting himself to the care of everything as belonging to the Lord, he should not neglect anything, even that which may have been cast aside or left uncared for. He should not be his own master, but should so think and act[22] in all things as one handed over by God into servitude to his like-minded brethren; 'but each in his own turn.'[23]

The Christian should not murmur[24] either because of the meagre care of his needs or because of fatiguing labors, since those entrusted with authority in these matters have the final decision over each. There should be no outburst, nor any angry demonstration or commotion,[25] nor should there be any distraction of mind from the realization of the presence of God.[26] The Christian ought to control his voice according to circumstances. He should neither give retort nor act boldly or contemptuously,[27] but in everything show moderation[28] and respect toward all.[29] He should not wink his eye slyly,

---

19 Cf. Rom. 14.21.
20 1 Cor. 9.25.
21 Cf. Acts 4.32.
22 Cf. 1 Cor. 9.19.
23 1 Cor. 15.23.
24 Cf. 1 Cor. 10.10.
25 Cf. Eph. 4.31.
26 Cf. Heb. 4.13.
27 Cf. Titus 3.2.
28 Cf. Phil. 4.5.
29 Cf. Rom. 2.10; 1 Peter 2.17.

nor use any other posture or gesture which grieves his brother or shows disdain.[30]

The Christian should not make a display of dress or shoes, as this is indeed idle ostentation.[31] He should use inexpensive clothing for his bodily needs. He should not spend anything beyond actual necessity or for mere extravagance. This is an abuse. He should not seek honor nor lay claim to the first place.[32] Each one ought to prefer all others to himself.[33] He ought not to be disobedient.[34] He who is idle, although able to work, should not eat;[35] moreover, he who is occupied with some task which is rightly intended for the glory of Christ ought to hold himself to a pursuit of work within his ability.[36] Each one, with the approval of his superiors, should, with reason and certainty, so do everything, even to eating and drinking, as serving the glory of God.[37] He should not change from one work to another without the approval of those who have been charged with the regulation of such matters, unless, perhaps, an unavoidable necessity should summon one unexpectedly to the aid of a helpless brother. Each one ought to remain at whatever work has been assigned him, without overstepping his own bounds to go on to tasks not prescribed, unless those entrusted with these matters judge that someone needs help. No one should be found going from one workshop to another. He should do nothing through rivalry or strife.

The Christian should not envy another's good repute, nor

---
30 Cf. Rom. 14.10.
31 Cf. Matt. 6.29; Luke 12.27.
32 Cf Mark. 9.34.
33 Cf. Phil. 2.3.
34 Cf. Titus 1.10.
35 Cf. 2 Thess. 3.10.
36 Cf. 1 Thess. 4.11.
37 Cf. 1 Cor. 10.31.

rejoice at the faults of anyone.[38] He must, in the love of Christ, be grieved and afflicted at the faults of his brother and rejoice at his virtuous deeds.[39] He should not be indifferent toward sinners, neither should he tolerate them in silence.[40] He who reproves should do so with all compassion in fear of God and with the view of correcting the sinner.[41] The one reproved or rebuked ought willingly to accept the correction, recognizing the benefit to himself. When one is accused, another ought not, before him or any others, to contradict the accuser. But, if at any time a charge should seem unreasonable to anyone, he ought in private to question the accuser and either convince him or be himself fully convinced.

Each one should conciliate, as far as he is able, anyone at variance with him. He should not hold past wrongs against the repentant sinner, but from his heart should pardon him.[42] He who says that he repents of his sin should not only feel remorse for the sin which he has committed, but should also bring forth fruits befitting repentance.[43] If he who has been corrected for his first sins and has been deemed worthy of pardon again falls, he prepares for himself a more wrathful judgment.[44] He who after the first and second admonition[45] remains in his fault should be reported to the superior, that perhaps he may be ashamed when further rebuked. But, if he does not even in this case correct himself, he must be cut off from the rest as a cause of scandal, and be looked upon

---

38 Cf. 1 Cor. 13.6.
39 Cf. 1 Cor. 12.26.
40 Cf. 1 Tim. 5.20.
41 Cf. 2 Tim. 4.2.
42 Cf. 2 Cor. 2.7.
43 Cf. Luke 3.8.
44 Cf. Heb. 10.26-27.
45 Cf. Titus 3.10.

as a heathen and a publican,[46] this for the safety of those zealous for obedience, according to the saying: 'When the impious fall, the just become fearful.'[47] But, all must also mourn for him as if a limb had been cut off from the body.

The sun must not go down on the wrath of a brother,[48] lest, perchance, the night of death come between the two and leave an inevitable charge for the day of judgment. He must not put off the time for his amendment,[49] because there is no certainty concerning the morrow, and because many, planning, have not reached the morrow. He must not be deluded by a full stomach, which often produces nightmares. He must not engage in excessive toil, achieving beyond sufficiency, according to the words of the Apostle: 'But having food and sufficient clothing, with these let us be content,'[50] because an abundance which exceeds the need presents an appearance of covetousness, but covetousness has the condemnation of idolatry.[51] He must not be fond of money,[52] nor treasure useless things which he does not need. He who draws nigh to God should welcome poverty in all things and be penetrated with the fear of God, according to him who said: 'Pierce thou my flesh with thy fear, for I am afraid of thy judgments.'[53] The Lord grant that you may receive with full confidence what I have said, and for the glory of God show forth fruits worthy of the Spirit, according to the will of God and with the assistance of our Lord Jesus Christ. Amen.

---

46 Cf. Matt. 18.17.
47 Prov. 29.16. The translation from the Latin Vulgate seems to be that of a somewhat different wording; St. Basil followed the Greek Septuagint.
48 Cf. Eph. 4.26.
49 Cf. Luke 12.40.
50 1 Tim. 6.8.
51 Cf. Col. 3.5.
52 Cf. Mark 10.23-24; Luke 18.24.
53 Ps. 119.120.

LETTERS   61

23. *Admonition to a Monk*[1]

There has come to me a man who says he despises the vanity of this life, the joys of which he has observed to be ephemeral, passing quickly away and merely furnishing material for eternal fire. He wishes to withdraw from a wretched and lamentable life, to forsake the pleasures of the flesh, and to travel for the future along the road that leads to the mansions of the Lord. Now, if he is really determined in his desire of a truly blessed manner of life, and has in his soul a noble and commendable longing—loving the Lord, our God, with his whole heart, with his whole strength, and with his whole mind—your Reverence[2] should warn him of the difficulties and hardships of the strait and narrow path, and confirm him in the hope of the now unseen blessings which, according to the promise, are reserved for those worthy of the Lord.

I therefore write to urge your incomparable[3] Perfection[4] in Christ to mold him, as far as possible, and to bring about without my assistance his renunciation according to God's pleasure, instructing him in the teachings of the holy Fathers as set forth by them in their writings. I urge you, then, to place before him all the best practices[5] of exact ascetic observance, and so to introduce him to that life that, having

---
1 This letter, written at Caesarea while St. Basil was a presbyter, seems to be an exhortation to his monks to train well a new recruit whom he is sending to them, rather than a personal admonition to any one monk.
2 *Theosebeías*—a title of address used by St. Basil, except in this letter, for bishops only.
3 *Asúnkriton*—a title of distinction used by St. Basil for both clergy and laity.
4 *Teleiótēta*—a title of address applied by St. Basil to clergy and laity.
5 Among the writings on the ascetic life ascribed to St. Basil is the *Book of Ascetic Discipline,* which is an exhortation to a renunciation of the world and contains specific directions for the monastic life.

voluntarily undertaken the contests of piety, subjecting himself to the kind yoke of the Lord, living his life in imitation of Him who became poor[6] and clothed Himself with flesh for us, and running according to his aim toward the prize of his heavenly calling, he may meet with approbation from the Lord. For, I put him off when he was eager to receive here the crown of the love of God, wishing to anoint him for such contests with the assistance of your Reverence, and to appoint as his trainer whomever of you he might request. Such a one would, through his earnest and blessed care, nobly train and bring to perfection an excellent wrestler, one wounding and overthrowing the world ruler of this darkness and the spiritual forces of wickedness, against whom, according to the blessed Apostle, is our wrestling.[7] Therefore, what I wished to do with your assistance, let your love in Christ do even without me.

24. *To Athanasius, Father of Athanasius, Bishop of Ancyra*[1]

I myself am convinced, nor do I think that your Excellency doubts it, that it is one of the most difficult, if not impossible, things, for the life of a man to be above slander. But, personally to provide no occasion to those keenly watching our actions or to those maliciously lying in wait for our slightest errors is both possible and characteristic of persons living wisely and according to the standards of piety. But, do

---
6 Cf. 2 Cor. 8.9.
7 Cf. Eph. 6.12.

---
1 Nothing is known of the elder Athanasius except what is given in this letter, which is a reply to slanders that had evidently been reported to St. Basil concerning Athanasius' treatment of his children. The letter was written before St. Basil's episcopate. Cf. Letter 25 n. 1.

not think that we are so easy-going and so credulous as to believe without investigation the accusations of chance persons. For, we bear in mind the spiritual maxim that we shall 'not receive the voice of a lie.'[2]

However, since you yourself who seriously pursue literature say that things seen are signs of things unseen, this is our opinion (and do not be offended if anything I say shall seem to be an instruction, for the weak things of the world and the foolish has God chosen;[3] and through these He frequently brings about the salvation of those who are saved). At all events, what I say and recommend is this: that we should be careful in fulfilling every word and every duty, and, according to the command of the Apostle, give offense to no one.[4] I hold that it is proper, when a man has sweated much in the acquiring of knowledge, and has administered the government of nations and cities, and has emulated the great virtues of his ancestors, for his life to be set before us as an example of virtue.

Of course, you ought not now to show only by word your love for your children, as you have long been showing it, indeed, ever since you became a father, nor to employ natural affection alone, which even brute beasts exhibit for their offspring, as you yourself have said and as experience proves. But, certainly, you should deliberately intensify your love in proportion to their increasing worthiness of your paternal prayers. It is not necessary, therefore, to persuade us of these things, for the testimony of actual facts is sufficient.

It is not out of place, however, for the sake of truth, to add that our brother Timotheus, the suffragan bishop, is not the one who reported the rumors to us. For, neither in

---

2 Cf. Ex. 23.1.
3 Cf. 1 Cor. 1.27-28.
4 Cf. 1 Cor. 6.3.

conversation nor in his letters has he been known to say anything slanderous, great or small, about you. Therefore, although we do not deny having heard reports, Timotheus was not the inventor of the slanders against you. But, at all events, when we hear anything, we shall at least, whatever else we do, follow the example of Alexander—keep one ear free for the accused.[5]

25. To Athanasius, Bishop of Ancyra[1]

Some coming to us from Ancyra—so many that it is not easy to enumerate them, but all agreeing in their accounts —reported to me that you, my dear Friend[2] (how can I speak of it without hurting you), do not mention us in a very pleasant manner nor in accordance with your usual character. Yet, you may be sure, nothing human astonishes me, nor should any defection be a complete surprise, as I have learned from long observing the weakness of human nature and its readiness to espouse the opposite cause. I do not, therefore, consider it of importance if your esteem of me has undergone somewhat of a change, and, instead of the honor of former times, reproaches and insults are now directed toward us. But, what impresses me as really incredible and monstrous is that you should be so disposed toward us as to be angered and embittered and should already even threat-

---

5 Cf. Plutarch, *Life of Alexander.*

1 This Athanasius was appointed to the see of Ancyra through the influence of Acacius, Bishop of Caesarea, a leader of the Homooeans. However, he himself acquired a reputation for orthodoxy. Cf. Greg. Nyss. *Contra Eunom.* 1.11.292. St. Basil speaks highly of him in Letter 29. This letter was written about the same time as the preceding one, before the spring of 368. Cf. Letter 29 n. 1.

2 *Kefalén*—used as a title by St. Basil for both clergymen and laymen.

en us with violence, according to the report of those who have heard you.

Now, as for the threats (the truth must be told), I indeed really laughed at them. In fact, I would be altogether childish if I feared such bogeys. But, this seemed to me both terrible and a matter for deep concern, that your Integrity,[3] whom we looked upon as one among the few being preserved for the consolation of the churches as a bulwark of sound doctrine and seed of the first and true love, should share to such an extent in the current mental attitude as to consider the blasphemies of chance-comers of greater weight than your long experience with us, and to be led without proof to suspect absurd reports to be true. Yet, why do I say 'suspect'? For, he who is vexed and threatens, as is reported concerning you, seems in some way to have displayed the wrath, not of one suspecting, but of a person already clearly and certainly persuaded.

Yet, as I have said, we trace the cause to the current course of thought. For, how much labor would it have been, admirable Sir, for you, in a brief letter, to have discussed confidentially with me any desired topic, or, if you would not entrust such matters to writing, to have summoned me to you? But, if you found it absolutely necessary to speak out, and the difficulty of restraining your wrath did not permit of delay, surely it would have been possible for you to use as a messenger of your words to us some one who is a close friend and disposed to keep secret matters confidential. But, now, who visits you for any need whatsoever whose ears are not ringing with the accusation that we are writing and composing certain abominations? Those who report your speeches word for word say that you use this very expression. Although I have looked upon this matter from every possible viewpoint,

---

[3] *Akribeian*—used as a title of address by St. Basil for the clergy alone.

nothing any longer frees me from a feeling of powerlessness.

As a consequence, even the thought has come to me that some heretic has maliciously affixed my name to his own writings, grieving your Rectitude,[4] and causing you to utter that speech. Surely, not because of my writings[5] against those who dared to say that God the Son was unlike in substance to God the Father, or against those who blasphemously said that the Holy Spirit was a thing created and made, would you permit yourself to bring forward this reproach, you who have taken part in those great and famous argumentations for the sake of right doctrine. But, you yourself would free us of this anxiety, if you would be willing to declare frankly the matters which have moved you to such anger against us.

26. To Caesarius, Brother of Gregory[1]

Thanks be to God, who in your person has manifested His wondrous power by saving you from such a terrible death, and preserving you both for your country and for us, your relatives. It remains for us, indeed, not to be ungrateful nor unworthy of so great a bounty. On the contrary, we are convinced that we should proclaim according to

---

4 *Orthótēta*—a title of address used by St. Basil for both clergymen and laymen.
5 St. Basil's dogmatic works are: *Against Eunomius*, written in 363 or 364 in three books, to which have been added two others probably belonging to Didymus the Blind; and *On the Holy Spirit*, written about 375.

---

1 Caesarius was the youngest brother of St. Gregory of Nazianzus. A narrow escape from death in an earthquake on October 10, 368, had occasioned this letter from St. Basil. Shortly after receiving it, Caesarius retired from the world. This letter was written in 368.

our power the miracles of God, extolling in song this loving kindness which we have experienced in deed, and we should show our gratitude not only by word but also by deed, becoming such as we should be as beneficiaries of the wonders performed in your regard.

And we urge a still better service of God with an increasing and augmenting fear of Him, and an advancement toward perfection, in order that we may prove ourselves prudent stewards of the life for which the goodness of God has preserved us. For, if we all are commanded to present 'ourselves to God as those who have come to life from the dead,'[2] how much more of an obligation is it not for one who has been lifted up from the gates of death? This injunction would be successfully carried out, I believe, if we were willing always to keep the same disposition of mind as we had at the time of danger. For, assuredly, in some degree we realized the vanity of life as well as the unreliability and instability of human affairs, which changed so easily. And, in all likelihood, we felt contrition for our past faults, and promised that, for the future, if we were saved we would serve God with watchful exactitude. If the impending danger of death inspired us with such reflections, I am indeed convinced that, at that time, you arrived at either these or similar considerations.

Consequently, we stand responsible for the payment of an urgent debt. As I am delighted exceedingly with God's gift and am also concerned about the future, I have had the boldness to remind your Perfection of these matters. It rests with you to receive our words aright and kindly, as you have indeed been accustomed to do in our conversations with each other.

---

2 Rom. 6.13.

27 To Eusebius, Bishop of Samosata[1]

When, by the grace of God and the aid of your prayers, I seemed to recover somewhat from my sickness and had gathered strength, the winter came, confining us indoors and compelling us at the same time to remain in our country. In fact, even if we had had a much milder winter than usual, it still would have been sufficient to hinder me not only from traveling during the season, but even from a possible venturing forth from my room.

Yet, it is no small privilege for me to be held worthy of conversing with your Reverence by letters, and to rest in the anticipation of your replies. Should the season permit it, however, and the span of life for us remain unbroken, and the famine not make our journey impracticable, with the help of your prayers we would quickly fulfill our desires. And if on our arrival we should find you at home, we would in all leisure enjoy the benefit of your treasured wisdom.

28. A Letter of Condolence to the Church of Neo-Caesarea[1]

Truly, that which has befallen you demanded our presence, that we might pay to the full with you, our closest friends, the honors due to a blessed man, and might share with you, at the sight of your greater sorrow, the dejection caused by

---

[1] This is the first of twenty-two letters addressed by St. Basil to his lifelong friend, Eusebius, Bishop of Samosata (about 260 miles from Caesarea), between 360 and 373. Cf. Theodoret, *Ecc. Hist.* 4.15 and 5.4. It is of no importance except as one of the numerous letters testifying to St. Basil's almost continual state of ill health. It was written in the spring of 368; cf. Schäfer, *op. cit.* 34.

---

[1] This letter is assumed to have been written at the death of Musonius, Bishop of Neo-Caesarea, of whom St. Basil speaks in Letter 210. It was written in the spring of 368; cf. Schäfer, *loc. cit.*

your misfortune, and, also, that we might with you make necessary plans. But, since many things prevented our meeting in person, our only recourse was to share the present sorrows with you by letter.

The remarkable endowments of the man, which especially caused us to consider that his loss was unendurable, could not be enumerated within the limits of a letter; besides, it is untimely to bring forward a discourse on the great number of his noble deeds, so prostrate is our soul with grief. For, what deed of his is such that it would either escape our memory or be considered worthy of being passed over in silence? Yet, to tell them all at one time would be impossible, and to mention them in part would, I fear, be a betrayal of the truth. A man has departed this life, one who has conspicuously surpassed all those about him in all human virtues, a mainstay of his country, an ornament of the churches, a pillar and support of truth, a solid foundation of faith in Christ, a sure protector of his friends, a most invincible foe of his opponents, a guardian of the laws of the Fathers, and an enemy to innovations. He showed in himself the ancient characteristics of the Church, fashioning the church under his charge according to its ancient constitution as after some sacred pattern, so that his associates seemed to live with those who shone like stars two hundred years ago and more.

Thus, the man brought forth nothing of his own nor any discovery of a more recent mind but, according to the blessing of Moses, he knew how to bring forth from the innermost goodly treasure of his heart 'the oldest of the old and the old apart from the new coming on.'[2] Thus, he was deemed worthy of precedence in the assemblies of the bishops, not because of age but by common consent he enjoyed the first place, being above all in the age of his wisdom. And for the

---
2 Cf. Lev. 26.10.

measure of the value of such leading, no one who looks upon you need search further. For, you alone of all, or certainly, among the few we know, spent a life unshaken by the waves under his pilotage in the midst of such a great storm and stress of affairs. In fact, the squalls of heretical gusts which bring drownings and shipwreck to changeable souls did not affect you. And grant that they may never touch them, O Master of all, who didst give the favor of tranquillity in the highest degree to Gregory,[3] Thy servant, who from the beginning made firm the foundation of the Church.

Do not you yourselves lose that tranquillity in this present time, and do not, by lamenting excessively and by giving yourselves up to sadness, afford the opportunity of constraining you to those lying in wait. But, if it is absolutely necessary to lament (which I, indeed, do not say, lest in this respect we be like those who have no hope[4]), do you, if it seems best, appoint a leader for yourselves and in a more orderly manner bewail with him the sad event as a funeral chorus.

Furthermore, even if this man did not reach extreme old age, yet as far as regards the period of his charge over you, he did not have an incomplete life. And he was united with his body long enough to manifest his strength of soul in his sufferings. Perchance, some one of you may assume that time brings on an increase of fellow feeling and an augmentation of love, and that no occasion of satiety comes to the long experienced, so that you feel the loss more deeply in proportion to the length of time in which you have enjoyed his kindness. Yet, to the pious, even the shadow of a just body is worthy of all honor. Would that many of you were of this opinion! I say myself that you must not be negligent regarding him, but I advise you to bear your grief with moderation. At all

---
[3] Gregory Thaumaturgus.
[4] Cf. 1 Thess. 4.13.

events, nothing that can be said by those lamenting the loss is unknown to me.

A tongue is silent, one that flooded our ears like a torrent, and a heart, whose depth hitherto no one was able to sound, now more unsubstantial than a dream, humanly speaking, has flown away. Who could more keenly foresee the future than he? Who else, of such a firm and steadfast disposition of soul as he, was able to accomplish his tasks more swiftly than the lightning? O city afflicted already by many calamities, but, in truth, by none so injured in the very vitals of its life! How your ornament has faded. The church has become mute, the assemblies are sad of countenance, the sacred council longs for its leader. The mystical doctrines await an interpreter; sons, their father; old men, their companion; magistrates, their leader; the people, their champion; those lacking livelihood, their foster father. All call upon him, each in his own affliction and with his own appropriate name, and each raises a lament suitable and proper to himself.

But, whither is my speech carried by the comfort of tears? Shall we not recover from our sorrow? Shall we not be masters of ourselves? Shall we not look to our common Master, who has permitted each of His saints to minister to his own generation, recalling him to Himself again at the proper moment? Now, in the present circumstances, be mindful of his words who always, when he had called you to an assembly, gave express orders to you, saying: 'Beware of the dogs, beware of the evil workers.'[5] The dogs are many. Why do I say dogs? Of a truth, they are fierce wolves, concealing their deception under the appearance of sheep, and scattering the flock of Christ throughout the whole world. Against these you, under the care of a watchful shepherd, must be on your guard. To seek him is your duty when you have purified

---

5 Phil. 3.2.

your souls of all contention and ambition. But to reveal him is the work of the Lord, who from the time of Gregory, the great leader of your church, until this blessed man, has given one after another, always fitting them together as precious stones into a setting, and so has favored you with the wondrous beauty of your church. Therefore, we must not despair of their successors. The Lord knows His own, and He may lead into your midst those, perhaps, whom we do not expect.

Although I wished long since to bring my words to an end, the grief in my heart does not permit it. But I conjure you, by the Fathers, by the true Faith, and by this blessed man, to rouse your souls, each one judging as his own the present concerns and considering that he will have the first benefit, whatever the outcome of the affair may be. Do not thrust off to a neighbor the care of the public interests, as generally happens, for then, since each one in his own mind regards the matters as of no importance, all through their negligence unconsciously draw upon themselves a personal evil.

Accept these words with all good will, either as the expression of your neighbors' sympathy, or of the fellowship of those who share the same faith, or even, as is truer, of the fellowship of those obeying the law of love and shunning the danger of silence. Be persuaded that you are our glory, just as we also are yours, till the day of the Lord, and that through the shepherd that will be given you we shall be either still more closely united with you in the bonds of love or be subjected to a complete separation. May this never happen! And by the grace of God it will not; nor would I myself now speak anything offensive. But, this we wish you to know, that, even if we did not have this blessed man co-operating with us for the peace of the churches on account of certain preconceptions, as he himself declared to us, nevertheless, with God as my witness and also those men who have had experience of us, we declare that on no occasion did we fail in our agreement in doctrine and in our summons to him as a partner of the contests against the heretics.

29. *A Letter of Condolence to the Church of Ancyra*[1]

The distressing report of your sad misfortune shocked us for a long time into silence. But, since we have somewhat recovered from the speechlessness which we suffered as do men who have been struck deaf by a mighty burst of thunder, we cannot, in the midst of our mourning over the occurrence, refrain from sending you a letter. We do this, not so much for your consolation (for what words could ever be found that would be able to heal such a great affliction), but to reveal to you by this message, as far as is possible, the grief of our hearts, for which we would need, indeed, the lamentations of Jeremias or of some other blessed man who has bitterly bewailed a tremendous calamity.

In truth, a man, the pillar and support of the Church, has fallen, or, rather, having gone from us, has been raised up to a blessed life. Now, there is no slight chance that many, having this prop snatched from under them, may fall, and that the corruption of some may become manifest. A mouth has been closed which impartially spoke frankly and graciously for the edification of the brethren. Gone are the counsels of a mind which truly moved in God. O how frequently (for I must accuse myself) have I been indignant with him, because, being wholly absorbed in his desire 'to depart and be with Christ,' he did not prefer for our sakes

---

[1] The death of Athanasius, Bishop of Ancyra, called forth this letter of consolation. It was written in the spring of 368; cf. Schäfer, *loc. cit.*

'to stay on in the flesh.'² To whom for the future can we entrust the cares of the churches? Whom can we take as a sharer of our sorrows and of our joys? O terrible and miserable loneliness! How truly have we become like to a pelican of the wilderness!³

But, assuredly, the members of the Church joined as with one soul under his leadership and bound together into a union of affection and true fellowship are both firmly preserved by those bonds of peace in a spiritual union, and will always be thus protected, if God bestows upon us this grace —that the works that blessed soul undertook for the churches of God remain firm and immovable. However, there is no slight danger that, because of some chance contention, strifes and contentions may spring up again at the election of the new leader and overturn at once all past labor.

30. To Eusebius, Bishop of Samosata[1]

If I should enumerate, one after another, all the causes which have kept me at home until the present time, even though I was exceedingly eager to visit your Reverence, I would produce a story of interminable length. I omit mention of my continual illnesses, of the burden of the winter season, and of the constant succession of business affairs, which are well known and are already familiar to your Perfection. But, now, because of my sins, I have been bereft of the only consolation which I have had in this life, my mother.[2] And do not smile because at my age I lament my

---
2 Cf. Phil. 1.23.24.
3 Cf. Ps. 102.7.

1 This letter was written in the summer of 368; Schäfer, *loc. cit.*
2 St. Emmelia.

orphanhood, but pardon me for not bearing patiently the separation from a soul incomparable among those left behind. Again, therefore, my illness has recurred, and again I am confined to my bed, sorely distressed by my utter weakness, and momentarily all but expecting the appointed end of life.

Further, the churches are afflicted in much the same manner as my body, no good hope dawning upon their affairs that are constantly sinking to a lower level. In the meantime, however, Neo-Caesarea and Ancyra seem to have found successors to the departed and so far they have remained calm. At least, those plotting against us[3] have not been allowed, up to the present time, to do anything comparable to their wrath and bitterness. The reason for this we openly attribute to your intercessions for the churches. Therefore, do not grow weary of praying and importuning God for the churches. Salute with many greetings those deemed worthy to assist your Holiness.[4]

31. To Eusebius, Bishop of Samosata[1]

The famine has not yet released us from its grasp. Therefore, we must remain in the city both for the purpose of distributing aid[2] and for showing compassion for those in affliction. For this reason, I am not able even now to share the journey with my most revered[3] brother Hypatius, to

---

3 I.e., St. Basil and his church.
4 *Hosiótēti*—a title generally used by St. Basil only in addressing bishops.

---

1 This letter was written in the autumn of 368; cf. Schäfer, *loc. cit.*
2 Cf. Letter 91, in which the Eastern bishops count among the evils in their churches the appropriation by officials of funds destined for the relief of the poor.
3 *Aedesimōtátōi*—a title of distinction applied by St. Basil to both clergymen and laymen.

whom I have the right to give this name, not only as a title of respect, but because of the natural relationship existing between us, for we are of the same blood.

Your Honor is not unaware of the nature of the illness he suffers. It grieves us that he has been deprived of all hope of relief, since those who have the gift of healing have not been able to give him any alleviation with their accustomed remedies. Therefore, he again implores the aid of your prayers, and we, too, urge you to intercede for him in your usual manner, both because of your own compassion for the sick and for our sake who are interceding for him, and indeed, if possible, summon to yourself the most pious of the brothers, so that treatment may be procured for him under your very eyes. If this is impossible, then be so kind as to send him forward with letters and recommendations.

32. To the Master Sophronius[1]

Our brother Gregory,[2] the bishop, dearly beloved of God,[3] is sharing the benefit of these times. For he, also, in common with everyone else, suffers the buffetings of successive slanders

---

1 Sophronius was a native of Cappadocia and a school companion of St. Basil and St. Gregory, who became very prominent in the civil affairs of the country. In 365 he was appointed prefect of Constantinople as a reward for warning the Emperor Valens of the attempted usurpation by Procopius; cf. Amm. Marc. 25.9. He is known chiefly from the letters of St. Basil and St. Gregory, who were continually invoking his aid for various persons; cf. Letters 76, 96, 177, 180, 192, 272; also Greg. Naz., Letters 21, 22, 29, 37, 39, 135. This letter was written in 369.

2 St. Gregory of Nazianzus is meant here. As he was not a bishop at this time, Maran suggests that *ho episcopos* is a marginal gloss which crept into the text. This cannot refer to Gregory the Elder, because he did not adopt the monastic life.

3 *Theophiléstatos*—a title of distinction which St. Basil uses for bishops only.

showered upon him like unexpected blows. For, men who do not fear God and who are, perhaps, hard pressed by the greatness of their troubles now insolently threaten him on the ground that Caesarius[4] borrowed money from them.

The loss of the money is, indeed, not serious, for he long ago learned to despise riches; but, since the executors had received very little of Caesarius' wealth, his estate having fallen into the hands of slaves and of men no better in character than slaves, who freely divided among themselves the articles of most value, they, the executors, had very little left, and believed that this little belonged to no one. They, therefore, both of their own deliberate choice and because of the request of the departed, immediately used it for those in need. For, it is reported that he said when dying: 'I want the poor to have all my possessions'; therefore, as administrators of the will of Caesarius, they distributed this property with all expediency. And now, both the poverty of a Christian and the continual haranguings of demagogues encompass him.[5] So, it occurred to me to give an explanation to your Honor, so worthy of all praise, in order that you might discuss with the Prefect of the Treasury the matter of a reasonable solution concerning him, and at one and the same time show esteem for the man whom you have known of old, glorify the Lord who receives as done for Him whatever is done for His servants, and honor us, your special friend,

---
4 Gregory's brother; cf Letter 26. Caesarius had died, bequeathing all his property to the poor and leaving St. Gregory as executor. However, servants looted the house, so that St. Gregory found a comparatively small amount of money. Furthermore, a number of persons presented themselves shortly afterwards as creditors of the estate, and their claims, through incapable of proof, were paid. Others then came forward until no more were admitted. Then a lawsuit was threatened. To put an end to all this, St. Basil wrote this letter to Sophronius, seeking his aid. Cf. Greg. Naz., Letter 29.
5 I.e., St. Gregory, the priest, must deal with creditors and claimants.

and also might in your great wisdom devise a means of relief from these insulting and intolerable disturbances.

Surely, no one is so ignorant of Gregory as to suspect anything unseemly on his part, such as scheming in this affair because he was fond of money. The proof of his liberality is obvious. He has gladly given up the remainder of Caesarius' property to the Treasury, which possessions have been taken over, and the advocate of the Treasury answers those attacking him and demands proofs, for we ourselves are unfitted to attend to such matters. Your Excellency may ascertain that, as long as it was possible, no one went away from him without obtaining what he wished, but each one carried away without difficulty what he sought. As a result, many are sorry that they did not ask for more in the first place, and this has made the number of slanderers especially large. For, keeping in mind the example of the first recipients, one false claimant after another appears.

We urge your Dignity,[6] therefore, to take a stand against all these abuses, to hold back the flood, as it were, and entirely to break off the succession of evils. But, you are well aware of how you can aid in this matter, so that you need not wait for us to teach you the manner; because of our inexperience in world affairs we are ignorant in this case, also, of how we may obtain deliverance. Therefore, be yourself the counselor and administrator, devising, through your own great wisdom, the form of the aid.

---

6 *Semnótēta*—a title of address used by St. Basil for both clergymen and laymen.

33. To Aburgius[1]

Who, indeed, knows as well as you how to honor an old friendship, to revere virtue, and to share the sufferings of those in distress? So, when troubles, unendurable in any event, but especially contrary to his character, overtook our brother Gregory,[2] the bishop dearly beloved of God, we thought it best to flee to your protection and to try to obtain from you deliverance from these vexations. For, it is an intolerable situation that one to whom it is not natural nor desirable should be compelled to plead his own case in court, and that one who is poor should be importuned for money, and that one who had long ago decided to spend his life in retirement should be drawn into court and should be harangued by demagogues. Now, your own prudence should decide whether it will be useful to discuss the matter with the Prefect of the Treasury or with some other magistrate.

34. To Eusebius, Bishop of Samosata[1]

How can we be silent in the present circumstances? Or, since we are not able to endure it patiently, how can we speak adequately of the existing conditions, so that our utterance will not be like a groaning but rather like a lamenta-

---

[1] Aburgius was an influential lay compatriot of St. Basil, upon whom the latter frequently called for aid; cf. Letters 75, 147, 175, 196 (which was also attributed to St. Gregory of Nazianzus), and 304. The date of this letter is 369.

[2] As the difficulties referred to are those mentioned in the previous letter, it is clearly St. Gregory of Nazianzus, and not St. Gregory of Nyssa, who is meant. The words *tòn epíscopon* crept into the text from the marginal notes.

---

[1] This letter was written in the autumn of 369; cf. Schäfer, *loc. cit.*

tion sufficiently evidencing the seriousness of the evil? For, even Tarsus[2] is lost to us. And this is not the only calamity, although it is unbearable. Nay, more bitter than this is the fact that a city so great and so conveniently situated that it links together within itself the Isaurians, the Cilicians, the Cappadocians, and the Syrians has been so lost through the extreme folly of one or two men, while you delayed, and planned, and looked at one another. Therefore, in imitation of doctors (and I generally have a large number of illustrations of this kind at hand because of the illness which is ever with me) who, whenever the intensity of the pain is excessive, produce for the sick insensibility to suffering, it would be an excellent practice in the case of our own souls to join in prayer for insensibility to evils, so as not to be oppressed by intolerable pains. Nevertheless, although we are in such affliction, we experience one consolation—when looking to your Clemency[3] the thought and memory of you calms the grief of our soul. For, just as to our eyes some relief is afforded by turning back to the blues and greens after having looked intently at brilliant objects, so also to our souls the memory of your gentleness and graciousness is like some gentle touch effacing the pain, especially when we consider that you have fulfilled your duty as completely as is in your power. By these means you have adequately shown to us men, if we judge the matter reasonably, that nothing has been lost through your fault. Great, too, is the reward which you have won from God for yourself because of your

---

2 Sylvanus, Metropolitan of Tarsus, had died, and through the neglect of the bishops his successor was an Arian. However, many of the priests remained orthodox and in friendly communication with St. Basil. Cf. Letter 114.

3 *Hēmerótēta*—a title of address used by St. Basil for clergymen and laymen.

zeal for that which is honorable. May the Lord graciously preserve you to us and to His churches for the improvement of our lives and the amendment of our souls, and may He deem us worthy of the benefit of seeing you again.

35. *Without an Address, in Behalf of Leontius*[1]

I have already written to you and shall often write even more concerning many persons on the ground that they are kinsmen of mine. For, the needy are always with us, nor are we able to deny them a favor. Besides, no one is dearer to me nor more able to give me relief by his prosperity than my most revered brother, Leontius. So, treat his household as if you were coming to me myself, not in the state of poverty in which I now am with God, but as though I had obtained some wealth and was possessed of lands. For, it is evident you would not make me a poor man, but would guard my present possessions, or even augment my wealth. This, then, we entreat you to do in the case of the household of the aforementioned man. And for this you will receive from me the customary reward—a prayer to the holy God for your labors—a reward for your honesty, and goodness, and forestalling care of those in need.

---

1 Written before St. Basil's episcopate, asking that justice be done in the assessments to Leontius, the same to whom Letter 21 was addressed.

36. Without an Address, for Assistance[1]

It has long been known to your Nobility, I think, that the presbyter of this place is my foster brother. What else, then, must I say to persuade your Excellency to look kindly upon him and to aid him in his affairs? Indeed, if you love me, as you assuredly do, then clearly you will wish to relieve with all means in your power those whom I love more than myself. What, then, is it that I request? That the assessment[2] formerly given be maintained for him. For, he indeed labors not a little in rendering service to us for our subsistence, because we, as you yourself know, possess nothing of our own, but are aided by the resources of our friends and relatives. Therefore, look upon the household of my brother as mine, or, rather, as your own; and, in return for the good done for him, God will provide for both you and your household and your whole family His customary assistance. But, realize that it is my special concern that this man suffer no mistreatment in the assessment.

37. Without an Address, for a Foster Brother[1]

I am already viewing with suspicion the number of my letters. Indeed, against my will and because I cannot endure the annoyance of people begging us, I am forced to cry out. Nevertheless, I write, since I can devise no other method of escape than to give letters each time to those asking for them.

---

1 Similar to the preceding and written at the same time.
2 Cf. Justin, *Apol.* 1.34.

---

1 Similar to the two preceding and of the same date.

Consequently, I fear lest, since many are carrying letters to you, this brother may be considered one of the many. I acknowledge that I have many friends and kinsmen in my native land and that I myself am placed in the position of a father[2] because of this dignity to which the Lord has appointed me. But, I have only this one foster brother, the son of my nurse, and I pray that his household in which I was reared may continue under the same terms of assessment as before, in order that the presence of your Modesty, which benefits all, may not become an occasion of grief for him. However, I am, even at the present time, still supported by this household, since I have nothing of my own but am sustained by the resources of my loved ones; therefore, I entreat you to have consideration for the family in which I was brought up, inasmuch as you are preserving the necessities for my subsistence. And, in return for these favors, may God deem you worthy of eternal rest.

At any rate, I wish this fact, the truest of all, to be known to your Modesty, that the majority of his slaves accrued to him from us, as a recompense provided by our parents for our sustenance. Yet, the recompense is not altogether a gift, but a loan for life. Therefore, if he is involved in any serious trouble concerning them,[3] he may return them to us and we shall become again, in another manner, liable for payments and taxes.

---
2 Maran considers this to refer to his presbyterate, not to his episcopate.
3 I.e., if the assessment is increased because of the slaves, the man may return them to St. Basil, who will himself then be responsible for the increased taxes.

38. To His Brother Gregory, concerning the Difference between Substance and Person[1]

Since, at present, many persons treating of the doctrines relating to the mystery [of the Trinity] make no distinction between the general term of 'substance' and the word 'person,' they fall into the same presumption, thinking that it makes no difference whether they say 'substance' or 'person.' For this reason, too, some of those who accept such expressions without examination are satisfied to speak of 'one person' in God, just as they say 'one substance'; contrariwise, those admitting the three persons believe that they must, because of this admission, declare also the division of substances into the same number. Therefore, in order that you may not be led to embrace similar errors, I have written a short explanation of this as a reminder for you. Now, to put it briefly, the meaning of these words is as follows.

Some nouns denominating several objects and objects differing in number have a more or less general signification, as 'man.' For, in saying 'man,' a person by means of the name points out the common nature but does not describe by this word a definite man, one specifically known by that name. For, 'man' is no more Peter than Andrew, John, or James. Therefore, the common quality of that which is signified, since it refers likewise to all those grouped under the same

---

[1] This letter, an important explanation of the difference between *ousía* (substance) and *hypóstasis* (person), is also found among the works of St. Gregory of Nyssa addressed to his brother, St. Peter of Sebaste. However, both from manuscript evidence and for stylistic reasons, as well as from the fact that it was referred to in the Council of Chalcedon as a letter of St. Basil's, it has in general been assigned to him, and no modern scholar has questioned its Basilian authorship. It was written either in 369 or 370. Cf. Letter 8 n. 1, for the definitions of the terminology employed by St. Basil in speaking of the Blessed Trinity.

name, has need of a specific characterization through which we shall recognize, not man in general, but Peter or John.

Other nouns have a more particular meaning through which is considered not the common nature in the object indicated but its individual quality, and this distinctive quality it does not share with other objects of the same nature, as Paul or Timothy. For, such a word refers now not to the common nature but, departing from the collective significance, it sets forth through the names used a meaning of certain definite objects. Whenever, therefore, in the case of two or more objects of the same nature, as Paul and Silvanus and Timothy, a name is sought for the substance of man, a person will not give one word for substance in the case of Paul, another in the case of Silvanus, and still another in the case of Timothy; but, whatever words portray the substance of Paul, these will also be proper for the others. Moreover, they who are designated by the same name with regard to their substance are consubstantial with each other. Whenever anyone, after having learned the common characteristic, turns his consideration to individual qualities through which one thing is distinguished from another, no longer will the cognitive name of each one agree in all respects with that of the others, even if in certain points it is found to have the common characteristic.

This, therefore, is our explanation. That which is spoken of in the specific sense is signified by the word 'person' [*hypóstasis*]. For, because of the indefiniteness of the term, he who says 'man' has introduced through our hearing some vague idea, so that, although the nature is manifested by the name, that which subsists in the nature and is specifically designated by the name is not indicated. On the other hand, he who says 'Paul' has shown the subsistent nature of the object signified by the name. This, then, is the 'person' [*hypó-*

stasis]. It is not the indefinite notion of 'substance' [*ousía*], which creates no definite image because of the generality of its significance, but it is that which, through the specific qualities evident in it, restricts and defines in a certain object the general and indefinite, as is often done in many places in Scripture and especially in the story of Job.[2] In the beginning of the narrative about him, the general term 'man' is used; then, immediately, that thought is limited to what is particular by adding 'a certain.' However, as to the description of the substance nothing is said, since it makes no contribution to the proposed object of the discourse; but the 'certain' one is characterized by specific marks, such as situation, traits of character, and the external characteristics which serve to differentiate him and set him apart from the general notion. Consequently, by all these means—the name, the place, the particular qualities of soul, and the exterior characteristics seen in him—a clear description is made of the man whose story is given. On the other hand, if the meaning of substance were being given, there would have been no mention of the aforesaid matters in the explanation of its nature. In fact, the term used would have been the same as in mentioning Baldad the Sauhite, Sophar the Minnaean, and each of the other men referred to in the story.[3]

Accordingly, you will not err if you transfer to divine doctrines this principle of differentiation between substance and person which you have recognized in their relation to human affairs. Whatever your judgment suggests and however it suggests as to the essence of the Father (for it is im-

---

2 Cf. Job 1.1: 'There was a man in the land of Hus, whose name was Job, and that man was simple and upright, and fearing God, and avoiding evil.'
3 Cf. Job 2.11: 'Now when Job's three friends heard all the evil that had befallen him, they came every one from his own place, Eliphaz the Themanite, and Baldad the Suhite, and Sophar the Naamathite.

possible to superimpose any definite concept upon the immaterial because of our persuasion that it is above every concept), this you will hold for the Son and likewise for the Holy Spirit. For, the term 'Being Uncreated and Incomprehensible' is one and the same in meaning regarding the Father and the Son and the Holy Spirit. For, one is not more incomprehensible and uncreated, and the other less. But, since it is necessary, in the case of the Trinity, to keep a clear distinction [of persons] by means of individualizing marks, we shall not include in the determining individual mark that which is observed to be common, such as the attribute I mention of being uncreated or of being beyond all apprehension, or any other such. We shall seek only the qualities by which the concept of each shall be clearly and sharply distinguished from that concept obtained when they are contemplated together.

Therefore, it seems well to me to follow up the discussion in this way. Everything good which comes to us from the divine power we say is the action of grace working all things in all, as the Apostle says: 'But all these things are the work of one and the same Spirit, who divides to everyone according as he will.'[4] Moreover, when we inquire if the abundant blessings thus accruing to the worthy have their source in the Holy Spirit alone, again we are guided by the Scripture to the belief that the Only-begotten God is the author and cause of the abundance of blessings wrought in us through the Spirit. For, that all things were made through Him and stand together in Him, we have been taught by Holy Scripture.[5] Furthermore, when we have been lifted up to that conception, again being led on by the divinely inspired guidance, we are taught that through this power all

---
4 1 Cor. 12.11.
5 Cf. John 1.3; also, Col. 1.17.

things are brought from non-existence into existence, but that is not done indeed even by this power without a beginning. Still, there is a certain power subsisting without generation and without beginning, which is the principle of the principle of all things which exist. For, from the Father is the Son, through whom are all things and with whom the Holy Spirit is always inseparably associated. In fact, it is not possible for one not previously enlightened by the Spirit to arrive at a conception of the Son. Since, therefore, the Holy Spirit from whom all the abundance of benefits pours out upon the creature is linked with the Son with whom He is inseparably comprehended, and has His existence dependent on the Father as a principle, from whom He also proceeds, this He has as the distinguishing mark of the individuality of His person, namely, that He is made known after the Son and with the Son and that He subsists from the Father.

Now, the Son, who through Himself and with Himself makes known the Spirit which proceeds from the Father and who alone shines forth as the Only-begotten from the Unbegotten Light, shares in common with the Father or with the Holy Spirit none of the peculiar marks by which the Son is known, but He alone is recognized by the marks just mentioned. Furthermore, the supreme God alone has a certain special mark of His person by which He is known, namely, that He is the Father and subsists from no other principle; and, again, through this mark He Himself is also individually recognized. On this account we say that in the general quality of substance the distinguishing marks observed in the Trinity through which the individuality of the persons as handed down in the faith is presented are distinct and not shared, since each person is comprehended separately by its own characteristic marks. As a consequence, through the marks just mentioned, the distinction of persons is attained, but, regarding the attribute of infinity and incomprehensibility, and that of being uncreated and of being circumscribed within no space, and in all other such attributes, there is no difference in the life-producing nature—I mean in the case of the Father and of the Son and of the Holy Spirit—but there is observed a certain constant and uninterrupted sharing in them. Through whatever thoughts one apprehends the majesty of any one of the persons which we believe to be in the Blessed Trinity, through the same thoughts he will advance in precisely the same way, viewing the glory in the Father and in the Son and in the Holy Spirit, since the intelligence does not tread on a gap between the Father and the Son and the Holy Spirit. For, there is nothing which intrudes itself between these persons, and nothing else subsisting beyond the divine nature that is able to separate it from itself through the interposition of something not belonging to it, nor is there a void due to any space lacking person, which causes the harmony of the divine substance to gape open, severing the continuity by the insertion of the void. But, he who has apprehended the Father has both apprehended Him in Himself and has also included the Son in the concept. And he who has received the Son has not separated the Holy Spirit from the Son, but, consistently according to the order and conjointly according to their nature, he has imaged to himself his belief, which is a blending at the same time of the three persons. And he who has mentioned only the Spirit has embraced with It by this admission Him from whom the Spirit proceeds. And since He is the Spirit of Christ and from God, as Paul[6] says, just as he who has grasped one end of a chain also draws along with him the other end, so he who

---

6 Cf. Rom. 8.9: 'But if anyone does not have the Spirit of Christ, he does not belong to Christ.'

draws the Spirit, as the Prophet[7] says, through Him draws along both the Son and the Father. And if he would truly apprehend the Son, he will hold Him on both sides, on one, indeed, bringing His Father along with Him, and on the other His own Spirit. For, neither will it be possible for Him who exists eternally in the Father to be cut off from the Father, nor will He who works all things in the Spirit ever be parted from His own Spirit. Similarly, he who receives the Father also virtually receives along with Him both the Son and the Spirit. For, it is impossible in any way to think of a severance or a division, so that the Son is considered apart from the Father, or the Spirit is separated from the Son; but there is found in them a certain inexpressible and incomprehensible union and distinction, since neither the difference of the persons breaks the continuity of the nature, nor the common attribute of substance dissolves the individual character of their distinctive marks. But, do not wonder if we say that the same thing is both joined and separated and if, as in a riddle, we contrive something both strange and incredible, a conjoined separation and a separated union. Nay, unless one listens to the explanation contentiously and haughtily, it is possible for him to find such a condition in the things which are perceived.

Receive my explanation, indeed, as an illustration and a shadow of the truth, not as the truth itself of the matters. For, it is impossible that what is observed in illustrations be capable of exact adaptation to that for which the need of illustration is admitted. Why, then, do we say that that which is separated and at the same time united is inferred by analogy from the things which appear to our senses? In spring, at various times you have beheld the brilliance of the

---

7 A misinterpretation, perhaps intentional, of Ps. 119.131: *'eilkusa pneûma,'*—'I drew breath' or 'I panted.'

bow in the clouds—I mean the arc which common speech is accustomed to call the 'rainbow.' Those experienced in these matters say that it is formed at a time when some moisture is mixed in with the air. The force of the wind presses into rain the damp and thick vapors which have already become cloudy. And they say that the rainbow is formed in this way. When the sunbeam stealing obliquely through the compact and opaque cloudy mass rests its circle veritcally on some cloud, there is produced, as it were, a certain bending and return of the light upon itself, since the brightness is returned in the opposite direction from the moist and gleaming particles. For, since it is the nature of the flame-like sparks, if they fall upon any smooth surface, to be reflected again to themselves, and since the shape of the sun produced by the ray on the moist and smooth particle of the air is circular, the shape of the solar circle necessarily is outlined by the reflected brightness, then, in the air lying around the cloud. Now, this brightness is both continuous with itself and is broken up. For, being of many colors and shapes it is imperceptibly intermingled with the varied hues of the dye, stealing unawares from our eyes the point of contact of the different colors with each other. As a result, between the blue-green and the flame-color, or the flame-color and the purple, or that and the amber, the space which both mixes and separates the two colors cannot be discerned. For, when the rays of all colors are seen at the same time they are distinct, and yet, by concealing the points of their contact with each other, they also elude our scrutiny, so that it is impossible to find out how far the red color or the green of the radiance extends, and from what point it begins to be no longer such as it is perceived in the distinct parts.[8]

---

8 St. Basil seems to be ignorant of the order of the colors of the spectrum. But the Greek terms for the colors are vague, and no one of the equivalents used in the translation is really certain.

Accordingly, as in the illustration we clearly discern the different colors and yet cannot detect by observation the lines of separation of one from the other, consider, I pray, that it is possible also to draw inferences concerning the divine dogmas, to reason that the specific qualities of the persons, like any one of the brilliant colors which appear in the rainbow, flash in each of those persons which we believe to be in the Holy Trinity, but that no distinction is observed in the peculiar character of the nature of one as compared with the other. Yet, in the common property of the substance, the distinguishing individual qualities of each shine forth. For, even there in the illustration it was one substance which flashed forth that many-colored light, the one which was reflected through the solar ray, but the brilliance of the bow which appeared was of many kinds. Reason also teaches us through the created object not to feel disturbed in the discussions about doctrine when, falling upon facts hard to understand, we become dizzy at the acceptance of the matters discussed. For, just as in the case of those things which are seen by the eyes, experience seemed better than a theory of causation, so also, in the case of the dogmas which transcend our comprehension, faith is mightier than the direct apprehension through reasoning, since it teaches both that which is separated in person and that which is united in substance. Since, therefore, our discussion has considered on the one hand that which is common to the persons of the Blessed Trinity, and on the other, what is peculiar to each, we may say that the substance is the common attribute, but the person is the specific quality of each.

Yet, some may think that the doctrine of the person as thus set forth does not agree with the thought expressed in the writings of the Apostle, in which he says concerning the Lord that He is the 'brightness of his glory and the image of his person.'⁹ For, if we have explained that 'person' is the combination of the specific qualities in each [member of the Trinity] and it is admitted, as in the case of the Father, that that which is observed of an individualizing nature is something through which He alone is known, and in the same manner a like belief is held concerning the Only-begotten, how does the Scripture in this passage ascribe the name of 'person' to the Father alone, and say that the Son is a form 'of his person,' characterized not by His own, but by the distinguishing marks of the Father? For, if the person is the special sign of the existence of each member and, further, it is admitted that being 'unbegotten' is peculiar to the Father, but the Son has been formed by the attributes peculiar to the Father, then no longer, as it seems, does it remain to the Father exclusively to be called the 'Unbegotten' in the sense of Himself alone, if, indeed, the existence of the Only-begotten is characterized by the property peculiar to the Father.

But, we may say this, that the expression fulfills in this passage another purpose of the Apostle, and looking toward that aim he used these words, saying: 'the brightness of his glory and the image of his person.' Now, if one carefully considers it, he will not find that it conflicts with the statement made by us, but that it supports the meaning of a certain particular idea. For, the statement of the Apostle does not elaborate on how the persons are distinguished from each other by the marks appearing in them, but how the true sonship and the inseparable and intimate relationship of the Son with the Father is apprehended. For, he did not say 'who being the glory of the Father,' although this is the truth, but, neglecting this as being already admitted, in teaching us to consider not one form of glory in the Father and

---

9 Cf. Heb. 1.3., where St. Paul uses the word *'hypóstasis'* (person)

another in the Son, he defines the glory of the Only-begotten as 'the brightness of the glory of the Father,' establishing from the illustration of the light the inseparable inclusion of the Son in our idea of the Father. For, as the brightness is from the flame, and not, indeed, a radiance coming after the flame, but at the same time that the flame is enkindled the light also flashes forth, so also he wishes the Son to be considered as from the Father, not, indeed, for the Only-begotten to be separated by some dimensional interval from the existence of the Father, but for that which is from the principle always to be understood together with the principle.

Therefore, in the same manner, as if explaining the idea set forth before, he says: 'and the image of his person,' guiding us by means of illustrations pertaining to the body to the perception of the invisible. For, although the body exists entirely in form, there is one meaning of 'form' and another of 'body,' and no one giving the definition of either of these would make use of one definition for the other. However, even if by reason you could separate the figure from the body, nature does not admit the separation, but the one is considered conjointly with the other. And so the Apostle thinks that, even though the doctrine of faith teaches that the difference of persons is unconfused and distinct, nevertheless, it is necessary to present, through his words just quoted, the close connection and, as it were, the congenital union of the Only-begotten with the Father, not because the Only-begotten also does not exist in person[10] but because He does not admit any intervening space in His oneness with the Father. Consequently, he who has looked intently at the image of the Only-begotten through the eyes of his soul also arrives at an

---

10 I.e., not in the sense that the relationship between the Father and Son is merely a figure of speech and that the Father and the Son are not distinct Persons.

understanding of the 'person' of the Father; yet, the individuality observed in them is neither interchanged nor intermingled so that we pretend begottenness as an attribute of the Father and unbegottenness as an attribute of the Son, but so that, if we separate one from the other, which is impossible, we comprehend the remaining one by Himself alone. For, it is impossible, when naming the Son, not to think also of the Father, since this appellation naturally suggests the Father, also.

Since, therefore, he who has seen the Son sees also the Father, as the Lord says in the Gospels,[11] on this account the Apostle asserts that the Only-begotten is 'the image of the person' of the Father. And in order that the thought may be more clearly perceived, we shall also include in our discussion other words of the Apostle in which he says that the Son is an 'image of the invisible God,'[12] and, again, 'an image of his goodness,'[13] not because the image differs from the archetype as far as concerns the meaning of invisibility and goodness, but in order that it may be shown that it is identical with the original although it is something else. For, the meaning of 'image' would not be preserved unless in all respects it would be clearly and exactly similar to the archetype. Certainly, then, he who has perceived the beauty of the image arrives at an understanding of the archetype. And he who has conceived in his mind the 'form,' as it were, of the Son conceives an 'image of his [Father's] person,' in looking at the latter through the former, since he does not behold the unbegottenness of the Father in the representation (for surely, then, the Son would be wholly the same and not some one else), but observing closely the unbegotten beauty in the

---
11 Cf. John 14.9.
12 Col. 1.15.
13 Wisd. 7.26. These words are ascribed to Solomon.

Begotten. For, as he who has noticed in a clean mirror the reflection of a form has a clear knowledge of the face reflected, so he who has learned to know the Son has received in his heart the 'image of his [Father's] person' through the knowledge of the Son. For, all the attributes of the Father are beheld in the Son, and all the attributes of the Son belong also to the Father, since both the whole Son remains in the Father and has the whole Father in Himself.[14] Therefore, the person of the Son becomes, as it were, the form and face of the knowledge of the Father, and the person of the Father is known in the form of the Son, although the individuality observed in them remains for the clear distinction of their persons.[15]

39. Julian to Basil[1]

'Thou comest not as a messenger of war,' the proverb[2] says, but I would add from the comedy,[3] 'O messenger of

---

14 Cf. John 14.10.
15 Thus St. Basil expresses the orthodoxy of the Trinity in one phrase: *mía ousía, treis hypostáseis* (one substance, three persons). Never again in his writings does he use *'hypóstasis'* in its earlier sense as equivalent to *'ousía.'* Cf. Athan., *Orat. contra Arianos.* 3.64 and 4.33.

---

1 The Emperor Julian was a student at Athens when St. Basil was there, but nothing is known of their relations with each other except what has been assumed from this and the two following letters. Letter 39 is found among the letters of the Emperor Julian, but the Basil to whom it is addressed is not St. Basil. It was first introduced among St. Basil's letters by Claude Morel in 1618; it is not contained in any of the manuscripts of letters. Furthermore, it speaks of the recipient as versed in court diplomacy, and St. Basil certainly was not. The date of its composition must be shortly after Julian became emperor, in the winter of 361-362, since at that period alone can it be said that he had any leisure. Cf. Bessières, *op. cit.* 344; for contrary opinion, cf. W. C. Wright, *Julian,* in L.C.L. II xli.
2 Plato, *Legg.* 4.702D; *Phaedr.* 242B.
3 Aristotle, *Plut.* 268.

golden words.' Come, then, prove this by your deeds, and hasten to us, for you will come as a friend to a friend.[4]

Regular and constant occupation in affairs of state seems to be somehow burdensome to those who make it subordinate to their principal interest,[5] but those sharing in my responsibility are, I am convinced, honorable and intelligent, and entirely reliable in all respects; therefore I grant myself some relaxation, so that it is possible even to take a holiday without neglecting anything. For, our life together is not spent in mere court diplomacy—of which I think you have hitherto had experience—through which men, although praising, feel more hatred than they would ever feel against their bitterest enemies. On the contrary, we, who both refute and censure each other with becoming frankness whenever it is necessary, love one another no less than do the closest companions. So, it is possible for us[6] (may there be no envy!), while relaxing, to pursue our studies; and while studying, not to be distressed; and to sleep undisturbed, since, when I am awake, I do not bestir myself for my own sake more, in all probability, than for the sake of everyone else.

I have, perhaps, wearied and overwhelmed you with this idle chatter, being somewhat stupid (for I have been praising myself like Astydamas[7]), but I have sent this letter in order that I may persuade you that your presence, inasmuch as it is that of a sensible man, will be of some advantage to us rather than a waste of time.

Hasten, then, as I have said, and make use of a state

---

4 Cf. Plato, *Menexen.* 247B.
5 Julian is intimating that his first interest is his studies.
6 I.e., to himself, the Emperor.
7 An Athenian tragic poet of the fourth century B.C. He wrote a laudatory inscription to be carved upon a pedestal of a bust of himself which the people had voted in his honor, and Philemon, the poet, gibed him. See Philemon, frag. 190 (Kock).

conveyance.⁸ When you have spent as much time with us as you please, you will be taken by us, as is proper, wherever you wish to go.

40. Julian to Basil¹

Although up to the present time we have shown the gentleness and kindliness natural from childhood, nevertheless we have gathered in all peoples under the sun as our subjects. For, lo! every nation of barbarians as far as the boundaries of the ocean has come, bringing gifts and placing them at our feet, as also have the Sagadares, who live along the Danube,² that comely, parti-colored, beetle-shaped folk, wild in aspect, and unlike human beings in appearance. These at present are prostrate at my feet, promising to do whatever is due to my sovereignty. And not only by this alone am I drawn on, but I must speedily seize the country of the Persians and subdue the renowned Sapor, the grandson of Darius, until he becomes tributary and pays taxes to me. At the same

---

8 The privilege of free transport at the expense of the State, granted to ecclesiastics by Constantine in 314, was revoked by Julian in 362 (*Codex Theodos.* 8.5.12), who reserved to himself the right to make exceptions as a special mark of his favor. Cf. Wright, Introd. to Vol. 3, L.C.L. edition of *Julian*.

1 This letter and the following have been considered unauthentic even from Byzantine times. The manuscript tradition does not support their authenticity; besides, Letter 40 is written to St. Basil as to a person of influence at Caesarea, whereas St. Basil was at that time in seclusion at Pontus, not yet a presbyter; and Letter 41 is, in diction and subject matter, entirely unworthy of St. Basil. Moreover, the two letters form a pair and, if Letter 40 falls, then Letter 41 must go with it. The assumed date is June or July, 362.

2 Julian always uses the name 'Ister' for the Danube; cf. Wright, *op. cit.* III xlii.

time I must despoil the neighboring lands of both the Indians and Saracens, until all these become tributaries and tax-payers, holding second rank to me in my empire.

But you yourself have shown arrogance beyond the capacity of all these, claiming to have put on piety, but covering yourself with shamelessness, everywhere spreading abroad the report that I have become unworthy of the sovereignty of the Romans. Do you not yourself, indeed, know that I am the descendant of that mighty ruler Constantius?

Although we know these things about you, we have not changed in the previous esteem which you and I shared in our youth. But, in a spirit of gentleness, I decree that you send me one thousand pounds of gold to be given while I am on the highway passing through Caesarea, since I am going at great speed to the Persian War. If you do not do this, I am ready to destroy the whole country of Caesarea, to overthrow the beautiful structures erected long ago, and to build throughout the country both temples and statues of the gods, so as to persuade all men to yield to the emperor of the Romans and not to exalt themselves. Therefore, send to me safely by a servant who is faithful to you the gold already referred to, counted out, weighed by scale, steelyard, and balance, and duly measured, then sealed with your signet, so that I, recognizing at length, even though late, the inevitable state of affairs,[3] may be gentle toward you in your failings. But what I have read I have understood and condemned.[4]

---

3 Julian had urgent business—the Persian War—ahead of him. Hence, if he received the money, he would leave Basil free.
4 Cf. last sentence in Letter 41. There is little manuscript authority for either remark.

41. Basil to Julian, in Answer[1]

Inconsequential are the vaunted deeds of your present high fortune. Miserable, also, is your boasted valor directed against us, yet not against us but against yourself. On my part, I shudder whenever I recall that you are invested with the purple and that your unworthy head is adorned with a crown; for all this without piety is not honorable, but renders your reign dishonored. Yet, since you have returned and have become exceedingly great, although, indeed, wicked spirits and those which hate all good raised you to this, you have begun not only to be presumptuous above all human kind, but also to exalt yourself above God, and to mock the Church, the mother and nurse of all, by informing me, the most unworthy of men, that I should despatch to you a thousand pounds of gold.

While the weight of the gold did not astound me, even though it was exceedingly great, still it caused me to weep bitterly at your extraordinarily swift fall. For, I recalled how your Honor and I together had studied the sacred and most excellent literature. We both read the holy and divinely inspired Scriptures, and at that time nothing escaped you. Now, however, you have become disordered in mind, beset by so much pride. You knew before yesterday, most Serene Sir,[3] that we are not ruled by greed for money, but now your letter demands that we send you a thousand pounds of gold. Therefore, be willing, most Serene Sir, to spare us who possess so little that, if we should wish to eat today, there would not be

---

1 Cf. Letter 40 n. 1. For a fuller discussion of the authenticity of Letter 41, cf. Sister Agnes Clare Way, 'The Authenticity of Letter 41 in the Julio-Basilian Correspondence,' *American Journal of Philology* 51 (1930) 67-69.

2 Julian returned to Constantinople from Gaul on Dec. 11, 361, becoming Emperor on the death of Constantius.

enough for us. For the art of cooking is very properly neglected in our house, and the knives of the cooks do not come in contact with blood. Our principal foods, in which lies our abundance, consist of leafy vegetables with very coarse bread and sour wine. As a result, our faculties are not so stupified by gluttony that they direct our actions foolishly.

Lausus, your much admired tribune, loyal to your interests, announced this also to me, that a certain woman approached your Serenity[4] after the loss of her son through poisoning, and that you decreed that poisoners should not be tolerated anywhere,[5] and that, if there were any, they should be executed, or only those should be saved who would combat wild beasts. And this so rightly decreed by you has seemed strange to me, since it is altogether ridiculous that you should attempt to allay such great sufferings with these trivial remedies.[6] For, since you have insulted God, you assume in vain the care of widows and orphans. In fact, the one step is an act of madness and peril, and the other the action of a compassionate and merciful man.

It is a serious matter for us, being but a private citizen, to speak thus to an emperor, but it will seem more grievous for you to speak to God. For, no one will appear as mediator between God and man. Yet, what you have read you have not understood; for, if you understood, you would not have condemned.

---

3 *Galēnótate*—a title of distinction not found in St. Basil's authentic letters.
4 *Galēnótētos*—a title of address not found in St. Basil's authentic letters.
5 Cf. St. Cyprian, Letter 15: '*legibus nostris bene atque utiliter censuistis delatores* non esse.'
6 The Greek word for 'poison' also means 'drugs' or 'remedies.' There seems to be a play on the two meanings.
7 Cf. Soz. 5.18, where the closing words of Letter 40 are attributed to Julian as addressed 'to the bishops,' and the closing words of Letter 41 are ascribed to these bishops in answer to Julian. Cf. also note 4 of the preceding letter.

42. To Chilo, His Pupil[1]

I shall become responsible for your salvation, my true brother, if you willingly accept our counsels as to your line of conduct, especially in those matters wherein you yourself have urged us to advise you. For, many have dared to begin the solitary life, but few, perhaps, have labored to bring it to a worthy end. By no means is the fulfillment in the mere intention, but in the fulfilling we have the fruit of our labors. For those, therefore, who do not hasten toward the accomplishment of their aim and who undertake the life of the monk only as far as the beginning, there is no profit; nevertheless, they abandon their purpose, a ridiculous act, for which they are accused by those on the outside of cowardice and indecision. Concerning such people the Lord says: 'For who, wishing to build a house, does not sit down first and calculate the outlays that are necessary, whether he has the means to complete it? Lest after he has laid the foundation and is not able to finish, . . . they begin to mock him saying, "This man began to build and was not able to finish!" '[2] Therefore, let the beginning contain the germ of zealous progress toward virtue. For, the most noble athlete, Paul, desiring that we should not be careless because of our previous good deeds, but should go forward day by day, says: 'Forgetting what is behind, I strain forward to what is before, I press on towards the goal, to the prize of God's heavenly call.'[3] Such is the whole life

---

1 No ancient manuscripts of the letters of St. Basil contain Letter 42. Moreover, a note found beside the letter in the Codex Regius 2895 reads: 'Some attribute this letter to the holy Nilus.' Cf. Bessieres, *op. cit.* 344. Furthermore, it appears in several manuscripts of the homilies, and should properly be considered among homilies rather than among letters. It is supposed to have been written before the time of St. Basil's episcopate.
2 Cf. Luke 14.28-30. The quotation is given almost verbatim, but *'oekon'* replaces *'púrgon'* of the Septuagint.
3 Phil. 3.13-14.

of man. Not content with the things that have gone before, he is supported not by things past, but rather by the things to come. Why, what does it profit a man to have dined well yesterday, if today his natural hunger does not find food for its proper satisfaction? Likewise, there is no gain for the soul from yesterday's virtue, if that virtue is deprived of today's just actions. 'For, as I find you,' He says, 'so shall I judge you.'[4]

Therefore, the labor of the just is fruitless, and even the way of the sinner is blameless, if followed by change, in the one from better to worse, and, in the other, from worse to better. This can also be understood from Ezechiel[5] as from the Lord teaching in person. 'For if,' he says, 'the just man, turning himself away from his justice, do iniquity, I shall not remember his justices which he formerly did, but he shall die in his sin.' And he also says this about the sinner: 'If turning away from his sin he shall do justice, he shall surely live.'[6] For, where were the great labors of His servant Moses, since the contradiction of a moment cancelled his entrance to the land of promise? And where was the close association of Giezi with Eliseus, since the former brought leprosy[7] on himself by his love of money. Also, what profit to Solomon were his vast store of wisdom and his great devotion toward God in his previous life, since later, because of his infatuation for women, he fell into idolatry? And not even his lofty position left the blessed David blameless for his sin against the wife of Uriah.[8] Sufficient also was the example of the fall of Judas from better to worse for the salvation of him

---
4 Cf. Ezech. 7.3.
5 Cf. Ezech. 18.24.
6 Cf. Ezech. 18.27-28.
7 Cf. 4 Kings 5.
8 Bathsheba.

who lives his life according to God. Judas, though he was a disciple of Christ for such a long time, later sold his Teacher for a little gain and by his labors prepared a rope for himself.

Therefore, be this known to you, brother, that not he who begins well is perfect, but he who ends well is approved by God.

Do not, then, give sleep to your eyes, brother, nor slumber to your eyelids,[9] that you may be saved as the doe from the noose and as the bird from the snare.[10] For, behold, you are going through the midst of the snares and walking about a lofty wall from which a misstep is not without danger for one who falls. Therefore, do not strive to reach immediately the highest perfection of the ascetic life; especially, do not be self-confident, lest, through inexperience, you fall from the heights of asceticism; it is better to advance little by little. Therefore, gradually steal away from the pleasures of life, utterly destroying every worldly habit of yours, lest, having aroused all your sensual desires at once, you should bring upon yourself a multitude of temptations. But, when with all your might you have prevailed over one passion of pleasure, gird yourself against another, and thus you will prevail in good time over all such pleasures. For, indeed, the name of pleasure is one, but the accompanying circumstances are various. Therefore, brother, be first of all patient in the face of every trial. But, by what sort of temptation is the faithful man proved? By losses of worldly possessions, by accusations, by false representations, by disobediences, by evil reports, by persecutions. By these and similar tests is the faithful man proved.

Secondly, be also quiet, not precipitate in speech, not

---

9 Cf. Ps. 132.4.
10 Cf. Ps. 124.7.

quarrelsome, not contentious, not conceited, not desirous to explain but to believe; be not talkative, but be ever ready to learn rather than to teach. Do not busy yourself about worldly affairs, from which no profit accrues to you. For, it is said: 'That my mouth may not speak the works of men.'[11] He who willingly talks of the deeds of sinners readily arouses desires of pleasure in himself. Rather, be occupied about the life of the just, for thus you will find profit for yourself. Do not be ostentatious, visiting houses in the villages, but flee these as snares of the soul. And if anyone through his great piety invites you to his house on various pretexts, let such a one learn to be guided by the faith of the centurion, who, when Jesus was hastening to him in order to work a cure, besought Him not to come, saying: 'Lord, I am not worthy that thou shouldst come under my roof; but only say the word, and my servant will be healed.'[12] And when Jesus answered him: 'Go thy way; as thou hast believed, so be it done to thee,'[13] the servant was cured from that hour. Be this known to you, therefore, brother, that not the presence of Christ, but the faith of him who asked, freed the sick man. So it is also now; if you pray in whatever place you are, and the sick person believes that he will be aided by your prayers, all things will result according to his will.

Furthermore, you shall not love your relatives more than the Lord. 'For he who loves,' He says, 'father or mother or brothers more than me is not worthy of me.'[14] What does this precept of the Lord mean? 'If anyone,' He says, 'does not carry his cross, and follow me, he cannot be my disciple.'[15] If you would die with Christ to your relatives according to

---

11 Ps. 16.4.
12 Matt. 8.8.
13 Matt. 8.13.
14 Cf. Matt. 10.37.
15 Cf. Luke 14.27.

the flesh, why do you wish to be among them again? And if what you have destroyed for Christ you build up again for your relatives, you make yourself an apostate. Therefore, you should not withdraw from your dwelling place because of the need of your relatives, for, in departing from your place of living, you will perhaps depart from your way of life.[16] Do not be a lover of the crowd, nor of your country, nor of your fellow citizens, but of solitude, remaining in it always unwaveringly, believing that prayer and the singing of psalms are your work. And do not neglect reading, especially of the New Testament, because harm often arises from reading the Old Testament, not because harmful things were written, but because the minds of those who are harmed are weak. All bread is nourishing, but to the sick it may be hurtful. So, also, all Scripture is divinely inspired and useful, and there is nothing unclean[17] in it, except it be unclean to him who thinks it is unclean. 'But test all things; hold fast that which is good. Keep yourself from every kind of evil,'[18] for 'all things are lawful, but not all things are expedient.'[19] Therefore, be not a stumbling-block[20] in any way to those with whom you meet; be cheerful, a lover of the brethren,[21] gentle, humble; do not forfeit the aim of hospitality[22] by seeking extravagant foods, but be content with what is at hand, and take nothing more from anyone than what the daily needs of the solitary life require. And, especially, shun gold

---

16 The play upon *tópos* (place) and *trópos* (character) cannot be exactly reproduced in English.
17 Cf. 2 Tim. 3.16.
18 1 Thess. 5.21-22. The quotation is in the exact words of the Scripture, but the verbs have been made singular.
19 Cf. 1 Cor. 6.12.
20 Cf. 1 Cor. 10.32.
21 Cf. 1 Peter 3.8.
22 The free offerings of the pious, on which the monks depended. Their gluttony would discourage entertainment.

as an enemy of the soul, the father of sin, and the servant of the Devil. Do not make yourself liable to the charge of avarice[23] under the pretext of serving the poor. If anyone brings you money for the needy, and you know that there are some in want, advise him to whom the money belongs to carry it himself to his needy brothers, lest at some time the acceptance of money should sully your conscience.

Flee pleasures; seek to attain self-control; train the body indeed by labor; and accustom the soul to trials. Regarding the separation of body and soul as deliverance from all evil, await eternal blessings for the enjoyment of which all the saints have been made partakers. Unceasingly set against the suggestions of the Devil your pious reasoning, balancing it as on a pair of scales, and continuing with your reasoning until the fall of the pan; especially whenever the evil thought arises and says: 'What is the advantage to you of living in this place? What profit is it to you to retire from the society of men? Do you not know that those appointed by God as bishops of the churches of God live customarily among men, and without intermission they hold the spiritual assemblies which greatly benefit those who attend? For there the difficult sayings of the Proverbs are laid open, the teachings of the Apostles are unfolded, the thoughts contained in the Gospels expounded, discourses on God are heard, and there are held conferences of spiritual brothers, who by the mere sight of their person occasion great profit to those meeting them. But, you have made yourself a stranger to such good influences, and sit here becoming like the wild beasts. For, you see here a vast solitude, entire absence of social intercourse, a lack of instruction, an estrangement from brethren, and great idleness of spirit in regard to the precept of God.'

When, therefore, the evil thought rises up and wishes to

---

23 I.e., by collecting alms 'for the poor' too diligently.

break your determination by such numerous and specious pretexts of this kind, set against it, by pious reflections, your experience of the matter in hand, saying: 'You tell me that the things of the world are good. It is on that account that I have moved here, since I judge myself unworthy of the good things of this world. For, evils have been mingled with the good things of the world—the evils preponderating. Once, indeed, when I was attending the spiritual assemblies, I met at length with great difficulty one brother who, it seemed, feared the Lord, but who was prevailed upon by the Devil. I heard from him clever speeches and fictitious tales told for the deception of those conversing with him. And, after him, I ran into many thieves, robbers, and oppressors. I saw the shameful sight of drunkards, and the blood of the oppressed. I looked upon the beauty of women, which tortured my self-control. And, though I fled the act of fornication, I sullied my virginity through the thought of my heart. I also heard many words profitable to my soul, but in none of the teachers did I find virtue worthy of his words. And, after this, I heard innumerable tragedies, which insinuated themselves into the mind by corrupt songs. Again, I heard the lyre sweetly sounding, the beat of the dancers' feet, the voice of the buffoons, much folly and ribald wit, and the outcry of an unspeakably large crowd. I saw the tears of the robbed, the distress of those led away by tyranny, the shrieks of the tortured. And I looked, and, lo! it was not a spiritual assembly, but a wind-swept and storm-tossed sea, striving to cover all alike with its waves.[24]

'Tell me, O evil thought, demon both of transient sensual

---

24 St. Gregory of Nyssa describes a similar scene of the vices in Palestine in his letter on Pilgrimages. Because of the similarity of the descriptions and because St. Basil is known to have visited Palestine (cf. Letter 223.2) Maran, *op. cit.*, suggests that St. Basil is describing conditions in the Holy Land.

pleasures and of vanities, what profit is it to me to see and hear these things, since I have not strength to aid the wronged, nor am I allowed either to succor the weak or to correct the erring; nay, perhaps I am destined to destroy myself as well? For, as a little pool of clear water is blotted out by a great storm of wind and dust, so the good deeds which we are accustomed to do in life are covered over by the mass of evils. Indeed, the tragedies recounting pleasures and joys are like stakes set up by worldlings in their hearts, so that the purity of their psalmody may be dimmed. And the wailings and lamentations of men wronged by their fellow men are introduced to show the endurance of the poor. What profit, therefore, is this for me, or is it manifestly harmful to my soul?

'So, for this reason I flee to the mountains "as a sparrow out of the snare of the fowlers."[25] For, I have been delivered as a sparrow. And I pass my life, O evil thought, in this solitude in which the Lord dwelt. Here is the oak of Mambre;[26] here is the ladder leading to heaven and the companies of angels which Jacob saw; here is the desert in which the people, having been purified, were given the laws, and, thus entering the land of promise, saw God. Here is Mount Carmel on which Elias, taking up his abode, was well-pleasing to God. Here is the plain into which Esdras withdrew and at the command of God produced his divinely inspired books. Here is the desert in which the blessed John ate locusts and preached penance to men. Here is the Mount of Olives which Christ ascended to pray, teaching us how to pray. Here is Christ, the lover of solitude. For, He says: "Where two or three are gathered together for my sake, there am I

---
25 Cf. Ps. 124.7.
26 Cf. Gen. 13.18; 18.1.

in the midst of them."²⁷ Here is the narrow and close way that leads to life.²⁸ Here are the teachers and prophets, "wandering in deserts, mountains, caves, and holes in the earth."²⁹ Here are apostles and evangelists, and monks living as citizens of the desert.

'Now, I have willingly accepted these things that I may receive the rewards which were promised to the martyrs of Christ and to all the other saints, and that I may truly say: "For the sake of the words of thy lips I have kept hard ways."³⁰ For, I know that Abraham, the beloved of God, obeyed the voice of God and settled in the solitude; that Isaac was oppressed; that Jacob, the patriarch, lived in a foreign land; the chaste Joseph was sold; the three steadfast youths resisted fire; Daniel twice was thrown into the den of lions; the outspoken Jeremias was condemned to a dungeon of filth; Isaias, the beholder of hidden things, was sawed in pieces; Israel was taken captive; John denounced adultery and was beheaded; and the martyrs of Christ were destroyed. Indeed, why do I speak at length when even the Saviour Himself was crucified for us, in order that by His death He might make us live and might anoint and draw us all to endurance. To Him and to the Father and to the Holy Spirit I press on. I strive to be found a true son, having judged myself unworthy of the good things of the world, indeed unworthy not on account of the world, but the world made unworthy on account of me.'

Therefore, considering these things within yourself, and zealously bringing them to fulfillment, as has been said to you, struggle until death for the sake of truth. For, even Christ

---
27 Matt. 18.20.
28 Cf. Matt. 7.14.
29 Heb. 11.38.
30 Ps. 16.4.

became obedient unto death.³¹ Moreover, the Apostle³² also says: 'Take heed lest perhaps there be in any of you an evil heart that would turn away from the living God.' But exhort one another, each edifying the other, while it is still called today. For, 'today' means the whole time of our life. If you thus conduct your life, brother, you will not only save yourself, but will also gladden us and glorify God forever and ever. Amen.

43. Admonition to the Young[1]

You who live a faithful solitary life and practice piety, observe and learn the way of life, according to the Gospel—subjection of the body, lowliness of spirit, purity of thought, and control of anger. When pressed into service[2] for the Lord's sake, do still more; when defrauded, abstain from lawsuits; when hated, love; when persecuted, endure; when slandered, pray. Be dead to sin; be crucified for God; transfer all your care to the Lord, that you may procure that end where there are hosts of angels, assemblies of first-born, thrones of apostles, seats of prophets, sceptres of patriarchs, crowns of martyrs, and praises of righteous men. Be eager to be yourself numbered with these just ones in Jesus Christ, our Lord. To Him be glory forever. Amen.

---
31 Cf. Phil. 2.8.
32 Cf. Heb. 3.12-13; 1 Thess. 5.11. A fusion of the two quotations, almost verbatim according to the Greek text.

1 Like the preceding with which it is usually considered, this letter is found in none of the manuscripts of letters, but it appears in the Paris edition of letters of 1618, numbered 2, between Letters 42 and 44. It is found in some manuscripts of the homilies, and was probably taken from them. Cf. Bessières, *op. cit.* 344.
2 Cf. Matt. 5.41.

44. To a Fallen Monk[1]

We do not say, 'Rejoice,' for there is no rejoicing for the wicked. Nay, disbelief still holds me fast, nor does my mind conceive so heinous an offense and so great a crime as you have committed, if the facts are really as they now appear to all. I wonder how such great wisdom was swallowed up; how such great strictness of life became relaxed; whence came such blindness that enwrapped you; how, without taking thought of anything at all, you wrought such terrible and such great destruction of souls. If this report is true, you have both consigned your own soul to the abyss and you have weakened the fervor of all who hear of this impiety. You have been a traitor to the faith; you have failed in the struggle for good. Therefore, I grieve for you. What priest, hearing the sad story, will not lament? What ecclesiastic does not strike his breast? What layman is not saddened? What ascetic does not mourn? Perchance, even the sun has been darkened at your fall and the powers of the heavens have been made to totter because of your destruction. Even the rocks, devoid of feeling, have wept at your madness; even your enemies have lamented over your lawlessness.

O appalling hardness! O strange cruelty! You did not fear God, nor did you reverence men, nor feel shame before your friends, but you have suffered shipwreck of all things at once; of all alike you have stripped yourself. Therefore, again I grieve for you, wretched man! You who were announcing your ardor for the kingdom have fallen from the

---

1 As in the case of Letter 42, no ancient manuscript of the correspondence of St. Basil contains this letter. The family Ac alone recognizes it. It was first edited at Venice in 1535 with Letter 42. A few of the important manuscripts of homilies contain it, but, as it is not in the general tradition of manuscripts of homilies in which **Letters 45** and **46** are found, it is considered as not even belonging to the homilies.

kingdom. You who were inspiring all with a reverence for the doctrine did not have the fear of God before your eyes. You who preach holiness are found to be polluted. You who glory in poverty are caught stealing money. You who through your guidance point out the punishment of God have drawn down chastisement upon yourself. How shall I bewail you? How shall I grieve for you? How has the morning star, rising early, fallen and been shattered upon the earth? The two ears of everyone who hears of it will ring. How did the Nazarite[2] who shone brighter than gold become darker than soot? The worthy son of Sion,[3] how did he become an unclean vessel? The remembrance of him whose knowledge of the Holy Scripture was talked about by all has today passed away with the echo of their voices. He who was quick of apprehension has perished quickly. He who had a manifold mind perpetrated a multifold offense. For those who were helped by your teaching have been injured by your destruction. Those who lent their ears to your instructions have closed their ears at your destruction. But I, lamenting and downcast, utterly despairing, eating ashes like bread and throwing sackcloth over my wound—I thus recount all your praises, or, rather, I draw up a funeral oration; I continue unconsolable and neglected, because consolation has been hidden from my eyes, and it is not possible for me to apply a salve nor oil nor a bandage, for my wound is painful. How shall I be healed?

If, then, any hope of salvation is still left to you, if any slight remembrance of God, if any desire for future rewards, if any fear of the punishments reserved for the unrepentant, come back quickly to sobriety; raise your eyes to the heavens; return to your senses; cease your wickedness; shake off the

---

2 Cf. Lam. 4.7-8.
3 Cf. Osee 8.8.

drunkenness that has drenched you; stand up against him who has overthrown you. Have the strength to rise up from the earth. Remember the Good Shepherd, how He will pursue and deliver you. And if there be but 'two legs, or the tip of an ear,'[4] leap back from him who has wounded you. Remember the compassion of God, how He heals with olive oil and wine. Do not despair of salvation. Recall the memory of what has been written, how he that falleth rises again, and he that is turned away turns again,[5] he that has been smitten is healed, he that is caught by wild beasts escapes, and he that confesses is not rejected. The Lord does not wish the death of the sinner, but that he return and live.[6] Be not contemptuous[7] as one who has fallen into the depths of sins.

There is still time for patience, time for forbearance, time for healing, time for amendment. Have you slipped? Rise up. Have you sinned? Cease. Do not stand in the way of sinners,[8] but turn aside; for then you will be saved when turning back you bewail your sins. In fact, from labors there is health; from sweat, salvation. So take heed, lest, in wishing to keep your contracts with others, you transgress your covenants with God which you confessed before many witnesses.[9] Do not, therefore, because of certain human considerations, hesitate to come to me. For, receiving my dead, I shall lament; I shall care for him; 'I shall weep bitterly for the devastation of the daughter of my people.'[10] All welcome you; all will aid you in your sufferings. Do not lose heart; be mindful of the days of old. There is salvation; there is amendment. Have courage; do not despair. There is no law which passes sentence

---

4 Cf. Amos. 3.12.
5 Cf. Jer. 8.4.
6 Cf. Ezech. 18.32.
7 Cf. Prov. 18.3.
8 Cf. Ps. 1.1.
9 Cf. 1 Tim. 6.12.
10 Cf. Isa. 22.4.

of death without pity, but grace, exceeding the chastisement, awaits the amendment. Not yet have the doors been closed; the Bridegroom listens; sin is not the master. Again take up the struggle; do not draw back, but pity yourself and all of us in Jesus Christ, our Lord, to whom be glory and might, now and forever, for ages of ages. Amen.

45. To a Fallen Monk[1]

A twofold fear has permeated the innermost depths of my mind because of the report concerning you. For, either a certain unsympathetic mood takes precedence, laying me open to a charge of harshness, or again, when I desire to pity and to be indulgent, your infirmities change my friendly attitude of mind. For this reason, even when I began to compose this letter of mine, I nerved my stiffening hand indeed by reasoning, but my face, which was downcast because of my distress over you, I was not able to alter; such great feeling of shame for you poured over me that immediately the line of my mouth fell as my lips parted with a sob. Alas! What shall I write? What shall I think, baffled as I am?

If I recall your previous life of vanity, when wealth and petty mundane glory surrounded you, I shudder. At that time,

---

1 The authenticity of Letters 45 and 46 has been questioned by a number of scholars. Yet, a careful study of the pros and cons, and especially of the testimony of M. Bessières, *op. cit.* 346ff., tends to support the opinion that they were written by St. Basil. However, they probably belong among the homilies rather than among the letters. Bessières' opinion is based, in the first place, upon the fact that they have the almost unanimous tradition of the manuscripts of letters; secondly, they have a very solid tradition in the manuscripts of homilies; thirdly, Letter 46 was translated into Latin by Rufinus as a homily; and lastly, the expressions and quotations used in Letter 46 are similar to the oratorical works of St. Basil; while Letter 45 has many traits in common with the Hexaemeron. Moreover, both have a Biblical coloring.

a crowd of flatterers and the transient pleasure of luxury with its obvious danger and unrighteous gains followed you. Indeed, on the one hand, fear of the magistrates dissipated your concern about salvation, and, on the other, turmoils in public affairs disturbed your home and constant misfortune caused your mind to return to Him who was able to aid you. Little by little, then, you began to study how you might seek the Saviour, who permits fears for your benefit, but delivers and protects you who in your security mock Him. And you were preparing yourself for a change to a holy way of life, contemptuously rejecting your very dangerous riches and denying yourself the comfort of a home and the company of a wife. Wholly uplifted, passing as a stranger and a pilgrim by fields and by cities, you hastened to Jerusalem. There I lived with you and deemed you happy because of your ascetic labors, when, continuously fasting through the cycles of the weeks, you meditated upon God, shunning at the same time the companionship of men on pretext of turning to a new life; when, conforming yourself to the exercise of silence and solitude, you avoided the distractions of civil affairs. You chastised your body with rough sackcloth; you bound your loins tightly with a stiff belt, patiently enduring the constriction of your bones. Through your abstemiousness, your sides became hollow and flabby as far back as the spine, and you utterly refused the use of an alleviating bandage. You drew in your flanks like a gourd, forcing them to cleave to the region of the kidneys. Then, ridding your flesh of all fat, with lofty purpose you dried the channels of your body, and by fasting compressed your stomach itself, so that you caused your ribs, like the eaves of a house, to cast a shadow over the region of your abdomen. So, with your whole body shrunken, you confessed to God during the hours of the night, and with streams of tears you drenched and smoothed down your beard.

But, why should I enumerate each separate detail? Remember the many saints whose lips you have greeted with a kiss; the many holy persons you have embraced; the many men who clasped your hands as undefiled; the many servants of God who ran like hirelings to clasp your knees.

And, after these things, what now? A slanderous report of adultery flies in all directions more swiftly than an arrow and wounds our ears, and with sharper point pierces our inmost heart. What sorcerer's cunning was so subtle as to bring you to such a destructive fall? What intricate nets of the Evil One entangled you, bringing to nought your steadfast practices of virtue? Where are the good reports of your labors? They are gone. For, must we not now distrust them? In consequence of the present evidence, how can we refuse to believe things up to now unseen, especially knowing you have bound by terrible oaths souls fleeing for refuge to God, when anything that is beyond 'yes' or 'no' is scrupulously attributed to the Devil?[2] Therefore, you have at the same time become liable for a ruinous perjury, and by bringing into contempt the distinctive characteristic of asceticism you have transmitted the disgrace even to the Apostles and to our Lord Himself. You have dishonored the glory of purity; you have mocked the profession of chastity. We have become a tragedy of captives, and our lives are being dramatized for Jews and Greeks.[3] You have impaired the spirit of the monks; you have forced fear and timidity upon the more cautious souls, who still wonder at the power of the Devil. You have per-

---
2 Cf. Matt. 5.37.
3 I.e., we monks in the role of captives are held up for ridicule by Jews and pagans. St. Basil uses the term 'Greeks' for the adherents of the old pagan religion.

verted the indifferent to an emulation of your licentiousness. As much as lies in you, you have destroyed the glory of Christ, who says: 'Take courage, I have overcome the world'⁴ and the ruler of it. You have mixed a cup of infamy for your fatherland. Truly you brought to accomplishment the words of the proverb: 'As a hart pierced to the liver.'⁵

But, what now? The tower of strength has not fallen, brother; the remedies of conversion have not been mocked; the city of refuge has not been closed. Do not remain in the depth of evil; do not subject yourself to the slayer of men. The Lord knows how to raise up those who have been thrown down. Do not flee afar, but hasten to us. Take up again the labors of your youth and by renewed virtuous actions destroy the sensuality and sordidness which made you grovel in the mire. Look up to the last day, which is so near to our life. Realize how even now the sons of Jews and Greeks are being drawn to the service of God, and once and for all cease denying the Saviour of the world, lest that most terrible sentence overtake you: 'I do not know who you are.'⁶

46. To a Fallen Virgin¹

Now is the time to utter aloud those words of the Prophet who said: 'Who will give water to my head, and a fountain of tears to my eyes, and I will weep for the slain of the daughter of my people?'² For, even if deep silence enfolds

---
4 John 16.33.
5 Cf. Prov 7.23. St. Basil gives the substance but not the exact words of the Septuagint. The Douay version is somewhat different.
6 Cf. Luke 13.27.

1 Cf. Letter 45 n. 1.
2 Cf. Jer. 9.1. (Septuagint). St. Basil omits the words, 'for this my people, day and night,' after 'weep.'

them and they lie dispossessed once and for all of their sense by the horrible deed (for by the deadly blow they have been deprived already of the very awareness of their condition), still we must not tearlessly disregard so great a fall. For, if Jeremias judged those whose bodies were smitten in war worthy of innumerable laments, what should be said regarding so terrible a disaster to souls? 'Thy slain,' it is said, 'are not slain by the sword, and thy dead are not dead in battle.'[3] But, I bewail the sharp sting which causes real death, that is, grievous sin, and the fiery darts of the Evil One, barbarously burning soul and body alike.

Surely, the laws of God would groan mightily at beholding such guilt upon earth, since they were ever forbidding and crying out of old, indeed: 'Thou shalt not covet thy neighbor's wife';[4] and, through the holy Gospels: 'Anyone who even looks with lust at a woman has already committed adultery with her in his heart.'[5] But, they now behold the Lord's bride herself, whose head is Christ, fearlessly committing adultery, at which the very spirits of the saints would lament: Phinehas the zealous, because he can no longer take the lance in his hand and with physical punishment avenge the defilement; and John the Baptist, because he is not able to leave his heavenly abode as he left the desert and to hasten to rebuke the transgression, and, if he should need to endure any suffering, rather to lose his head than his freedom of speech. Now, if like the blessed Abel,[6] John himself, 'though he is dead, yet speaks' to us, even now he cries out and shouts more loudly than he did then concerning Herodias: 'It is not lawful for thee to have her.'[7] At any rate, even

---

[3] Cf. Isa. 22.2.
[4] Deut. 5.21.
[5] Cf. Matt. 5.28 (St. Basil quotes almost verbatim)
[6] Cf. Heb. 11.4.
[7] Matt. 14.4.

though the body of John according to the law of nature has accepted the divine sentence, and his tongue is silent, yet 'the word of God is not bound.'[8] For, if he, because the marriage of a fellow servant was set at naught, exercised his freedom of speech even to death, how would he feel when he beheld such insolence concerning the sacred bridal chamber of the Lord?

But you have thrown off the yoke of that divine union; you have fled the undefiled bridal chamber of the true king, have shamefully fallen into that disgraceful and sacrilegious seduction, and, since you may in no way escape this bitter charge, and as there is no means or method by which you may hide this horror, you rush recklessly on. Then, inasmuch as a sinner, on falling into the depths of sin, becomes thereafter contemptuous, you deny those covenants with your true Bridegroom, protesting that you neither are nor ever promised to be a virgin; you who both received and made show of many declarations of virginity.

Recall your glorious profession which you made before God, the angels, and men.[9] Remember the august company, the holy chorus of virgins, the assembly of the Lord, and the Church of saints. Call to mind, also, your grandmother, old in Christ, but still young and strong in virtue, and your mother, vying with her in the Lord and striving by new and unusual toils to destroy former habits. Remember, also, your sister, who is likewise both imitating and aspiring to surpass them, and who by the advantage of her virginity is outstripping the virtuous actions of her elders and is industriously summoning, both by word and by life, you her sister, as she thought, to a contest of like eagerness. Recall these, and also the angelic chorus singing with them to God, the spiritual

---
8 2 Tim. 2.9.
9 Cf. 1 Tim. 6.12.

life in the flesh, and the heavenly life on earth. Remember your unperturbed days, your enlightened nights, your spiritual songs, the melodious chanting of psalms, the holy prayers, the pure and undefiled bed, the procession of virgins, the temperate table, and you yourself saying fervent prayers that your virginity be kept unstained.

Where, now, is that dignified appearance, and where the well-ordered disposition, the simple clothing becoming to a virgin, the beautiful blush of modesty, and the seemly pallor which blooms through self-control and watchings, and has a radiance more charming than any fresh complexion? How often in your prayers to keep your virginity unspotted did you, perhaps, shed tears? And how many letters did you write to holy men, through which you asked them to pray earnestly for you, not in order that you might attain human marriage, much less this disgraceful corruption, but in order that you might not fall away from the Lord Jesus? And how often did you receive gifts from your Bridegroom? And why should I even mention the honors received through Him from His ministers? The companionship with virgins? The processions with them? The salutations from them? The praises of your virginity? The virginal blessings?[10] The letters written to you as a virgin? But, now, having received a little breath of 'the spirit of the air, which now works on the unbelievers,'[11] you have denied all those things; and that precious and highly prized possession you have exchanged for a brief pleasure, which indeed satisfies[12] for a time, but later will be found more bitter than gall.

In his grief over these things, who would not say: 'How is the faithful city, Sion, become a harlot?'[13] And how would

---
10 The sacerdotal benedictions given to nuns by the priests.
11 Cf. Eph. 2.2.
12 Literally, 'oils your throat.
13 Cf. Isa. 1.21.

not the Lord[14] Himself say to any one of those who are now walking about in the spirit of Jeremias: 'Hast thou seen what things the virgin of Israel hath done to me? I espoused her to myself in faith and in purity, in justice and judgment, and in mercy and in commiserations, as I promised to her through Osee, the prophet. But she has loved strangers; and while I, her husband, am living, she is called an adulteress, and does not to fear to be with another man.' And that, then, does the friend of the bride who gave her to her husband, the holy and blessed Paul, say, both that Paul of old and the Paul of to-day, under whom as mediator and teacher you left the paternal home and were united with the Lord?[15] Would not each in a state of intense grief over such an evil say: 'For the fear which I feared hath come upon me; and that which I was afraid of hath befallen me'?[16] 'For I betrothed you to one spouse, that I might present you a chaste virgin to Christ'[17] and 'I feared always lest, as the serpent seduced Eve by his guile, so your minds may at some time be corrupted.'[18] On this account I always tried with innumerable holy diversions to restrain the tumult of your passions, and with numberless safeguards to watch over the bride of the Lord, and I always described the life of the unmarried, say-

---

14 These quoted words are adapted from three sources: Jer. 18.13, 'Therefore thus saith the Lord: Ask among the nations: Who hath heard such horrible things, as the virgin of Israel hath done to excess?'; Osee 2.19, 'And I will espouse thee to me forever; and I will espouse thee to me in justice, and judgment, and in mercy, and in commiserations'; Rom. 7.3, 'Therefore while her husband is alive, she will be called an adulteress if she be with another man; but if her husband dies, she is set free from the law of the husband, so that she is not an adulteress if she has been with another man.'
15 The two Pauls to whom St. Basil is referring are Paul, a priest who received her when she took her vows, and St. Paul.
16 Job 3.25 (almost verbatim from the Septuagint). The rest of the quotations in the assumed rebuke of Paul, the priest, are taken from St. Paul's Epistles.
17 Cf. 2 Cor. 11.2.
18 Cf. 2 Cor. 11.3.

ing that truly the 'unmarried woman alone thinks about the things of the Lord, that she may be holy in body and in spirit.'[19] I set forth the dignity of virginity, and, addressing you as 'the temple of God,'[20] I tried as it were to give wings to your eagerness, raising you up to Jesus; and I strove to aid you by fear of evil not to fall, saying: 'If anyone destroys the temple of God, him will God destroy.'[21] Indeed, I also added the security that might come from my prayers if by some means 'your body and soul and spirit might be preserved sound, blameless at the coming of our Lord Jesus Christ.'[22] But, in all these things I spent myself in vain for you, and the end of those sweet labors proved bitter to me; and I have to lament again over her in whom I should have rejoiced. For, lo! you were deceived by the serpent, more bitterly than Eve. Not only was 'your mind corrupted,'[23] but even your very body as well; and even that terrible horror, which I hesitate to mention, and yet am not able to pass over in silence (for it is as a burning and flaming fire in my bones, and I am completely weakened and am not able to endure), taking 'the members of Christ, you have made them members of a harlot.'[24]

This alone among all evils is without comparison; this is a new act of shamelessness in life. 'Pass over,' the Lord says, 'to the isles of Cethim, and see; and send into Cedar, and consider diligently, . . . if there hath been done anything like this, if a nation hath changed their gods, and indeed they are not gods.'[25] But, the virgin 'has changed her glory,' and her glory is in her shame. 'Heaven was amazed at

---

19 Cf. 1 Cor. 7.34.
20 Cf. 1 Cor. 3.16.
21 1 Cor. 3.17.
22 Cf. 1 Thess. 5.23.
23 Cf. 2 Cor. 11.3.
24 Cf. 1 Cor. 6.15.
25 Cf. Jer. 2.10-11.

this,' and the earth 'shuddered more violently than ever before.' And now, too, the Lord says: 'My virgin has done two evils; she has forsaken me,' the true and holy Bridegroom of holy souls, and she has fled to an impious and lawless destroyer of soul and body alike. She departed from God her Saviour, and she 'yielded her members as slaves of uncleanness and iniquity,' 'and she forgot me, and went after her lover,' from whom she will receive no good.[26]

'It were better for him if a millstone were hung about his neck and he were thrown into the sea, than that anyone should cause the virgin of the Lord to sin.'[27] Was any surly slave so mad as to throw himself upon his master's bed? Or what robber was ever led on to such folly as to lay violent hands upon the very offerings made to God—not lifeless vessels, but living bodies possessing an indwelling soul made to the image of God? Of whom since time began has it been heard that he dared in the midst of the city and at high noon to draw the figures of unclean swine upon the statue of the king? If anyone violates a human marriage, he dies without pity in the presence of two or three witnesses. 'How much worse punishments do you think he deserves who has trodden under foot the Son of God,' and has corrupted the virgin vowed to Him and has insulted the spirit of virginity?[28] 'But she was willing,' he [the corrupter] says; 'and I did not force her against her will.' Why, that abandoned Egyptian mistress herself was madly in love with the fair Joseph, but the madness of the licentious woman did not overcome the virtue of the chaste man; not even when she laid violent hands upon him was he forced into sin. 'But this,' he says, 'had been determined by that woman, and she was no longer

---

26 A fusion and adaptation of Jer. 2.12.13, Rom. 6.19, and Osee 2.13 (Septuagint).
27 Cf. Luke 17.2.
28 Cf. Heb. 10.29.

a virgin; and if I had not been willing, she would have been corrupted by another.' 'For indeed,' it is said, 'the Son of man must be betrayed, but woe to that man by whom He was betrayed';[29] and 'it must needs be that scandals come, but woe to that man through whom they come.'[30]

In addition to these things, 'Shall not he that falleth rise again? and he that is turned away, shall he not turn again?'[31] Why, then, is the virgin 'turned away with a stubborn revolting,' even though she heard Christ, her Spouse, saying through Jeremias: 'And when she had committed all these fornications, I said: Return to me, and she did not return'?[32] 'Is there no balm in Galaad? or is there no physician there? Why, then, is not the wound of the daughter of my people closed?'[33] Indeed, many safeguards against the evil would you find in the divine Scripture, and many remedies which from destruction bring salvation: the mysteries of death and resurrection; the words of the terrible judgment and everlasting punishment; the doctrines of repentance and the forgiveness of sin; those innumerable examples of conversion; the drachma, the sheep, the son who spent his livelihood with harlots, was lost and found, was dead and alive again.[34] Let us use these safeguards against evil; through them, let us heal our soul.

But, take thought of the last day (for, indeed, not you alone will live an eternal life), the distress, the suffocation, the hour of death, the instant sentence of God, the angels hastening on, the soul in the midst of these things terribly disturbed, bitterly scourged by a guilty conscience and pite-

---

29 Cf. Mark 14.21.
30 Cf. Matt. 18.7.
31 Jer. 8.4.
32 Jer. 3.7 (Septuagint). The Douay version reads: 'done all these things,' instead of 'committed all these fornications.'
33 Jer. 8.22.
34 Cf. Luke 15.

ously turning now to earthly things, and now to the inexorable necessity of that long life to come. Picture in your mind, I pray, the final end of human life, when the Son of God will come in His glory with His angels. For, He 'shall come and shall not keep silence,'[35] when He comes to judge the living and the dead and to give to each according to his deed, when that trumpet sending forth a great and terrible call shall awaken all who through the ages have been sleeping. 'And they who have done good shall come forth unto resurrection of life; but they who have done evil unto resurrection of judgment.'[36] Recall Daniel's[37] divine vision, how he brings the judgment before our eyes. 'I beheld,' he says, 'till thrones were placed, and the Ancient of days sat; his garment was white as snow, and the hair of his head like clean wool . . .,[38] the wheels of it like a burning fire. A swift stream of fire issued forth from before him; thousands of thousands ministered to him, and ten thousand times a hundred thousand stood before him; the judgment sat, and the books were opened,' revealing clearly in the hearing of all the angels and men the good things, the bad, the seen, the hidden, the actions, the words, the thoughts, all things at once. How must those who have lived wickedly be affected by these things? Where, then, will that soul hide itself, which is suddenly exposed, filled with shame, before the eyes of so many spectators? With what sort of body will it endure those countless and insupportable scourgings, where there is unquenchable fire, and the worm[39] punishes without end, the dark and horrible abyss of Hades, the bitter wailings, violent screaming, weeping and gnashing of teeth, and horrors which have no end?

---

35 Cf. Ps. 49.3.
36 John 5.29.
37 Dan. 7.9-10.
38 St. Basil omits 'his throne like flames of fire.
39 Cf. Mark 9.44, 46, 48.

Nor is there after death any relief from these woes, nor any method or device of escaping the bitter punishments.

It is possible now to avoid them. While we are able, let us lift up ourselves from our fall, let us not despair of our salvation, if only we depart from our sins. Jesus Christ came into the world to save sinners. 'Come, let us adore and fall down and weep before Him.'[40] The Word calling us to repentance cries out and exclaims: 'Come to Me, all you who labor and are burdened, and I will give you rest.'[41] Therefore, there is a way of salvation, if only we will it. Death prevailing has swallowed us up, but be assured that God has again wiped away every tear from the face of all who repent.[42] 'The Lord is faithful in all His words.'[43] He does not deceive when He says: 'If your sins be as scarlet, they shall be made as white as snow; and if they be red as crimson, they shall be white as wool.'[44] The great Physician of souls is ready to cure your suffering; He is the ready liberator, not of you alone, but of all those enslaved by sin. His words, pronounced by that sweet and saving mouth, are: 'It is not the healthy who need a physician, but they who are sick. . . . For I have come to call sinners to repentance, 'not the just.'[45] What, therefore, is your excuse, or that of any other person, since He utters these words? The Lord wishes to free you from the pain of the wound, and to show you light after darkness. The Good Shepherd, leaving those that have not strayed, seeks you. If you will surrender yourself, He will not hold back, nor will He in His kindness disdain to lift you up on His own shoulders, rejoicing that He has found His sheep that was lost.

---

40 Cf. Ps. 95.6.
41 Matt. 11.28.
42 Cf. Isa. 25.8 (Septuagint). The Douay version differs somewhat in text.
43 Cf. Ps. 145.17.
44 Isa. 1.18.
45 Matt. 9.12-13.

The Father stands and awaits your return from your wandering. Only turn to Him and, while you are still afar off, He will run and fall upon your neck, and with loving embraces will enfold you, now cleansed by your repentance. And He will put the best robe on your soul which has stripped off the old man with his works; and He will put a ring on your hands, washed of the blood of death; and He will put shoes on your feet, since they have turned from the way of evil to the course of the gospel of peace. And He will announce a day of joy and gladness for His own, both angels and men, and will celebrate in every way your salvation. He says: 'Amen I say to you that there is joy in heaven before God over one sinner who repents.'[46] And if any one of those who seem to stand shall bring a charge that you have been quickly received, the good Father Himself will answer for you and say: 'But it is fit that we should make merry and be glad, for this My daughter was dead and is come to life again; she was lost and is found.'[47]

47. *To Gregory, His Companion*[1]

'Who will give me wings like a dove?'[2] Or how can my old age be renewed, so that I may be able to visit your

---
46 Cf. Luke 15.7.
47 Cf. Luke 15.32.

---
1 Letters 47-291 inclusive form the second main division of St. Basil's letters according to the Benedictine arrangement. They are the letters written during his episcopate. The present letter was written at the death of Eusebius, Archbishop of Caesarea, in 370, and St. Basil, who had really directed the affairs of the see for some years, was the ablest of all possible candidates. St. Basil himself, understanding the difficulties of the time and realizing that he was the most fit to deal with the situation, was eager for the office. He had summoned St. Gregory, his friend, to Caesarea on the plea of his own illness, but St. Gregory

Charity,[3] there to satisfy the longing which I have of seeing you and to tell you the sorrows of my soul, and thus through you to find some solace for my afflictions? For, at the death of the blessed Bishop Eusebius[4] we were seized with no little fear that, perchance, those who are ever lying in wait for the church of our metropolis and desiring to fill it with the tares of heresy would grasp the opportunity of rooting out of the souls of men by their wicked teachings the piety planted with much trouble, and would destroy its unity, as they have done in many churches. Then, when letters also came to us from the clergy, urging us not to be negligent at such a time, taking thought, I recalled your charity and upright faith, and the zeal which you ever had for the churches of God.

Therefore, I have sent Eustathius, my beloved[5] fellow deacon, to appeal to your Grace and to entreat you to add this imminent task to all your former labors for the churches. And this not only to comfort my old age by a conference with you but to restore the widely proclaimed piety of the true Church by helping us (if, indeed, we should be considered worthy to share with you in the good work) to give it a

---

refused to come. The Benedictine editors and Tillemont, *Mémoires pour servir à l'histoire ecclésiastique des six premiers siècles* 9 (Paris 1643-1712) 658, assign the letter to the elder Gregory, writing through the younger Gregory to Eusebius of Samosata. One reason for this is that St. Basil was not an old man and both the writer and the addressee of this letter were old. Again, the elder Gregory was instrumental in securing St. Basil's election. He had Eusebius come from Samosata to make the third bishop necessary for the consecration, while he himself had to be carried to the church from his bed of sickness. This letter also appears as Letter 42 among those of Gregory of Nazianzus.

2 Ps. 55.6.
3 *Agápēn*—a title of address used by St. Basil in speaking to bishops.
4 On the death of Dianius in 362, Eusebius had been elected Bishop of Caesarea through the counsels and influence of the elder Gregory. It was Eusebius who had ordained St. Basil to the presbyterate, and at first chafed because of the activity and success of his more able subordinate.
5 *Agapētós*—a title of distinction used by St. Basil for both clergymen and laymen.

pastor according to the Lord's will, one who is able to guide His people aright. For, we have before our eyes a man whom you also know well. If we should be considered worthy to secure him, I know that we shall appear before God with much confidence, and shall bestow the greatest benefit on the people who have called upon us. But, I entreat you once again and often no longer to hesitate but to visit us, starting before the hardships of the winter season begin.

48. To Eusebius, Bishop of Samosata[1]

It was with great difficulty that we were able to secure a carrier for this letter to your Reverence. For, the people of our country cringe so beneath the winter that they do not have the least courage to venture out of their houses. In fact, we have been covered with such a heavy snowfall that for two months we have been in hiding, buried with the very houses. Assuredly, then, understanding both our Cappadocian[2] timidity and natural sluggishness, you will pardon us for not writing sooner and informing your Honor of the affairs at Antioch. It is, no doubt, to no purpose to make these matters known to you at this late hour, since you have probably learned of them long ago. However, considering it no trouble to tell you even things known to you, we have sent the letter in care of our reader. So much for these matters.

Constantinople has for a long time had Demophilus,[3] as they themselves will tell you, and as others also assuredly have

---

[1] This letter was written in the spring of 371.
[2] The Cappadocians were notorious for their bad character. Together with the Cretans and Cilicians, they were accounted the 'three worst kappas.'
[3] Demophilus was elected bishop by the Arians in 370 to fill the see left vacant by the death of Eudoxius.

announced to your Holiness. Indeed, a certain pretense of true faith and piety on his part is commonly reported by those coming from there, all with the same account. As a result, even the parts of the city which were at variance have united, and some of the neighboring bishops have accepted the union. Furthermore, our own people have shown themselves no better than we had expected of them. For, when they arrived, just in the wake of your departure, they said and did many distressing things, and finally departed, confirming their schism.[4] At all events, it is evident to no one except God whether the condition will improve and whether they will cease their evil-doing. Such, then, is the present situation.

The rest of the Church is, by the grace of God, enjoying tranquillity, and is likewise praying to see you with us again in the spring, and to be reinvigorated by your sound teaching. As for me, my physical health is no better than usual.

49. To Arcadius, the Bishop[1]

I gave thanks to the holy God on reading your Reverence's[2] letter; and I pray both that I may be worthy of the hope which you entertain of us, and that you may obtain the perfect reward for the honor which you bestow on us in the name of our Lord Jesus Christ. We were delighted beyond measure that, upon yourself assuming a charge becoming to a Christian, you had erected a home for the glory of the name of Christ, truly loving, as it is written, 'the beauty of the house

---
4 Letters 98, 141, and 282 also tell of the troubles St. Basil encountered after he became bishop.

---
1 This letter was written shortly after St. Basil's elevation to the episcopate.
2 *Eulabeías*—a title of address used by St. Basil for clergymen only.

of the Lord.³ Doing so, you have provided for yourself the heavenly mansion which is prepared in the place of rest for those who love the name of the Lord. If we are able to find relics of martyrs anywhere, we beg that we also may contribute to your undertaking. For, if 'the just shall be in everlasting remembrance,'⁴ surely we shall be sharers of the good remembrance which will be given to you by the saint.

50. To Bishop Innocent[1]

Who is more fit than your Reverence in the Lord to inspire courage in the cowardly and arouse the sluggish. You have also manifested your excellence in all perfections, in being willing to descend to our Lowliness, proving yourself a true disciple of Him who said: 'But I am in your midst,' not as he who reclines at table but 'as he who serves.'[2] For, you yourself deigned to serve to us your spiritual joy, to lift up our souls by your esteemed letter, and to throw around us, like infant children, as it were, the arms of your greatness.

Therefore, pray, we beg of your noble soul, that we may be worthy to be aided by your great strength, receiving voice

---

3 Cf. Ps. 26.8.
4 Ps. 112.6.

---

1 St. Basil's authorship of Letters 50 and 81 is denied by J. Wittig, 'Studien zur Geschichte des Papstes Innocenz I und der Papstwahlen des 5 Jahrhunderts,' *Theol. Quartalschrift* 84 (1902) 388-439. He offers very convincing evidence that both are letters of St. John Chrysostom to Pope Innocent. The Benedictine editors consider Letter 50 the work of St. Basil and reject as an error the addition 'of Rome' to the title found in many editions. They support their contention with the statement that Damasus was Bishop of Rome at the time of St. Basil, and they assign the letter to the beginning of his episcopate.
2 Luke 22.27.

and wisdom to venture to answer you who are led by the Holy Spirit. And, since we hear that you are His friend and true glorifier, we avow our deep thankfulness for your firm and unwavering love for God. In our prayers we beg of the Lord that our place may be with the true adorers, among whom assuredly your Perfection stands, as does that great and true bishop[3] who fills all the world with admiration for himself.

51. To Bishop Bosporius[1]

How deeply, think you, was my soul pained on hearing of that slander poured out against me by some of those who do not fear the Judge who will 'destroy all that speak a lie'?[2] As a result, your affectionate words kept me sleepless nearly the whole night, so firmly had grief fastened upon my inmost heart. For, truly, according to Solomon, 'slander humbles a man';[3] and no one is so insensible to pain as not, when made a prey of lying mouths, to suffer in soul and be bowed down to the earth. But, I must indeed bear up under all things, endure all things, leaving vengeance to the Lord, who will not disregard us, since it is said: 'He that oppresseth the poor, upbraideth his Maker.'[4] Nevertheless, those who have framed this new tale of blasphemy against us seem

---
3 The identity of this bishop is unknown.
---
1 Bosporius was Bishop of Colonia in Cappadocia Secunda and St. Basil's close friend. This letter is a defense against a slanderous report that St. Basil had anathematized Bishop Dianius, his friend, who had subscribed to the Creed of Ariminum. It was written in 370.
2 Ps. 5.7.
3 Cf. Eccle. 7.8.
4 Prov. 14.31.

utterly to disbelieve the Lord, who has declared that on the day of judgment we shall give an account of even every idle word.[5]

But, tell me, did I anathematize the most blessed[6] Dianius? This is the charge against us. Where, or when? In whose presence? On what pretext? By mere spoken words, or in writing? Following the example of others, or as the originator and author of the daring act? Oh, the shamelessness of those who speak so glibly of every matter! Oh, the contempt for the judgments of God! Unless to their fabrication they add this monstrosity, also, that I was some time so demented that I did not know what I was saying. For, as long as I was possessed of my senses, I know that I did no such thing, nor did I wish in the first place so to do. But, on the contrary, I am conscious of this, that from my earliest years I grew up with a great love for him. I used to look with admiration upon the man, so majestic to behold, so magnificent, and possessed of such great priestly dignity of form. And when I reached the age of reason, then I recognized the virtues of his soul. And I rejoiced in his company, perceiving the simplicity, the nobility, and the generosity of his disposition, and all the other virtues characteristic of the man—his meekness of spirit, his magnanimity combined with gentleness, his propriety, his mildness of temper, his cheerfulness and affability seasoned with dignity. Therefore, I counted him among the most eminent in virtue.

However, toward the end of his life (for I will not conceal the truth), I, together with many in our native land who fear the Lord, suffered intolerable grief on his account because he had subscribed to the creed introduced from Con-

---
5 Cf. Matt. 12.36.
6 *Makariótaton*—a title of distinction used by St. Basil only for bishops.

stantinople by George and his followers.⁷ Then, when he had already fallen into his last illness, being, through his mildness of disposition and his spirit of fairness, so willing in his paternal affection to completely satisfy all, he summoned us. He said that, with the Lord as his witness, in the simplicity of his heart he had agreed to the document from Constantinople, but he had accepted nothing in rejection of the faith set forth by the holy Fathers at Nicaea, nor was he at heart otherwise than he had been when he had first received it. On the contrary, he even prayed that he might not be separated from the lot of those three hundred and eighteen blessed bishops who had announced the sacred doctrine to the world. Consequently, we, at this assurance, blotting out all doubt from our hearts, as you yourself know, entered in communion with him and ceased grieving.

Such, indeed, were our relations with the man. If anyone should say that he is aware of any wicked slander against him on our part, let him not babble furtively like a slave, but openly confront and fearlessly refute us.

---

7 The Homoean Creed of Ariminum revised at Nica and accepted in 360 at the Acacian Synod of Constantinople. 'George is, presumably, the George, Bishop of Laodicea, who at Seleucia opposed the Acacians, but who appears afterwards to have become reconciled to that party, and to have joined them in persecuting the Catholics of Constantinople'— Jackson. Cf. Letter 251.

52. To the Canonesses[1]

Our brother Bosporius,[2] a bishop dearly beloved of God,

---

1 Canonesses were women of the early Church who lived a life of piety and followed a definite rule of life. They differed from nuns in that they did not take the vows of poverty, chastity, and obedience. The date of this letter is 370, in the beginning of St. Basil's episcopate.
2 Cf. Letter 51.

by his more favorable report concerning your piety, gave us as much joy as the distressing rumor which resounded about our ears had previously pained us. For, he said, by the grace of God, all those rumors spread abroad were fabrications of men not accurately understanding the truth about you. But, he adds that he found among you such slanders against us, indeed, as might be spoken by those who do not expect, on the day of His just retribution, to render an account to the Judge even of every idle word.[3] Therefore, I gave thanks to the Lord both because I myself was set right concerning my damaging opinion of you which, as it seems, I had accepted from the slanders of men, and also because I heard that you, upon receiving the favorable affirmation of our brother, had laid aside your false suspicions of us.

In those matters in which the latter presented to you his own opinion he, at the same time, fully expressed ours. For, we are both of one mind concerning the faith, both being heirs of the same Fathers, who previously at Nicaea proclaimed publicly the great doctrine of our religion. Although this doctrine is entirely free from misrepresentation in other respects, yet there are certain persons who never have accepted the word 'consubstantial,' which had been ill received by some. These might be justly blamed and yet again be considered worthy of pardon. For, to refuse to follow the Fathers and to refuse to regard their word as of greater authority than their own opinion is an arrogance deserving of reproach. On the other hand, to hold in suspicion that word which is discredited by others, perhaps, seems to free them somewhat from the charge. For, in truth, those who assembled in the case of Paul of Samosata[4] complained of

---

[3] Cf. Matt. 12.36.
[4] The two Antiochene synods of A.D. 264 and 269. To enforce their decisions against Paul of Samosata, recourse was had to the pagan Aurelian.

the word on the ground that it was not clear. Now, they said that the word 'consubstantial' set before the mind an idea both of substance and derivatives in such a manner that the substance, when divided into parts, gives to the parts into which it was divided the name of 'consubstantial.' This idea has some ground in the case of bronze and the money made from it, but in reference to God the Father and God the Son, substance is not considered anterior, nor is it considered as superimposed on both. In fact, to think or to say this is something more than impiety. For, what could be anterior to the Unbegotten? And by this blasphemy even the faith in the Father and the Son is destroyed, since objects subsisting from one and the same thing are related as brothers to each other.[5]

And, since at that time some were saying that the Son was brought from non-existence into existence, the word 'consubstantial' was added to destroy this irreverence. For, the union of the Son with the Father is without time and without interruption. Moreover, the preceding words prove that this was the thought of these men. For, after they had said light from light, and that the Son was begotten and not made from the substance of the Father, they brought in 'consubstantial' over and above these attributes, indicating that whatever meaning of light is attributed to the Father, the same will also be appropriate for the Son. For, true light will show no variation from true light according to the very conception of light. Therefore, since the Father is light without beginning, and the Son light begotten, but one is light and the other is light, they rightly say 'consubstantial' in order that they may show the equal dignity of their nature. For, cognate objects are not said to be consub-

---

5 A *reductio ad absurdum*. The doctrine of 'Likeness of Substance' was devised to get rid of this very notion.

stantial, as some assume. But, when the cause and that which has its existence from the cause are of the same nature, they are said to be consubstantial.

The same word also corrects the error of Sabellius.[6] For, it destroys the identity of person [*hypóstasis*] and introduces a perfect idea of the persons. Now, nothing is in itself consubstantial with itself, but one thing is consubstantial with another. Hence, the expression is a good and legitimate one, since it defines the individuality of the persons and shows the invariability of the nature.

But, when we learn that the Son is from the substance of the Father, begotten and not made, let us not fall into material ideas of the process. For, the substance was not separated from the Father and formed into the Son; nor did it engender by fluxion, nor by the putting forth of shoots,[7] as plants produce their fruits, but the manner of the divine generation is incapable of expression and of comprehension by human reason. Yet, truly, it is characteristic of a lowly and carnal mind to compare the eternal with the perishable and transient, and to think that, as corporeal things beget, so God does in like manner. In reference to religion, we ought to take our arguments from the contraries, saying that, since the mortal concerns are thus, the immortal Being is not thus. Assuredly, we must not deny the divine generation, nor sully our minds with carnal thoughts.

Moreover, the Holy Spirit is numbered with the Father and the Son, because He also is above the created object, and His rank is as we have learned it in the Gospel from our Lord, who said: 'Go, baptizing in the name of the Father,

---

6 Cf. Letter 9 n. 5.
7 Cf. Luke 21.30.

and of the Son, and of the Holy Spirit.'[8] But, the one who places Him before the Son, or says that He is older than the Father, opposes God's command and is a stranger to sound faith, since he does not preserve the form of the Doxology which he received, but invents for himself a novelty in order to be pleasing to men. Now, if He [the Spirit] is anterior to God, He is not from God. For, it is written: 'But the Spirit is of God.'[9] And, if He is from God, how is He older than He from whom He is? And what madness also is it, since the Unbegotten is one, to say that something else is anterior to the Unbegotten! Moreover, He is not before the Only-begotten,[10] for there is no intervening space between the Son and the Father. And, if He is not from God, but is through Christ, He does not exist at all. Therefore, the innovation about the rank [of the Holy Spirit] contains a rejection of His very existence and is a denial of the whole faith. It is equally impious to reduce Him to the level of a creature, or to place Him above either the Son or the Father whether according to time or to rank.

These, indeed, are the subjects about which I heard that your Reverences were inquiring, and, if the Lord should grant that we meet with each other, perhaps we may say something more on these points. We ourselves may also receive some certainty from you on matters about which we are inquiring.

---

8 Cf. Matt. 28.19.
9 Cf. 1 Cor. 2.12.
10 Cf. Letter 38, where St. Basil argues this point.

53. To the Suffragan Bishops[1]

The disgracefulness of this hitherto-considered-incredible matter about which I am writing, and which consequently has become the subject of suspicion and common conversation, has filled my soul with grief. Therefore, let him who is conscious of guilt receive my words on this subject as a remedy; anyone who is not guilty, as a precaution; and anyone who is indifferent—I pray that such may not be found among you—as a solemn protest.

What is it that I mean? There is a rumor that some of you receive money from those you ordain, covering this over with the name of piety,[2] thus making the fault worse. For, if anyone does evil under the pretense of good, he is deserving of a twofold punishment, because he not only does evil, but also uses the good as an accomplice, so to say, for committing the sin. If this be so, it must not be done in the future, but must be corrected. For, it is necessary to say to him who receives the money what the Apostles said to the man who wished to pay in order to buy a participation in the Holy Spirit: 'Thy money go to destruction with thee.'[3] In fact, he who through ignorance wishes to buy is less guilty than he who sells the gift of God, making it a business transaction. And, if you sell what you have received as a gift, you will be deprived of its grace, as if you had been sold

---

[1] The suffragan bishops were a grade of the clergy between bishops and priests. The Benedictine editors say that, since suffragan bishops do not have the power of ordination, the letter is addressed to the bishops subject to St. Basil. Although the authenticity of this letter has been questioned by Schäfer, *op. cit.* 5ff, it is not lacking in the earliest manuscripts of the letters. It was written in the beginning of his episcopate.
[2] I.e., piety on the part of the contributor.
[3] Acts 8.20.

to Satan. Furthermore, you are introducing into the Church, where we have been entrusted with the Body and Blood of Christ, the bartering of material for spiritual things. Therefore, this must not be done. This, I say, is the artifice. They think they do not sin because the money is received not before, but after, the ordination. But, any receiving, whensoever it may be, is receiving.

Now, I urge, forsake this way to revenue, or rather, this road leading to hell, and do not, by defiling your hands with such gains, make yourselves unworthy of celebrating the sacred mysteries. But, pardon me; at first I speak as one not believing, and then I threaten as one persuaded. If after this my letter anyone shall do any such thing, he shall withdraw from the altars in this diocese and seek a place where he may be able to buy and sell again the gift of God. For we and the churches of God do not have such a custom.[4]

After adding one more statement, I shall stop. This practice is born of avarice. And avarice is the root of all evils, and is called idolatry.[5] Do not, therefore, for the sake of a little money, honor idols above Christ. And again, do not imitate Judas, handing over for gain a second time Him who was once crucified for us. For, both the lands and the hands of those who receive these fruits will be called Haceldama.[6]

---
4 Cf. 1 Cor. 11.16.
5 Cf. Col. 3.5.
6 Cf. Acts 1.18-19.

54. To the Suffragan Bishops[1]

It grieves me exceedingly that the canons of the Fathers have now fallen into disuse, and that all exact observance has been banished from the churches. I fear that, since this indifference is steadily growing, the affairs of the Church will sink gradually into utter ruin. The practice formerly observed in the churches of God was to admit subdeacons[2] for the service of the Church only after a most thorough investigation. Their whole manner of life was closely inquired into, whether or not they were scoffers, or drunkards, or quarrelsome, or if they were moderating their youthful spirits so as to be able to attain 'the holiness without which no man will see the Lord.'[3] This scrutiny was made by the presbyters and the deacons who lived with them, and was in turn reported to the suffragan bishops, who, after receiving the votes of those who were really witnesses and notifying the

---

1 The authenticity of this letter assigned to one of the early years of St. Basil's episcopate has been questioned by Schäfer, *op. cit.* 5ff. It contains instructions for admission to ordination, and claims that many have been presenting themselves as candidates to escape conscription. But, in St. Basil's time the clergy were not exempt from conscription, Schäfer claims; moreover, the word '*epinémēsis*' is used for a period of time only in a later age. Bessières, however, does not find it lacking in any of the earliest manuscripts of St. Basil's letters.

2 The Greek Church acknowledges the following orders: bishops, priests, deacons, subdeacons, readers, acolytes, exorcists, and porters. Of these, the priesthood, including bishops, and the diaconate alone are regarded as major orders. This seems to have been true at least from the time of the Synod of Laodicea (about the middle of the fourth century). In the Latin Church, the priesthood, including the bishops, the diaconate, and subdiaconate are the major or 'sacred orders,' so called because they have immediate reference to what is consecrated. It is interesting to note that St. Basil in this letter considers the subdiaconate as one of the sacred orders. The earliest historical mention of the subdiaconate seems to be in the letter of Pope Cornelius (255) to Fabius of Antioch, in which he states that there are among the Roman clergy forty-six priests, seven deacons, and seven subdeacons.

3 Heb. 12.14.

bishop, then enrolled the subdeacons as members of the clergy.⁴

But, now, in the first place, you, disregarding us and not deigning to notify us, have yourselves assumed all authority. In the next place, becoming careless in the matter, you have permitted presbyters and deacons, acting through motives of affection due either to kinship or to some other friendly relationship, to introduce without due examination any unworthy men they wished into the Church. Therefore, many subdeacons have been numbered in each village, but not one worthy of the service of the altar,⁵ as you yourselves testify, since you are at a loss for men in the elections.

Since, then, I see that the matter is already becoming an incurable condition, especially at this time when very many, in fear of induction into the army, are forcing their way into the subdiaconate, I am compelled to revive again the canons of the Fathers. Moreover, I enjoin upon you to send me the registration of the subdeacons of each village, and to say by whom each has been introduced and what manner of life he is leading. And you yourselves also keep the registration in your own possession, so that you may compare your records with those preserved by us, and also so that it may not be possible for anyone illegally to enroll himself whenever he wishes. Of course, if some were brought in by presbyters after the first year of the indiction,⁶ these fall back among the laity. And make the examination of these men over again, and if they are indeed worthy, let them be admitted by your vote. Purge the Church yet more, driving out of it the unworthy. In the future, examine and admit,

---
4 Cf. note 2. For testing of candidates, cf. St. Cyprian, Letter 68.
5 I.e., few, if any, of the subdeacons are worthy of being raised to the diaconate or priesthood.
6 The indictions were conventional periods of fifteen years, the first of which began in the reign of Constantine the Great.

indeed, the deserving, but do not enroll them before you have reported to us; or else, realize that he who has been admitted to the subdiaconate without our consent will still be a layman.

55. To Paregorius, a Presbyter[1]

I read your letter with all patience, and I am amazed that, although you could have defended yourself before us briefly and easily by your actions, you prefer to persist in the situation causing the charges against you, and attempt to cure the incurable by long speeches. We are neither the first nor the only ones, Paregorius, who decreed that women should not live with men. Why, read the canon published by our holy Fathers in the Synod of Nicaea which clearly forbids the introduction of women into the household.[2] The honor of celibacy lies in this—namely, in the separation from companionship with women. But, if anyone professing celibacy in name conducts himself as those who are married, he is evidently seeking the honor of virginity in name but is not abstaining from unbecoming indulgence.

Therefore, you ought, in proportion as you say that you are free from all carnal passion, so much the more readily to yield to our demand. For, neither do I believe that a

---

[1] This letter, like the two preceding, is assigned to the early period of St. Basil's episcopate, and, like them, its authenticity has been called into question by Schäfer, *op. cit.* However, it, too, is supported by the manuscript tradition.

[2] *Syneisaktoe*—women admitted to the homes of priests to look after the household duties. Scandals naturally arose therefrom, and prohibitive measures were passed at various councils, the earliest at the Council of Elvira in 305. The Canon (III) of Nicaea, to which St. Basil refers, only allowed the introduction of a mother, a sister, or an aunt, if their character was above suspicion.

seventy-year-old man lives with a woman for the sake of passion, nor have we made this decision on the ground that some abominable act has been committed, but because we have been taught by the Apostle that we 'should not put a stumbling-block or a hindrance in our brother's way.'³ Yet, we know that an act honorably performed by some is to others an occasion of sin. For this reason, following the command of the holy Fathers, we have ordered you to separate from the woman.

Why, then, do you make charges against the suffragan bishop and recall his former enmity? And why do you censure us as having ears ready to believe slanders? Why do you not rather blame yourself for not consenting to give up the companionship of the woman? Put her out of your house, therefore, and settle her in a monastery. Let her be with virgins, and you be served by men, in order that the name of God may not be reviled on your account. Until you do this, the innumerable excuses which you write in your letters will be of no avail, but you will die suspended, and you will give the Lord a reason for your idleness. And if you dare, without correcting yourself, to cling to your priestly duties, you will be anathema to all the people, and they who receive you will be excommunicated throughout the whole Church.

56. To Pergamius[1]

I am naturally forgetful, and the multiplicity of business affairs which has fallen to my lot is augmenting my natural

---

3 Rom. 14.13 (Septuagint).

1 Pergamius seems to have been a lay person of importance, but nothing is definitely known about him. This letter was written at the beginning of St. Basil's episcopate.

weakness. Therefore, even though I do not remember that I have received a letter from your Nobility, I am persuaded that you sent us one, for surely you would not tell us a falsehood. Yet, that I have not answered is not my fault, but his who did not demand an answer. Now, however, this letter is going to you, not only making a complete apology for the past, but also offering an opportunity for a second salutation. Therefore, when you write to us, do not suppose that you are introducing a second series of letters, but that you are paying the debt owed for the present one. For, really, even though our letter is an exchange for your former letter, yet, since it is more than twice the length of yours, it will satisfy for both purposes. Do you see to what sophistry idleness impels us?

But, as for you, most noble Sir, cease to introduce in a few words great charges, charges which involve, certainly, the utmost wickedness. For, forgetfulness of friends and contempts arising from power embrace all evils together. In fact, if we do not love according to the command of the Lord, neither do we retain that distinctive character that has been imposed upon us. And if we, rendered vain, are filled with empty conceit and false pretense, we fall into the sin of the Devil from which there is no escape. Therefore, if you used these words because you had such a feeling toward us, pray that we may escape the evil which you found in our character. But, if your tongue came upon the words by force of habit and without deliberation, we shall console ourselves and urge your Excellency to add evidence from our deeds. Yet, realize this well, that the present anxiety has become an occasion of humiliation for us. Consequently, we shall forget you only when we shall fail to know ourselves. Furthermore, never make want of leisure an indication of character or of an evil disposition.

57. To Meletius, Bishop of Antioch[1]

If the intensity of the joy with which you inspire us as often as you write were at all evident to your Reverence, I know that you would never have passed by any pretext offered you for writing. On the contrary, you would have contrived many excuses for sending us letters on every occasion, since you know the reward reserved by our loving Master for relieving the afflicted. For, everything here is replete with grief, and the thought of your Holiness is our only refuge from these evils. This thought is brought to us more vividly in your correspondence, letters full of all wisdom and grace. As a result, whenever we take your letter into our hands, first we notice its length, and we love it the more in proportion as it surpasses the usual length. Then we read it through, and we are always delighted with every word that meets our eyes. But, we are disappointed when we approach the end, so good is everything that you say in your letters! For, that is good which overflows from a good heart.

But, if we should be considered worthy because of your prayers not only to meet you in person while we are upon earth, but also to receive from your living voice beneficial instructions or provisions for the journey of our present and future life, we would esteem this the greatest of blessings, and regard it as the prelude of God's favor toward us. Indeed, we would already be following our desire if our brothers, most true and beloved in all respects, had not detained us. Now, in order that I may not, through my letter, make public

---

[1] Meletius had been exiled from Antioch in 364 because of his orthodoxy, although he was not in full communion with the Catholics. This letter was written in 371. St. Basil's statement that the Church of Caesarea was still in an unfortunate state confirms this date.

their plan, I have described it to my brother Theophrastus,[2] so that he may explain it in detail to your Excellency.

58. To Gregory, His Brother[1]

How can I argue with you by letter? How can I upbraid, as it deserves, your simplicity in all matters? Who, tell me, ever falls a third time into the same snares? Who falls a third time into the same trap? Even a brute beast would scarcely suffer that to happen to it. You forged one letter and brought it to me as from the most revered bishop, our common uncle, deceiving me, for I know not what purpose. I received it as sent by the bishop through you. Why should I not? In my excessive joy I showed it to many of my friends. I gave thanks to God. The forgery was exposed, since the bishop himself denied it with his own voice. We were put to shame because of it. Involved in the disgrace of fraud, falsehood, and deceit, we prayed that the earth might open for us. Again they gave me a second letter as dispatched by the bishop himself to me through your servant Asterius. Not even that one had the bishop himself really sent, as the most revered brother, Anthimus,[2] has announced to us. Once more,

---

2 Perhaps the deacon, Theophrastus, who died shortly after Easter, 372; cf. Letter 95. According to the Benedictine editors, the intentions referred to here are the plans to bring about the peace of the whole Church.

---

1 St. Basil's uncle, Bishop Gregory, had been in sympathy with the disaffected suffragans in their troubles with St. Basil. To effect a reconciliation between the two, St. Gregory of Nyssa went so far as to forge several letters in the uncle's name. The forgery was naturally found out, and the breach between the two was bridged only with great difficulty. This letter was written in 371.
2 Bishop of Tyana, at odds with St. Basil. Cf. Letters 120, 121, 122, and 210.

Adamantius has come bringing a third one. How could I accept a letter sent through you or your household? I prayed that I might have a heart of stone, so as neither to remember the past nor to take notice of the present, but that I might bear every blow with head bowed down to the ground like the beasts. But, how much I suffer in my mind, since after a first and then a second experience, I can admit nothing without investigation.

I have written this to upbraid you for your simplicity—which I consider not only unbecoming in a Christian, but especially inappropriate at the present time—in order that for the future you may both watch over youself and spare me, since—for I must speak to you frankly—you are untrustworthy as a messenger in such matters. Yet, whoever they may be who wrote, we have answered them as was proper. Therefore, whether you yourself were laying this trap for me or had really received from the bishops the letter which you sent me, you have my answer. In fact, since you are our brother still mindful of the ties of nature, and do not look upon us as an enemy, you should have been otherwise concerned at the present, seeing that we have entered upon a life which, because it exceeds our strength, wears away our body and even afflicts our soul. Still, since you have in this way become involved in the warfare, you ought, therefore, to be at hand now and to share the troubles. 'For brethren,' it is said, 'are a help in the time of troubles.'[3]

But, if the most revered bishops really are willing to meet us, let them make known to us a definite place and time, and let them summon us through their own messengers. Though I do not refuse to meet my uncle, I will not consent to do so if the summons be not in proper form.

---
3 Cf. Eccli. 40.24.

59. To Gregory, His Uncle[1]

'I have kept silence. And shall I always keep silence and be content'[2] even longer to impose upon myself that most severe penalty of silence, neither myself writing nor hearing you salute me? For, since I have persisted in this grave decision until the present time, I think I may fittingly use the words of the Prophet: 'As a woman in labor I have been patient,'[3] always desiring either a public conference or a private talk with you, but failing always of my object because of my sins. I cannot ascribe to any other cause what has happened except that I am undoubtedly paying the penalty of my former sins by being alienated from your friendship—if, indeed, it is not a sacrilege to speak, in your case, of an alienation from any person, much more so from us, to whom from the beginning you have been a father.

But my sin, like some dense overspreading cloud, now has produced in me a lack of comprehension of all these things. For, when I consider that, except for my grief over the situation, nothing is being attained by it, how can I reasonably do otherwise than attribute the present condition to my defects? But, if my sins are the cause of what has happened, let this be the end of my difficulties; if some discipline was being administered, the purpose has assuredly been fulfilled. For, the time of punishment has not been short. And, therefore, being no longer able to contain myself, I have been the first to break silence, entreating you to be mindful both of us and of yourself who have shown for us

---

[1] Referring to the same trouble as the preceding letter and written at about the same time, in 371.
[2] Isa. 42.14 (Septuagint). The Douay translations seems to follow another text.
[3] *Ibid.*

during our whole life a solicitude beyond that which kinship calls for. And we now beg you, for our sake, to regard our city[4] with affection; at all events, not to alienate yourself from it on our account.

If, then, there is any consolation in Christ, if any communion of the Spirit, if any affection and compassion, fulfill our prayer. Put an end now to our sorrowing. Offer some beginning of brighter associations for the future. You yourself lead others to what is best, but do not yourself follow another to unfaithfulness. For, no physical trait has been considered so characteristic of anyone as are peace and gentleness characteristic of your soul. Assuredly, it would be proper for one such as you to draw others to himself and to cause all those who come near you to be permeated, as with the sweet odor of some perfume, with the excellence of your character. For, even if at present there is still some opposition, in a little while the value of peace will of itself be recognized. But, as long as dissensions arise out of slanders, suspicions will necessarily continue to grow worse. Truly, therefore, it is not becoming even for others to slight us, but, more than all these, for your Honor to do so. If we are, indeed, failing in some point, being admonished, we shall become better. But, this is impossible without a conference. And, if we are doing no wrong, why are we hated? This, therefore, I offer in my own defense.

As to what the churches, taking advantage of our disagreement, might say in their defense, but not for their good, it is better to pass over in silence. For, it is not in order to cause distress that I am writing thus, but that I may bring these distressing troubles to an end. Yet, nothing, I am

---
4 I.e., Caesarea. St. Basil, on being made Archbishop of Caesarea, was very anxious to have the support of the various bishops, among them Gregory, his uncle, who was in sympathy with the bishops of the opposition.

sure, has escaped your Intelligence,⁵ but with your deep understanding you might find out and inform others of much greater and more serious instances than we perceive. Indeed, you certainly have seen before we did the harm being done to the churches, and you are grieving more than we, since you have long ago been taught by the Lord not to despise even the least.⁶ The harm is not limited now to one or two men, but whole cities and districts share in the fruits of our misfortunes, to say nothing of what kind of reports concerning us will be made in the remoter regions. Therefore, it would be becoming to your Magnanimity⁷ to leave contention to others; nay, rather, to pluck it out of their hearts if it is possible, and by patience yourself to overcome the troubles. Now, while it is characteristic of every man to avenge himself when angry, yet, to be superior even to anger itself belongs only to you and those closely resembling you in virtue. However, I will not say that he who is angry with us is venting his wrath upon the innocent.

Therefore, either by your presence, or by letter, or by a summons to come to you, or by whatever means you may wish, comfort our soul. It is our prayer that your Reverence may be seen in our church, and may heal at once both us and the people by your very appearance and your gracious words. If, then, this is possible, well and good, but, if you should decide upon something else, we shall accept that. Only let us beg of you to make known to us without reserve what your Wisdom decides.

---

5 *Synesin*—a title of address generally used by St. Basil only for bishops.
6 Cf. Matt. 18.10.
7 *Megalopsuchia*—a title of address used by St. Basil for both clergy and laity, but not cited for other authors.

60. To Gregory, His Uncle[1]

I have always been glad to see my brother. In fact, why should I not, since he is my brother, and such a one? And at the present visit I have received him with the same affection, and have not in any way altered my love. God forbid that any such thing should happen as would make me forgetful of the ties of nature and hostile toward my relatives. On the contrary, I have deemed his presence a consolation in my physical infirmities and various spiritual sufferings. I also rejoiced much at receiving the letter which he brought from your Honor. For a considerable time I have been longing to hear from you, for no other reason than that we, too, might not add to our lives any sad tale of a mutual disagreement between the nearest of kin. This would indeed be a cause of pleasure to our enemies, but a misfortune to our friends, and it would displease God who has set up perfect love as a distinguishing mark of His disciples. Therefore, I am compelled to speak again, urging you to pray for us and to care for us in all things as your kinsman.

Since we ourselves are not able in our stupidity to understand the meaning of what is happening, we have decided to hold that as true which you have deigned to explain to us. But your Lordship[2] also must determine further appointments: our interview with each other, a suitable time, and a convenient place. If, then, your Dignity is actually willing to descend to our Lowliness and to exchange speech with us, whether you wish the conference to be in the presence of others or in private, we shall comply, since we have resolved upon this once and for all—to serve you in love,

---
1 Of the same subject matter and date as the preceding.
2 *Megalonoéas*—a title of address used by St. Basil for clergy and laymen, but not cited for other authors.

and by all means to do what is enjoined on us by your Reverence for the glory of God.

We have not required our most revered brother to tell us anything by word of mouth, because, formerly, his words could not be attested by the facts.

61. To Athanasius, Bishop of Alexandria[1]

I have read the letter of your Holiness in which you expressed your sorrow at the actions of the disreputable governor of Libya, and we have truly mourned for our country[2] because she is the mother and nurse of such evils. We have grieved, too, for Libya, our neighbor, since she shares in these evils and has been delivered up to the brutal practices of a man who spends his life in cruelty and in licentiousness. For such reasons, it would seem, the wise words of Ecclesiastes[3] were spoken: 'Woe to thee, O land, when thy king is a child' (and here is something even more stern), 'and when the princes eat' not at night, but they wanton at midday, lusting after unnatural unions more senselessly than beasts! Therefore, lashes from the just Judge await that man and they will be meted out in measure equal to that which he himself first inflicted upon God's saints.

As he has been made known to our Church by your Reverence's letter, all will, furthermore, consider him as one to be avoided, sharing neither fire nor water nor shelter with him, hoping, indeed, that there is some help for men who have thus won for themselves a common and unanimous

---
1 This, the first of St. Basil's six extant letters to the great St. Athanasius, is an answer to his letter announcing the excommunication of the governor of Libya, a native of Cappadocia. It was written in 371.
2 Cf. Homer, *Od.* 13.219.
3 Eccle. 10.16.

condemnation. Sufficient for him is his record and your letter itself which is read everywhere. We shall not cease showing it to all his relatives and friends, and to strangers. And, perhaps, even if the due penalties do not touch him at the present moment, as they did the Pharaoh,[4] at some later period they will bring to him a heavy and painful retribution.

62. A Letter of Consolation to the Church of Parnassus[1]

Following an old custom established by long observance and revealing to you the fruit of the Spirit, love in God, we are visiting your Reverence by letter, sharing with you both your grief at your bereavement and your solicitude for the affairs now at hand. Concerning your distressing troubles we say only this, that it is an opportune time for us to look to the precepts of the Apostle and not to grieve 'even as others who have no hope';[2] not to be insensible, of course, to what has happened, but, while conscious of our loss, not to be overcome by our grief. We should, on the other hand, consider our pastor happy in his death because he has laid aside his life at an age rich with years and has gone to his rest amid the greatest honors from the Lord.

Concerning all else we have this to recommend, that you should cast off all dejection, regain self-control, and rise to

---

4 An allusion to the plagues and the final destruction of the Pharaoh as described in Exodus.

---

1 This letter to the people of Parnassus (a town of Northern Cappadocia near the modern Tchikin Aghyl) on the death of their bishop, while ostensibly written for consolation, was in reality an exhortation to elect an orthodox bishop. They elected the orthodox Hypsis, but he was expelled by the Arians in 375. Cf. Letter 237. The date, according to Maran, *op. cit.* xvi, is 372, just before the visit of Valens which gave the Arians of this church so much power.

2 1 Thess. 4.13.

the necessary duty of caring for the Church, so that the holy God may give heed to His own flock and provide for you a shepherd according to His will, one who will govern you wisely.

63. To the Governor of Neo-Caesarea[1]

'The wise man, e'en though he dwells in a distant land, though I may never behold him with my eyes, I account my friend,' says the tragic poet Euripides.[2] If we say, therefore, even though we have never enjoyed the favor of personal acquaintance with your Excellency,[3] that we are your intimate friend, do not judge these words to be flattery. Our friendship has sprung from report that with mighty voice proclaimed your achievements to all men. Moreover, since meeting with the most revered Elpidius,[4] we have come to know you as well, and have been as utterly captivated by you, as if we had been associated with you for a long time, gaining knowledge of your virtues through long experience. For, the man could not stop telling us every detail about you—your nobility of soul, your loftiness of spirit, your gentleness of disposition, your experience in affairs, your prudence in judgment, your dignity blended with joyousness, your eloquence, and other qualities which he enumerated in his long conversation with us but which we cannot write without making our letter excessively long. How, then, could I help esteem-

---
1 A respectful salutation to the Governor of Neo-Caesarea, written in 371.
2 From an unknown play of Euripides. Cf. Nauck, *Trag. Graec. Frag.* No. 902. Similar expressions are found in Iamblichus, *De vita Pythag.* 33.237; Procop. Gaz., *Epist.* 154; and Cicero, *De nat. deorum* 1.44.121.
3 *Megalophuias*—a title of address used by St. Basil for the clergy and for laymen.
4 An Elpidius is also mentioned in Letters 64, 77, and 78.

ing such a man? Why, how could I even refrain from declaring aloud the emotions of my soul?

Therefore, accept the appellation,⁵ O admirable Sir, applied to you out of true and genuine friendship, for our practice is far from servile flattering. Keep us numbered among your friends, manifesting yourself to us by continual letters and consoling us for your absence.

64. To Hesychius[1]

There are many things which even from the beginning have bound me to your Honor—our common love of letters, which is proclaimed in many places by those who have made proof of it, and our long-standing friendship with that admirable man, Terentius.[2] Added to this is the conversation which we had with that thoroughly excellent man who fulfills the claim of every intimate relationship with us,[3] our most revered brother Elpidius.[4] He described all your virtuous qualities (and he, if anyone, is most able to discern and express in words the virtue of a man). He enkindled in us such a longing for you that we prayed you might some day stand upon our ancient hearth, in order that we might enjoy your splendid gifts not only by hearsay but also by experience.

---

5 I.e., of 'friend.

---

1 Nothing is known of Hesychius except such information as is found in this letter and in Letter 72. The date of this writing is the same as that of the preceding letter.
2 Terentius was a general and a count of the orthodox faith. Cf. Letters 99, 214, and 216.
3 Cf. Homer, *Iliad* 6.429-430: 'Nay, Hector, thou art to me father and queenly mother, thou art brother, and thou art my stalwart husband.'
4 Cf. preceding Letter 63 n. 3.

65. To Atarbius[1]

And what end will there be to our silence, if I, on the one hand, should claim the privileges of age and wait for you to take the initiative in offering salutations, while your Charity, on the other, should wish to persist in your sinister decision of maintaining silence? Yet, since I consider that defeat in matters of friendship has the force of victory, I admit that I am conceding to you the credit of seeming to have prevailed over my opinion. And I have been the first to start writing, knowing that charity 'bears with all things, endures all things,' nowhere 'seeks her own,' and therefore 'never fails.'[2] For, he who submits to his neighbor through charity is not humbled. Therefore, see to it that you yourself exhibit for the future, at least, the first and greatest fruit of the Spirit, which is charity.[3] Cast off the sullenness of an angry man which you are evincing by your silence, and regain joy in your heart, peace toward your like-minded brethren, and zeal and solicitude for the preservation of the churches of the Lord. In fact, be assured that, unless we resume a struggle for the churches equal to that which the opponents of sound doctrine maintain for their ruin and destruction, there will

---
1 Atarbius, whom Tillemont wrongly considered an Armenian bishop, was Bishop of Neo-Caesarea and probably a relative of St. Basil. Cf. Letter 210. Letters 126, 204, 207, and 210 contain information on the break between St. Basil and Atarbius, and on the efforts made by St. Basil to mend the breach and rescue Atarbius from his errors. That he was Bishop of Neo-Caesarea is evident from the fact that (1) he is so designated in some MSS. of St. Basil's Letters; (2) the character and circumstances of Atarbius, as depicted in Letter 126, entirely agree with those of the unnamed Bishop of Neo-Caesarea referred to in Letters 204, 207, and 210; (3) in the Acts of the Council of Constantinople he represents the Province of Pontus Palemoniacus, of which Neo-Caesarea was the metropolis.
2 Cf. 1 Cor. 13.5,7,8.
3 Cf. Gal. 5.22-23.

be nothing to hinder the truth from being swept away by enemies, and lost. Likewise, nothing will prevent our sharing the condemnation, unless, with all zeal and eagerness, in agreement with each other and in harmony with God, we show all possible care for the unity of the churches.

Therefore, I urge, cast out of your mind the thought that you stand in need of union with no one. For, it is not the spirit of one who walks in charity or fulfills the command of Christ to cut himself off from union with his brethren. At the same time I wish that your plan of action would be to consider that the evil of war[4] going on around is ever coming nearer to us, also, and if we, along with the others, share its abuse, we shall find no one sympathizing with us, because we have not in our time of peace offered to the wronged our contribution of sympathy.

66. To Athanasius, Bishop of Alexandria[1]

I think that the present order or, rather, to speak more truly, disorder of the churches, grieves no one else so much as your Honor. Indeed, in comparing the present with the past you can observe how utterly different from the former the existing conditions have become. You can also infer that, if our affairs continue sinking to a lower level with the same speed, there will be nothing to hinder the churches from being changed completely in a short time to some other form. Frequently, while alone, I have had this thought—if the perversion of the churches appears so piteous to us, what feeling about these matters must he have who has experienced the ancient tranquillity and unity in faith of the churches of the

---
4 I.e., the persecutions of Valens.

1 This letter was written in 371.

Lord?[2] Yet, as the greater part of the distress falls upon your Excellency, so we think that fittingly the greater share of the anxiety for the churches will be borne by your Wisdom.[3] I have also known and realized for a long time from the moderate understanding which I have of the affairs that the one way of sustaining our churches is union with the Western bishops. If they should be willing to show for the dioceses of our regions that zeal which they employed in the case of one or two of those in the West[4] who were discovered to be heretical, it would perhaps be of some advantage to our common interests, since our rulers are looking askance at the trustworthiness of the people, and the people everywhere are following their bishops[5] without question.

Now, who is more able than your Intelligence to accomplish this? Who is keener in comprehending the needs? Who is more practical in carrying out useful measures? Who is more sympathetic toward the affliction of his brethren? Who is more revered in the whole West than you by virtue of your venerable white hair? Leave to men some memorial worthy of your manner of life, O most honorable Father.[6] Adorn by this one work your numberless labors in behalf of religion. Send from the holy church subject to you to the bishops throughout the West some men strong in sound doctrine. Tell them of the calamities pressing upon us. Suggest some means of assistance. Become a Samuel to the

---

2 As St. Athanasius was about twenty-five years older than St. Basil, he could easily remember the peace in the Church before the outbreak of Arianism.

3 *Phronései*—a title of address used by St. Basil for clergymen and laymen.

4 On the margin of the Codex Regius Secundus is found this scholion: 'Concerning the bishops at Rome, Auxentius and those with him.'

5 The Benedictine editors consider that Valens is meant by *ton kratoúnton*, and not the rulers but the bishops by *autois*. It is in this sense that the passage has been translated.

6 *Timiótate*—a title of distinction generally applied by St. Basil to bishops.

churches. Share in the sufferings of the people who are being oppressed by war. Offer up prayers for peace. Beg of God the favor that He send upon His churches some remembrance of peace. I know that letters are weak instruments for advising in matters of such importance. You, however, do not need exhortation from others—no more, certainly, than the noblest athletes need the acclamation of boys; nor are we speaking to one who does not understand, but we are urging on the effort of a man who is already busily concerned.

In regard to the other affairs of the East you need, perhaps, the co-operation also of a greater number, and you must await the bishops from the West. Of course, the good condition of the Church at Antioch clearly depends upon your Reverence, who will restore some to order, silence others, and give back strength to the Church through unanimity.[7] Without doubt, you yourself understand more clearly than anyone else that, like the wisest doctors, you should begin the treatment in the most vital parts. And what could be more vital for the churches throughout the world than the Church at Antioch? If this Church should happen to return to unity, nothing would prevent it, as a sound head, from furnishing soundness to the whole body. And the infirmities of that city truly need your wisdom and evangelical sympathy. It is not only disunited by the heretics, but it is torn asunder by those who say that they are of the same mind with one another. Now,

---

7 St. Basil here refers to the schisms caused by the refusal of the Eustathian or Old Catholic party to recognize Meletius as bishop of the whole orthodox party. After the death of Eustathius, the Church at Antioch, the staunch support of orthodoxy, was rent with dissensions because of the election of several incompetent bishops. Then, Meletius was elected as a compromise candidate. He seems to have been neither entirely Nicene nor Arian, but he was esteemed by such men as St. John Chrysostom, St. Gregory Nazianzen, St. Gregory of Nyssa, St. Basil, and even his adversary St. Epiphanius. Most of the churches of the West and Egypt supported Paulinus, ordained in the Old Catholic party, but the East supported Meletius. Cf. St. Ambrose, Letter 13, which also deals with this same general topic.

to unite these and bring them together into the harmony of one body is the prerogative of Him alone who by His ineffable power grants even to dry bones a return to sinews and flesh. Assuredly, the Lord performs His great works through those worthy of Him. Again, therefore, we hope that in this instance, also, your Excellency will see fit to assume the administration of these important matters, so that you will settle the disorder of the people, make an end of the factional exercise of authority, subject all to one another in love, and give back to the Church her pristine strength.

67. To Athanasius, Bishop of Alexandria[1]

In my earlier letter to your Honor it seemed sufficient to me to declare this only—that all those comprising the holy Church at Antioch, who are strong in their faith, should be brought into agreement and unity. My purpose was to make clear that the many sections which have now been formed should unite with Bishop Meletius, dearly beloved of God. But, since this same beloved fellow deacon of ours, Dorotheus,[2] has asked for more definite information on these matters, we are, perforce, adding by way of explanation that both the whole East and we, who are in complete union with Meletius, pray and desire to see him governing the Church of the Lord. For, he is a man blameless in faith and incomparable in his manner of life, as well as being, so to say, the leader of the whole body of the Church, whereas all the rest are as segments of its members.

---

1 Concerning the same matter as the preceding and written at about the same time.
2 Dorotheus was a deacon of the Church at Antioch belonging to the party of Meletius. St. Basil used him on several occasions to carry letters. Cf. Letters 47, 50, 52, 61, 62, and 273.

As a consequence, it is entirely necessary and at the same time advantageous for some to be united with this man, as small streams unite with great rivers, and for some proper regulation to be made for the others which will bring peace to the people, and will be in accord with your intelligence and with your renowned skill and zeal. As your unsurpassed[3] Wisdom is not unaware, these same arrangements are already satisfactory on the whole to your co-religionists in the West, as the letter brought to us by the blessed Sylvanus[4] declares.

68. To Meletius, Bishop of Antioch[1]

Hitherto, we wished to keep the most pious[2] brother Dorotheus,[3] our fellow deacon, with us, so that at the end of our negotiations we might send him back to acquaint your Honor with the details of what has taken place. But, since we had long delayed, postponing matters from day to day, and since at the same time a certain plan occurred to us for action to be taken in our perplexity, we dispatched this same brother to meet your Holiness, personally to report everything, and to set forth our suggestion. Our purpose was that, if our ideas should appear to be useful, your Excellency should zealously strive for their realization.

Now, to put it briefly, the opinion has prevailed that this same brother of ours, Dorotheus, should go to Rome and

---

3 *Anhypérblēton*—a title of distinction which St. Basil uses for both clergymen and laymen.
4 The identity of Sylvanus cannot be determined.

1 The same Bishop Meletius of whom St. Basil speaks with such esteem in the preceding letter. Cf. also Letter 66 n. 4. The letter is of the same date as the preceding.
2 *Eulabéstaton*—a title of distinction used by St. Basil for the lower ranks of the clergy, but never for bishops.
3 Cf. Letter 67.

should induce some of the brethren from Italy to visit us, coming by sea in order that they may elude those who would try to hinder them. For, I have seen that those who have influence at court are not at all willing or able to make any mention of the exiles to the emperor, but they consider it a gain to see nothing worse happening in the churches. Therefore, if your Wisdom should think that the plan is good, you will condescend to write letters offering suggestions on the points[4] he should discuss and the persons with whom he should speak. And, so that your letter will have some authority, you will by all means include in it the names of those who are of like mind, even if they are not present. Conditions here are still in a state of uncertainty. Euippius[5] indeed has come, but he has not, as yet, made any disclosures. However, they are threatening an assembly of those people from both the Armenian Tetrapolis and from Cilicia who hold views similar to theirs.

69. To Athanasius, Bishop of Alexandria[1]

The opinion which we have had for a long time of your Honor is always being confirmed as time advances; rather, it is even strengthened by the accumulation of successive incidents. Although it is quite enough for most men to watch over their own responsibilities, this does not suffice for you. On the contrary, you have as great a care for all the churches

---

4 I.e., the deacon Dorotheus.
5 Euippius was a bishop with a tendency to Arianism, and St. Basil felt obligated to separate from communion with him. Cf. Letter 128. Although in 360 Eustathius of Sebaste had declared Euippius unworthy of the name of bishop, in 376 he united with him and recognized bishops and presbyters ordained by him. Cf. Letters 226, 239, 244, and 251.

---

1 This letter was written at about the same time as the preceding one.

as for the one particularly entrusted to you by our benign Lord. For, indeed, you never cease reasoning, admonishing, writing, and on every occasion sending the best counselors. And even now we have welcomed with much joy the most revered brother Peter, who was sent from the holy company of the clergy under your direction. We have approved the good intent of his journey, which he explains according to the commands of your Honor, winning over the rebellious and joining together those who have been torn asunder. Therefore, wishing to make some contribution to the effort in this affair, we thought a most suitable beginning for us in the undertaking would be to have recourse to your Perfection as to the head of all, and to regard you as counselor and guide of our actions. For this reason we have again sent to your Reverence the brother Dorotheus, deacon of the church subject to the most honorable Bishop Meletius, who has shown a goodly zeal concerning the right faith and is also desirous of seeing the peace of the churches. Following your advice, therefore (which you are able to make safer from error both by virtue of your age and experience in affairs and also because of the fact that you have the guidance of the Spirit beyond other men), he may at once undertake the work which we are eagerly pursuing.

You will, I am sure, receive him and look upon him with the eyes of peace, aiding him with the support of your prayers and furnishing him with letters for his journey Further, after having him associate with the zealous brethren there, you will guide him in the task set before him. It seemed to us to be worth while to write to the Bishop of Rome, asking him to examine our affairs and give us advice, so that, since it is difficult for men to be sent from Rome by a general synodical decree, he himself might have full authority in the matter, choosing men able to endure the hardships of travel and also competent through their gentleness and strength of character, to rebuke the perverse among us. They should be men who have an appropriate and effective manner of speech, and should understand thoroughly everything accomplished after the Council of Ariminum[2] for the dissolution of the measures taken there through compulsion. Furthermore, they should come quietly by sea without the knowledge of anyone, so as to arrive before the enemies of peace are aware of their coming.

Now, this, too, is the request of some here—and necessarily, as it appears to us, also—that they[3] eradicate the heresy of

---

2 On the Council of Ariminum or Rimini the *Catholic Encylopedia* says: 'The Council of Rimini was opened early in July, 359, with over four hundred bishops present. About eighty Semi-Arians, including Ursacius, Germinius, and Auxentius, withdrew from the orthodox bishops, the most eminent of whom was Restitutus of Carthage; Liberius, Eusebius, Dionysius, and others were still in exile. The two parties sent separate deputations to the Emperor, the orthodox asserting clearly their firm attachment to the faith of Nicaea, the Arian minority adhering to the imperial formula. But the inexperienced representatives of the orthodox majority allowed themselves to be deceived, and not only entered into communion with the heretical delegates, but even subscribed, at Nice in Thrace, a formula to the effect merely that the Son is like the Father according to the Scriptures (the words "in all things" being omitted). On their return to Rimini, they were met with the unanimous protests of their colleagues. But the threats of the consul Taurus, the remonstrances of the Semi-Arians against hindering peace between East and West for a word not contained in Scripture, their privations and their home-sickness—all combined to weaken the constancy of the orthodox bishops. And the last twenty were induced to subscribe when Ursacius had an addition made to the formula of Nice, declaring that the Son is not a creature like other creatures. Pope Liberius, having regained his liberty, rejected this formula, which was thereupon repudiated by many who had signed it. In view of the hasty manner of its adoption and lack of approbation by the Holy See, it could have no authority.'

3 I.e., the Romans, especially, proposed representatives. St. Basil was annoyed that Marcellus, whom he regarded as unorthodox, was, in the words of St. Jerome, 'fortified by communion with Julius and Athanasius, popes of Rome and Alexandria.' Cf. *De Vir Illust.* 86. According to Cardinal Newman, St. Athanasius upheld Marcellus 'to about A.D. 360,' but in his fourth oration against the Arians attacked him pointedly without naming him.

Marcellus[4] on the ground that it is dangerous, harmful, and hostile to the true faith. Up to the present time, in all the letters which they write, they never cease anathematizing the detestable Arius up and down and banishing him from the churches. But they seem to have brought no charge against Marcellus who has displayed an impiety diametrically opposed to that of Arius, has been sacrilegious as regards the very existence of the divinty of the Only-begotten, and has accepted in a wrong sense the expression, 'the Word.' He declares, indeed, that the Only-begotten was called the 'Word,' and that He came forth according to the need and the time, but had again returned to Him whence He had come forth, and that He neither existed before His procession nor does He subsist[5] after His return. Moreover, as a proof of this, the books containing that sinful writing are in our possession. But, in spite of all, they did not seem to discredit him in any way and they are guilty to this degree, that—in the beginning, in ignorance of the truth—they even received him into ecclesiastical communion. Therefore, the present circumstances demand that mention be made of this man in proper manner, so that men wanting an opportunity[6] may not have one, since those sound in faith are joined with your Holiness and the men who are wavering in the true faith are publicly exposed. As a result, we shall hereafter know those who are united with us, and not, as in a night battle, be unable to distinguish between friends and foes. We urge only that the deacon whom we mentioned before be sent

---

4 Cf. Letters 125 and 263 for St. Basil's opinion of the heretical doctrines of Marcellus of Ancyra. Marcellus had upheld the cause of orthodoxy at Nicaea. Later, however, when attacking the errors of Asterius, he was supposed to have taught that the Son had no real personality, but was merely an external manifestation of the Father.
5 I.e., does not exist in essence.
6 I.e., of following the heresy of Marcellus, as they could safely do so as long as he remained in good standing for orthodoxy.

out immediately on the first voyage, so that some of the things for which we prayed can be accomplished at least next year.

Now, this you yourself will understand even before we speak and you certainly will be careful that, when these men take charge, if God wills it, they will not start schisms in the churches, but will in every way draw together into unity those holding the same doctrines, even if they find some who have personal reasons for differences with each other. This is necessary, lest the orthodox people, revolting with their leaders, should be split into many factions. For there is need of zealous endeavor that everything be considered secondary to peace, and that before all else attention be given to the Church at Antioch, so that the sound part may not become weak by being divided on the question of the Persons.[7] Or, rather, you yourself will hereafter care for all these matters when, as we pray, with God's help you will find all entrusting to you the affairs pertaining to the present condition of the churches.

70. *Without Address, concerning a Synod*[1]

To renew bonds characteristic of the early love and again to restore to vigor the peace of the Fathers, the heavenly and saving gift of Christ, which has been dimmed by time, is for us both essential and advantageous, and it will be, I well know, a pleasure to your Christ-loving spirit. For, what could be more pleasing than to see men who are separated by such great distances bound in a union of love into one harmonious

---

7 I.e., of the Godhead.

1 This letter is considered by all, including Tillemont and the Benedictine editors, as addressed to Pope Damasus. It was written in the autumn of 371.

membership in the body of Christ? Almost the whole East, most honorable Father (and by the East I mean the regions from Illyricum to Egypt[2]) is being shaken by a mighty storm and flood. The old heresy sown by Arius, the enemy of truth, is now shamelessly springing up, like a bitter root that yields deadly fruit, and is finally prevailing. For, as a result of calumny and abuse, the champions of sound faith in each diocese have been banished from the Church, and the control of affairs has been handed over to those who are leading captive the souls of purest faith. We have awaited one solution of the difficulties—the visitation of your Mercifulness.[3] Indeed, in times past, your incredible charity has always attracted us and we for a short time regained strength in our soul because of the joyful report that we should have a visitation from you. But, we are utterly disappointed in our hope, and, being no longer able to endure, we have resorted to an exhortation by letter, asking you to rouse yourselves to our assistance and send some of the like-minded brethren either to reconcile those at variance or to restore to friendship the churches of God, or, at least, to make more evident to you those responsible for the confusion. This will also make it clear to you with whom you ought for the future to have communion.

We do not at all seek something new, but what has been customary both with the other blessed men of old,[4] who

---

2 Roughly, the two eastern prefectures of Diocletian and his successors.
3 *Eusplanchnias*—a title of address used by St. Basil for clergymen, but not found in the works of other authors.
4 The bishops of Rome. The Benedictine edition points out that the kindness of the bishops of Rome here mentioned by St. Basil is borne out by the evidence both of Dionysius, Bishop of Corinth (cf. Eusebius, *Hist. Eccl.* 4.23), of Dionysius of Alexandria (Dionysius to Sixtus II in Eusebius, *Hist. Eccl.* 7.5), and of Eusebius himself in his history. The troubles here referred to took place in the time of Gallienus, when the Scythians plundered Cappadocia and the neighboring countries (cf. Sozomen, *Eccl. Hist.* 2.6).

were dear to God, and especially with yourselves. We know from continuous tradition, and we have been taught by our fathers in their answers to our questions, and by letters still preserved among us, that the renowned Dionysius,[5] the most blessed bishop, who was conspicuous among you for the soundness of his faith and, in fact, for all virtues, visited our Church at Caesarea and consoled our fathers through letters, and also sent men to redeem the brethren from captivity. But, our affairs now are in a sadder and more difficult condition, and demand even more care. For, at present, we lament, not the overthrowing of earthly structures, but the seizing of the churches; we behold, not bodily slavery, but the enslavement of souls, effected daily by the fighters for heresy. Therefore, unless you will now rouse yourselves for our relief, you will in a short time find there are none to whom you may stretch your hand, since all things will be under the dominion of heresy.

71. Basil to Gregory[1]

I received the letter from your Reverence through the

---

[5] A Greek by birth, and consecrated July 22, 259, on the death of Sixtus II, during the persecution of Valerian. Nothing is recorded of him except his efforts against heresy.

[1] As St. Gregory of Nazianzus had refused to give his assistance for the election of St. Basil as bishop, so he later refused his support to St. Basil and would not accept any great responsibilities. He begged to be excused for remaining at Nazianzus on the ground that it was better for St. Basil's sake that there should be no suspicion of favor toward personal friends. Cf. Greg. Naz., Letter 45. The present letter, written in 371, is partly an answer to the letter from St. Gregory in which he announced this stand; partly a plea that St. Gregory would not heed the charges of heterodoxy which were being spread against him.

most revered brother Helenius;[2] and what you intimated to us he in person clearly explained. As to how we were affected on hearing it, you certainly can have no possible doubt. But, since we have decided to consider our love for you superior to every grievance, we have received even this as is befitting, and we pray to the holy God that during the days or hours remaining to us we may be preserved in the same disposition toward you as in the past. For, during that time we were conscious of having failed in nothing either great or small.

But, if that man[3] who at present is striving eagerly to pry into the life of the Christians[4] and who also thinks that associating with us brings him some dignity is inventing what he has not heard and is relating what he has not understood, it is no wonder. But, this is amazing and incredible—that of the brothers with you he has as listeners those who were the truest to me, and not as listeners only, but even, it seems, as disciples. At all events, even though under other circumstances it would be surprising that such a person should be the teacher and I the one disparaged, the unhappy state of affairs has taught us to be annoyed at nothing. In fact, because of our sins, more ignominious reports than these have for a long time been commonly made against us. For my part, indeed, if I have not yet given that man's brethren a proof of my beliefs concerning God, not even now have I any answer to give. For, how will a brief letter convince those whom a long life has not persuaded? But, if my former life is sufficient in itself, let the accusations of the slanderers

---

2 Hellenius was a surveyor of customs at Nazianzus, the confidential friend of both St. Basil and St. Gregory of Nazianzus. Besides delivering to St. Basil the message here referred to, we find him in 372 conveying a message from the bishops of Lesser Armenia. Cf. Letter 98.
3 St. Basil avoids mentioning the slanderer by name.
4 I.e., not entering into the brotherhood of Christians, but merely peering in.

be considered as nonsense. Yet, if we permit unbridled mouths and untaught minds to discuss whatever they may wish, and if we have ears ready to accept their statements, not only shall we ourselves receive wrong accounts of other's affairs, but others also of ours.

Now, the cause of this is the fact that we do not meet together, a situation which I have long urged should be avoided, but about which I am now silent through weariness. For, if, in accordance with our agreement of former days and with the care we now owe to our churches, we had passed a great part of the year with each other, we would not have given opening to the slanderers. But, if it seems best, dismiss these men from your mind, and be encouraged yourself to labor with us in the struggle which lies ahead, and with us to meet him who is making war against us. For, if you are only seen, you will check his assault, and you will separate those who are joining together to overthrow their fatherland by making known to them that you yourself, by the grace of God, are the leader of our assembly, and that you will close every iniquitous mouth that pours forth contempt against God. If this is done, the very circumstances will show who it is that is following you toward the good, and who is changing from one side to another and through cowardice betraying the word of truth. But, if the interests of the Church are betrayed, there is little reason for me to try to convince by words those who regard my worth as would men who have not yet learned to measure themselves. In fact, after a short time, by the grace of God, the arguments drawn from our actions will refute the slanders, since we expect to endure even greater sufferings,[5] perhaps, for the word of truth, but, if not, at least to be driven from our

---

5 Perhaps St. Basil is referring to martyrdom.

churches and our fatherlands.⁶ Even if nothing for which we hope shall happen, the judgment of Christ is not far off. Consequently, if you request a conference for the sake of the churches, I am ready to hasten wherever you may summon me, but if to end the slanders, I have no leisure at present to give an answer concerning them.

72. To Hesychius[1]

I know both your love for us and your zeal for good. Therefore, since I must appease my most beloved[2] son, Callisthenes,[3] I thought that I would more easily accomplish my earnest desire if you would share my solicitude. The man has been vexed at the most eloquent[4] Eustochius; and his vexation is just. He charges the latter's servants with insolent and mad acts against him. We are asking him to relent, to be satisfied with the fear with which he has inspired both those overbold men and their masters, and to put an end to the quarrel by granting pardon. For, in this way, two advantages will accrue to him—the respect of men and the approval of God —if he is willing to mingle forbearance with the fear aroused. Do you yourself, therefore, if you have any past friendship and intimacy with the man, beg of him this favor, and if you know any in the city who are able to appease him, take

---

6 Probably Caesarea, the place of his birth, and the Pontus, the region of his bringing up.

---

1 Cf. Letter 44, concerning Hesychius. This letter was written about 371.
2 *Potheinótaton*—a title of distinction used by St. Basil for clergy and laymen.
3 Callisthenes and Eustochius were both laymen of Cappadocia. Nothing is known of them except what has been learned from this and the following letters.
4 *Logiotátou*—a title of distinction used by St. Basil for laymen.

them as companions in our solicitude, telling them that the accomplishment of this will be especially gratifying to me.

And send back the fellow deacon when he has completed the business for which he was despatched. For, I am confused, when men have recourse to me, that I am unable to be of any help to them.

73. To Callisthenes[1]

I gave thanks to God on reading the letter of your Nobility: first, because I received a greeting from a man who chose to honor us, for, truly, we value most highly association with eminent men; secondly, because I had the pleasure of being kindly remembered. The sign of remembrance was the letter. When I received it and understood its purport, I marveled at how truly, according to the opinion of all, it bespoke paternal reverence. For the fact that a man, incensed and angered, and eager for vengeance against those who had vexed him, really put an end to a great part of his vehemence, and gave us authority in the affair, afforded the pleasure as of a father rejoicing over a spiritual son. In return for this, then, what else remains but to pray for blessings for you—that to friends you may be most pleasing, to enemies formidable, but by all alike respected, in order that even those who have failed in any of their proper duties, taking notice of your gentleness, may reproach themselves because they have wronged such a person as you.

Now, since you have ordered the servants brought to the scene of their disorderly conduct, I ask to know the object of your Excellency's demanding this. For, if you yourself will

---
[1] The Callisthenes mentioned in the preceding letter. This letter was written at about the same time and on the same subject as the preceding.

be present and will in person exact the penalty for the bold deeds, the slaves will certainly be at hand. In fact, what else can be done if you have already decided upon this? But, we do not know what further favor we shall receive, if we are not able to free the slaves from punishment. And, if in this case business on the way detains you, who will be there to receive the men? And who will punish them for you? But, if you are resolved that they shall come into your presence, and this has been decided once and for all, order them to come no farther than Sasima, and there show the gentleness and magnanimity of your character. For after you have taken in hand those who have provoked you, and have shown in this way that your dignity must not be treated with contempt, dismiss them unharmed, as we urged in our former letter, thus not only granting us a favor, but also receiving from God the recompense for your deeds.

And I say this, not because I think that the matters should be brought to an end in this way, but because I am yielding to your impetuosity and because I fear that some rawness of spirit may remain, and as even the simplest of remedies appear painful in the case of inflamed eyes, so now, also, our words may rouse your anger rather than calm it. Yet, to entrust the vengeance to us would be especially becoming and would avail to bring the greatest honor to you and to achieve the desirable respect for me among my friends and contemporaries. At any rate, even if you have sworn to give them up for punishment according to the laws, our censure is neither inferior as a legal remedy, nor is the divine law less honored than are the civil laws.

But, it would be possible that, if they were corrected here by our laws, in which you yourself also have the hope of salvation, you would be freed from the obligation of your oath, and they would pay a penalty commensurate with their sins.

But, I am again writing a long letter. For, in my great desire to persuade you, I cannot willingly leave unsaid any of the thoughts which come to my mind, fearing lest on that account my request may become ineffectual, because I have done my teaching inadequately. O most honorable and noble son of the Church, confirm both my hopes which I now place in you and the unanimous testimony of all concerning your graciousness and gentleness, and order the soldier to depart from us at once. As the matter stands, he has left undone no act of annoyance or of insolence, since he prefers to avoid grieving you rather than to hold all of us as his close friends.

74. To Martinianus[1]

How much, think you, would I esteem the opportunity of our some time meeting and conversing together at greater length, so that I may enjoy all your splendid qualities? For, if it is important as an evidence of culture 'to have seen the cities of men and to have learned their minds,'[2] association

---

[1] The identity of this Martinianus is not known beyond the fact that he was a personal friend of St. Basil. From the references in the letter to his great knowledge and extensive travels it may be inferred that he was a philosopher or a man of letters. Cf. W. M. Ramsay, 'Basil of Caesarea,' *Expositor* 5, Series 3 (1896) 54. St. Basil wrote this and the two following letters to obtain mediators with the emperor for his country. The policy of the Byzantine government was to divide the larger provinces so as to lessen the power of the provincial governors. It was now time for Cappadocia to be divided; and Valens' hatred of St. Basil caused him to leave the smaller section of the country to the metropolis, Caesarea. These letters, written in 371, are some of the poorest in the collection. St. Basil, however, showed his true greatness immediately after this when Valens came to Caesarea.

[2] Cf. *Odyssey* 1.3ff: 'Many were the men whose cities he saw and whose mind he learned, and many the woes he suffered in his heart upon the sea, seeking to win his own life and the return of his comrades.' Cf. also Horace, *De arte poetica* 142: 'Qui mores hominum multorum vidit et urbes.'

with you, I think, bestows this favor in a short time. In fact, what greater advantage is it for a person to see many men, one at a time, than to see one man who has acquired the experience of all men together? I would rather say that the benefit is greatest in whatever procures without fatigue an acquaintance with the beautiful, and gathers a knowledge of virtue free from admixture with evil. At all events, whether it is renowned deeds or words worthy of remembrance, or the laws and customs of the most excellent men, all are stored up in the treasury of your soul. Therefore, not only for a year, as Alcinous listened to Odysseus,[3] but for my whole life should I pray that I might listen to you, and that for this reason, at least, my life might be a long one, even though a burdensome one to me. Why in the world, then, am I writing now, when I ought to be present with you? Because my afflicted country urgently summons me to herself. You are not ignorant, most noble Sir, of what she has suffered—that certain veritable Maenads, evil spirits, have torn her asunder as they did Pentheus. In fact, they divide and redivide her like inexperienced doctors, making her wounds more painful because of their lack of experience. Now, since she is suffering because she has been cut to pieces, it is left to us to cure her ills, as it were. Therefore, the citizens have written urging us to come; it is necessary to present ourselves, not because we shall be of any assistance in the trouble, but to avoid the censure of desertion. For, you know how prone to hope are those who are in great straits, and prone at times also to find fault, always directing the blame to what has been disregarded.

Yet, for this same reason I wanted to meet you and to express my opinion, or rather to entreat you to consider some vigorous policy—one becoming to your high spirit—and not

---
3 Cf. *Odyssey* Bks. 7, 8, 9.

to neglect our country which has fallen on her knees, but to go to the court, saying with your accustomed frankness that they should not think that they have acquired two provinces instead of one. They have not brought in the second from some other country, but have acted almost the same as a person who, after he had gained possession of a horse or a cow, would cut it in two, and then think that he had two animals in place of the one. Yet, he did not make two; he even destroyed the one. Furthermore, say to those who are in authority that they do not in this way strengthen their dominions, for power lies not in number but in the state of their affairs. For, now, we certainly think that some, perhaps because of their ignorance of the truth, others, because they do not wish to cause grief by their words, and still others, because it is a matter of no concern to them, disregard what is happening. Therefore, if it would be possible for you to go to the emperor himself, that would be best for our affairs, and befitting the noble character of your life. And if it is especially hard, both because of the time of year, and because of your age which, as you yourself say, has an accompanying sluggishness, at least there is no labor involved in writing. Therefore, if you give aid through letters to your country, you will, first, be fully aware that you have failed in nothing that comes within your power; then, furthermore, you will offer sufficient consolation to the afflicted by the very fact of showing sympathy. Would that it had been possible for you to be at hand in these troubles and to see with your own eyes the sad condition itself. For, thus being moved by the very vividness of the sight, you would, perhaps, have given vent to some utterance befitting both your Lordship and the dejection of the city. But, at all events, do not refuse to believe us when we give our description. Or would we truly need a Simonides[4] or some other such lyric poet who knows how to bewail the sufferings in a striking manner? Yet, why do I say Simonides? I should have said Aeschylus,[5] or someone like him, who graphically portrayed a terrible calamity, wailing aloud with mighty voice.

For, those assemblies and speeches and conferences in the market place by men of high repute, and such things as formerly made our city famous, have gone from us. As a result, any man of learning and eloquence now would seem to approach the market place more rarely than those did formerly at Athens who were charged with dishonor or were unclean of hand. There has been introduced in place of these assemblies the crudeness of certain Scythians or Massagetae. And there is only the sound of demanding creditors and hounded debtors, and of men being beaten with whips. The galleries on each side, resounding with gloomy echoes, seem, as it were, to send forth their own voice, groaning over the things that are happening. The struggle for life itself does not permit us to take into account at all closed schools and torchless nights. For, the danger is not slight that, since those in power have been removed, everything will go down with them as with falling props. What words could adequately describe our evils? Some have fled, a part of our senate, and not the most inefficient part, preferring life exile to Podandus.[6] And when I say Podandus, imagine that I say the Laconian Ceades,[7]

---

[4] St. Basil is probably thinking of Simonides' lament on those who died at Thermopylae.
[5] St. Basil probably has in mind Aeschylus' *Seven Against Thebes* and the Orestean trilogy.
[6] Modern Podando, in southern Cappadocia, established by Valens as the captial of the new division of the province.
[7] The name given by the Spartans to the pit into which all condemned criminals were thrown. Cf. Pausanias 4.18.4; Thucydides 1.134; Strabo 8.367.

or any other natural pit you may have seen in the world, such places, in fact, which, because they exhale sickness-laden breezes, some men have instinctively called Charonian. Realize that the vileness of Podandus also is like that of some such place. Accordingly, of the three divisions of our citizens, some, rising up, flee with their wives and their household; others, the majority of the noblest in the city, are led away like captives, a pitiable sight to their friends but fulfilling the prayer of their enemies, if, of course, there has been anyone at all invoking so terrible a curse upon us. But, now, the third part is left. These, being not only unable to endure the abandonment of friends, but being at the same time exposed in their weakened condition to destitution, have grown tired of life itself.

We urge you to make these facts clear to all by your own voice, and by the righteous frankness of speech which you possess by virtue of your state of life, distinctly declaring this —that, unless they quickly change their plans, they will not have any to whom they may show clemency. At all events, you will either be of some assistance for the common welfare or you will have done what Solon[8] did, who, not being able to defend his abandoned citizens when the citadel had already been taken, put on his armor and sat down before the gates, making it very evident from his appearance that he did not agree to the things that were happening. Furthermore, I know this most positively, that, even if anyone would not now receive your opinion, a little later he will bestow on you the greatest praise for your good will and your wisdom, when he sees affairs turning out according to your prediction.

---

8 This story is related in Plutarch, *Solon* 30 and in Diogenes Laertius 1.49.

75. To Aburgius[1]

Although there are many qualities which make your character superior to that of others, nothing is so characteristically yours as zeal for your country. Moreover, because you make just returns to that country from which you are sprung, you have become so great that your fame is known throughout the whole world. This same country which brought you forth and nourished you has now returned to the incredible condition found in ancient tales, and no one coming into our city, not even one who is very well acquainted, would recognize it, so suddenly has it been transformed into a complete solitude. Even before this many of the magistrates were taken away from it, and, now, almost all have migrated to Podandus.[2] Those remaining, having been torn from them, have themselves fallen into utter despair, and all have been plunged into such a depth of despondency, as even to drain the city of inhabitants and to make the place a terrible solitude, a pitiable sight indeed to friends, but one that brings much joy and cheer to those who have been watching a long time for our fall. Who, then, will stretch out a hand to us? Or who will let fall a sympathetic tear over us, except your Clemency, who would feel sympathy even for another's city if it were enduring such sufferings, to say nothing of that one which brought you forth into life? If, therefore, you have any power, show it in our present need. At any rate, you have great influence with God, who has abandoned you under no circumstances, and has given many proofs of His benevolence.

---

[1] Another attempt to save Cappadocia from being divided into two provinces. Cf. Letter 74 n. 1. Letters 33, 147, 178, and 304 are also addressed to Aburgius. Cf. Letter 33 n. 1.

[2] See Letter 74 n. 6.

Only, may you be willing to rise to our aid, and to use the power which you possess for the assistance of your fellow citizens.

76. To the Master Sophronius[1]

Truly, the magnitude of the misfortunes which have overtaken our country was impelling me to go to court and describe not only to your Excellency but also to all others who possess the greatest influence in civil affairs the despondency which has overspread our city. But, since my physical condition and the care of the churches hold me back, I have been forced, meanwhile, to voice my lamentation to your Lordship in a letter. And I say that no ship at sea, overwhelmed by violent winds, has ever disappeared from sight so suddenly, no city destroyed by earthquakes or flooded by waters ever met with such total obliteration, as our city, swallowed up by this new administration of affairs, has suffered complete destruction. Our institutions have become a myth. The administration of our government is gone; the whole civil assembly, having abandoned its dwelling in the city in hopeless despair at the loss of its rulers, is wandering about the country. Now, even the marketing of the necessities of life has come to an end, and this city, which formerly gloried both in learned men and in all things else by which wealthy cities thrive, has become a most hideous spectacle. But, we thought, as we are in terrible straits, that the one solace was to deplore our sufferings to your Clemency, and to beseech you, if you have any power, to stretch out your hand to our city, which has already fallen to its knees. Now, the manner

---

[1] Another plea for help at the time of the division of Cappadocia, written at about the same time as the preceding letter. For Sophronius, cf. Letter 32 n. 1; also Letters 96, 177, 180, 193, and 272.

through which you may be of some benefit in the circumstances I myself am not able to suggest. No doubt, however, it will be easy for you to find a way because of your intelligence, and not difficult to use the means found because of the power given to you by God.

77. Without Address, concerning Therasius[1]

This one advantage we have enjoyed from the administration of the great Therasius—the continuous visits of your Eloquence to us. But, since we have been deprived of our ruler, we have likewise suffered the loss of this advantage. Yet, since favors once bestowed upon us by God remain steadfastly with us and though memory of them are present in the souls of each of us even though we are separated in body, let us at least continue to write and tell each other our needs, especially at the present time when the storm has offered this briefly enduring truce.

We still are hoping that you will not depart from the admirable[2] man, Therasius, but decide it proper to share such great cares with him, or, at least, that you will not accept unavailingly the opportunity which permits you to see your friends and be seen by them. Although I have much to say about many things, I have deferred them until our meeting, since I do not think that it is safe to entrust such matters to letters.

---

1 This letter was probably written to Elpidius, about whom the following letter was written. Therasius appears to have been the Governor of Cappadocia, who had been deposed because of slanderous charges brought against him. It is possible that Therasius is the governor in whose behalf St. Basil wrote to Sophronius, the Prefect of Constantinople, in 372. Cf. Letter 96. This letter is of about the same date as the preceding.
2 *Thaumasiōtātou*—a title of distinction used by St. Basil for clergymen and laymen.

78. Without Address, in Behalf of Elpidius[1]

Your kindly regard for our most revered companion Elpidius has not escaped our notice—how, with your customary sagacity, you gave the prefect an opportunity to show his benevolence. Therefore, through this letter we now urge you to make this favor perfect, reminding the prefect personally to put in charge of our country the man on whom depends nearly the whole care of our public interests. Consequently, you will be able to suggest many plausible reasons which will necessarily cause the prefect to order him to remain in our country. Now, in what condition our affairs are here, and how valuable the man is in our troubles, there is assuredly no need for us to explain, since you yourself with your intelligence understand it thoroughly.

79. To Eustathius, Bishop of Sebaste[1]

Even before I received your letter, I was aware of the distress which you feel for every soul and, especially, for our

---

[1] This letter was written at about the same time as the preceding.

[1] Eustathius was the Bishop of Sebaste (modern Sivas), a town of the Pontus and capital of Armenia Minor, from 357-380. He was regarded with suspicion by most schools of theology of his day because of his frequent change of opinion, but he had succeeded in securing and retaining the affection of St. Basil. He had expressed his great joy at St. Basil's elevation to the episcopate and offered to aid his friend in his new and responsible position. This letter shows that kindly relation which existed between the two men. Suggesting that St. Basil would need fellow helpers and counselors, Eustathius recommended certain persons, whom St. Basil later complained were but spies watching his every word and action, interpreting them in an evil way, and reporting them to their chief in an attempt to convict him of heresy. This was the beginning of a bitter struggle between the two which lasted until the death of St. Basil in 379. This letter was written about the year 371.

Lowliness, because I have been thrown into this conflict. And when I had received the letter from the most revered Eleusinius,[2] and had actually seen him present, I thanked God, who, through His spiritual aid, has granted us in our struggles for the cause of religion such an assistant and fellow soldier. And let it be known to your unsurpassed Reverence that, up to the present, we have suffered some attacks from high officials and these violent, since for personal reasons both the prefect[3] and the chamberlain[4] argued for our adversaries. Meanwhile, we have endured every attack unmoved, by the mercy of God, who is favoring us with the assistance of the Spirit and through Him has strengthened our weakness.

80. To Athanasius, Bishop of Alexandria[1]

The more the disorders of the Church increase, the more do we turn toward your Perfection, believing that the one consolation left to us in our dangers lies in your leadership. You, indeed, have saved us from this terrible storm by the power of your prayers and by your knowledge of how to give the best suggestions in our troubles. This is believed by all alike who even slightly know your Perfection by hearsay or by experience. Therefore, do not be remiss in praying for us and encouraging us by your letters. For, if you had realized

---

2 Known only from this letter. He was sent with this present letter, apparently to warn St. Basil of the approach of the Emperor Valens, and to express the fear he felt for the safety of Catholics, especially of St. Basil himself.
3 During the later Empire, the Pretorian Prefects lost their military power. Four prefects continued to be created, but they were civil rulers of the provinces.
4 A favorite eunuch placed in charge of the private apartments of the imperial palace.

---

1 Cf. Letter 61 n. 1.

the greatness of their benefit to us, you would never have let pass any opportunity of writing which was offered to you. And, if we should be accounted worthy, by the aid of your prayers, to see you, to enjoy noble gifts, and to add to the story of our life the meeting with your truly great and apostolic soul, we would assuredly consider that we had received from the loving kindness of God a consolation compensating for all we have suffered in our whole life.

81. To Bishop Innocent[1]

As I was delighted at receiving your Charity's letter, so in the same measure was I grieved because you have placed upon us a burden of responsibilities which exceeds our strength. For, how shall we be able, from so great a distance, to be in charge of such an important administration? Doubtless, as long as the Church possesses you, it rests, as it were, on its own supports. But, if the Lord makes some dispensation of your life, who as revered as you can I send out from here to care for the brethren? What you honorably and sensibly requested in your letter, desiring in your lifetime to see him who is to rule the chosen flock of the Lord after you, that the blessed Moses also desired and saw. Therefore, since the position is important and much talked of, and your work is well known to many, and since the times are difficult and in need of a mighty pilot in the face of the continual squalls and the floods rising up against the Church, I did not think it safe for my soul to treat the matter perfunctorily. Especially was I mindful of what you have written, that you

---

[1] This letter is assigned by Wittig to St. John Chrysostom. Cf. Letter 50 n. 1. The Benedictines ascribe it to St. Basil, written in 372.

intend to oppose me before the Lord, citing me for negligence concerning the churches.

In order, then, that I may not go to trial with you, but rather may find in you a companion in my defense before Christ, I looked around in the meeting of the presbyters in the city and chose as a most honorable vessel the offspring of the blessed Hermogenes,[2] who in the great Council[3] wrote the important and inviolable profession of faith. This man has been a presbyter of the Church for many years, is steadfast in character, fully acquainted with the canons, undeviating in faith, and has lived a life up to the present time of self-control and asceticism, even though the rigor of his austere living has already wasted away his flesh. He is poor and has no means of livelihood in this world, so that he does not even have enough bread, but together with the brethren who are associated with him makes a living by the work of his hands. It is my desire to send him.

If, then, you need such a man as this and not, rather, some younger person fit only to serve as a messenger and to fulfill routine secular duties, be so kind as to write me at the very first opportunity, in order that I may send you this man who is chosen of God, suitable for the work, and revered by those who come in contact with him. He also instructs his opponents with meekness. I could, indeed, have sent him out immediately, but, since you had first requested a man both honorable and beloved by me in other respects, but far inferior to the one mentioned above, I wished to make

---

2 He was the spiritual offspring of Hermogenes, who had ordained him. Hermogenes had been Bishop of Caesarea in Cappadocia and the predecessor of Dianius. Cf. Letters 244 and 263.

3 I.e., at Nicaea. St. Basil seems to forget that Leontius was present at Nicaea as Bishop of Caesarea. Hermogenes may have been present in lower orders and may have written the creed.

my opinion known to you, in order that, if you want a man of this calibre, you may either send, about the time of the fast, one of the brethren to take him along, or may write to us if you have no one able to endure the fatigue of a journey here.

82. To Athanasius, Bishop of Alexandria[1]

When we look into our affairs and perceive the difficulties by which every good action is restrained as if fettered by some chain, we fall into an absolute despair concerning ourselves. But, when again we look to your Grace and consider that our Lord has preserved you as the physician of the maladies in the churches, we resume our reflection and from the lapse into despair we rise up to the hope of better things. All the Church has been rent asunder, as your Wisdom does not fail to realize. And, no doubt, you see the situation on every side as from some lofty watchtower of your mind's contemplation, how, just as at sea, when many ships are sailing together, all at once they are dashed one against another by the violence of the waves and there is a shipwreck, partly because of the violent stirring up of the sea by an external cause, and partly because of the confusion produced by the sailors pushing and jostling one another. It suffices with this comparison to have done with the subject, since your Wisdom requires nothing more, and the situation permits me no freedom of speech. But, who is a capable pilot for these troubles? Who is to be trusted to rouse the Lord that He may rebuke the wind and sea?[2] Who else than he who from childhood bore up bravely in the struggles for religion?

---

1 According to Tillemont (note 60), the bishops here referred to are probably the Macedonians. This letter was written late in the year 371.
2 Cf. Luke 8.24.

Since, therefore, everything about us sound in faith is now truly hastening toward communion and union with those of the same faith, we have come confidently to request your Patience[3] to write a circular letter to all of us, advising us what we must do. For, they wish you, in this way, to take the initiative in their conferences pertaining to communion. Since, perhaps, they may appear to you subject to suspicion because of your recollection of the past, I wish, Father dearly beloved of God, you would do this: Send me the letters for the bishops, either through one of the faithful there, or through the brother Dorotheus,[4] our fellow deacon. After I have received them, I shall not give them out until I have the answers from the bishops; if I should fail to do this, 'I will be guilty of sin against thee' all the days of my life.[5] Assuredly, this declaration did not warrant more fear in him who was speaking of old to his father than it does in me who am now speaking to you, my spiritual father. But, if you absolutely reject this arrangement, at least free us from blame in this duty, since we have come to this embassy and mediation without deceit or artifice, only with a desire for peace and mutual harmony among us who agree in our beliefs about the Lord.

83. To an Assessor[1]

My acquaintance and personal contact with your Nobility

---

3 *Anexikakias*—used as a title only once by St. Basil.
4 The deacon employed so frequently by St. Basil as a messenger.
5 Cf. Gen. 43.9. Judah is speaking to his father Jacob. St. Basil has added the final words.

---

1 The assessor, like the censors at Rome, evaluated property and levied taxes. These assessors, or *censitores,* were appointed by the emperor for each province or smaller unit of territory. The letter was written in the year 372.

has been exceedingly brief, but my knowledge of you by repute, through which we are associated with many distinguished men, is neither slight nor unworthy of consideration. Now, whether you also have heard any chance mention of us, you yourself would know better than I. At all events, your reputation with us is as we have said. But, God has called you to an office which offers an occasion for kindness, one through which our country, completely beaten to the ground, can be restored. Therefore, I think that it is befitting for me to solicit your Excellency's attention, so that, hoping for a reward from God, you may think it worth while so to comport yourself, ameliorating the afflictions of the oppressed, as to merit an undying remembrance and become an heir of everlasting rest.

Now, since I have a certain piece of property around Chamanene, I beg you to guard it as your own. And do not wonder if I, having been taught friendship along with other virtues, and being mindful of him who said that a friend is another self,[2] call my friends' possessions my own. Accordingly, this property which belongs to him I commend to your Honor as my own. Furthermore, I urge you, after viewing the hardships of this household, to offer some consideration for the past, and for the future to make desirable this dwelling, which they now shun and abandon because of the amount of taxes imposed upon it. I myself will be eager, when I meet your Modesty, to discuss more fully all details.

---

[2] Pythagoras is supposed to have been the first to give us these words. They occur also in Aristotle, *Magna Moralia* 2.15 (*héteros egó*); and in Cicero, *Laelius* 21.80 (*alter idem*).

84. To an Official[1]

What I am about to write is almost incredible, but for the sake of truth it shall be written. And this it is—that, although I had every desire to converse with your Honor as frequently as possible, when I found the occasion for this letter I did not rush eagerly to avail myself of the unexpected opportunity, but hesitated and shrank back. Now, the wonder in this is that when the chance for which I had prayed presented itself, I did not welcome it. And the reason—that I am ashamed to write not purely out of friendship, but each time to seek remedy for some need. Still, this has occurred to me (and I hope that you, taking thought, will believe that we are engaging in this correspondence not more for the sake of business than out of friendship) that the manner of addressing officials should be somewhat different from that of addressing private individuals. We do not converse with a physician as we would with any chance comer, nor, assuredly, with an official as with a private individual, but we must endeavor to gain some benefit from the skill of the one and from the influence of the other. At all events, as the shadow under all circumstances follows those who walk in the sun, whether or not they themselves wish it, so also some advantage follows association with officials, namely, help for the afflicted.

Therefore, let the very act of greeting your Lordship fulfill the primary reason for our letter, and this, even if no pretext for writing were at hand, should in itself be considered a plausible justification. Accordingly, accept our salutation, most noble Sir, and may you be kept safe during all your life and pass from office to office, benefitting by your authority now one and again another. It is not only customary for

---

[1] The official addressed here is probably Elias, Governor of Cappadocia. The letter was written in 372. Cf., also, Letters 94 and 96.

me to speak thus, but it is also your due from those who have had ever so little experience of your excellent administration.

Now, after this prayer, receive also our petition. It is for a poor old man whom an imperial decree freed from public duties, but to whom, even before the emperor, old age itself gave the necessary exemption. And you yourself also confirmed this favor from the higher authority through respect, I am sure, for nature, and also, as it seems to me, through forethought for the public good, precluding possible danger to the public interests from a man suffering from senility. How is it, then, O admirable Sir, that you have unmindfully brought him back in another manner into the midst of affairs? For, since you have commanded his grandson, not yet four years old, to take his place in the Senate, what else is this if not dragging the old man out into public service anew in the person of his grandson? We ask you now to have compassion on both, and to release them in consideration of the pitiable circumstances attending each. For, the one neither saw nor knew his parents, because he was bereaved of both from the very cradle and reared by strangers, and the other has lived so long a life that he has escaped no form of misfortune. He beheld the untimely death of his son; he saw his house deprived of successors; and now, unless you bethink yourself of something worthy of your gentleness, he will see this consolation of his childlessness become for him an occasion of numberless evils. Surely, the boy will not be enrolled in the Senate, or levy taxes, or furnish provision money for the soldiers, but again the gray hairs of the wretched old man necessarily will be put to shame. Therefore, grant the favor, both consistent with the laws and in accordance with nature, commanding the one to be withdrawn until he has reached his majority and the other to be allowed to await his death at ease. Let others allege the excuse of continuous business and inexorable necessity. Certainly, it is not characteristic of you, even if the affairs of men press upon you, either to disregard those who fare ill, or to take no heed of the laws, or to refuse to yield to the appeals of friends.

85. Concerning the Fact That It Is Unnecessary to Take an Oath[1]

We do not cease protesting in every synod and urging in private conferences this matter—that, in the case of public taxes, collectors must not exact oaths of farmers. My last resort is to protest solemnly before God and man by letter concerning this same subject, that it is your duty to cease bringing death upon the souls of men, to contrive some other methods of exacting payment, and so to allow men to keep their souls unharmed. We are writing this to you, not on the ground that you need a verbal exhortation (for you have present with you inducements for fearing the Lord), but in order that through you all those who depend on you may be taught not to rouse the Holy One to anger, by evil practice reducing a forbidden act to a matter of indifference. For, men have no benefit at all from the oaths in the matter of exactions and they are taking upon their souls an admitted evil, since they become practiced in perjury, no longer striving to make the payment, but believing that the oath has been devised for them as a weapon of deceit and an opportunity for delay.

---
1 For a further elaboration on the sufferings of the Cappadocians under the heavy burden of taxation, cf. Letter 74. One feature of the system of taxation was the practice of putting the people under oath as to their inability to pay. This taking of oaths the Church condemned. The date of this letter is the year 372.

Should the Lord bring a swift retribution upon the perjurers, the collectors will have none to answer their summons, since the farmers will have been destroyed by divine vengeance. And, if the Master in His patience endures (and, as I previously said, those who have experienced the forbearance of the Lord often despise His goodness), let them not violate the law to no purpose,[2] nor provoke the wrath of God against themselves. We have said what our duty lays on us; the disobedient will see to the consequence.

86. To an Official[1]

I know that the greatest and principal care of your Honor is to comply in every way with the demands of justice, and the second, to benefit your friends and to exert yourself for those who have fled to your Lordship's protection. In this, therefore, we are in complete agreement on the present occasion. Now, the matter for which we are making intercession is just and a favor to us whom you have deigned to count among your friends, and is also the due of those who call on your Firmness[2] for assistance in the injuries which they have suffered.

Now, the grain, which was the only thing our most beloved brother Dorotheus possessed for the necessary sustenance of life, has been seized by some men of Brisi who were trusted to administer public affairs. Whether they used violence of themselves or were enjoined by others to do so, they are in no way blameless in the affair. For, why does he who is wick-

---

2 I.e., they will not escape their taxes even if they swear to their inability to pay them.

---

1 This letter was written in the same year as the preceding.
2 *Sterrótēta*—a title of address used by St. Basil for laymen only.

ed of himself do less wrong than he who serves for the wickedness of others? For those who suffer, the harm done is the same. We ask that this man receive again his grain from those who robbed him, and that they be not allowed to blame others for their brash deeds. And we shall esteem the favor from your Excellency, if you will be so kind as to grant it, as highly as if we were escaping the hardship of famine.

87. Without Address, concerning the Same Subject[1]

I am astonished that, when you were acting as mediator, so much wrong was perpetrated against our fellow presbyter[2] that he was despoiled of the only means of livelihood that he possessed. And the most terrible part of it is that they who dared to do this laid the responsibility for what they had done upon you, whose duty it even was, far from permitting such a thing to happen, to prevent it with all your strength in the case of all men; certainly, if not all, at least in the case of our presbyters and of those who are of the same mind with us and are proceeding along the same road of piety. Therefore, if you have any care to relieve us, see that the things which have been done are set right. For, you are able, with the help of God, to correct both these matters and still greater for whomever you may wish. I have written also to the governor of the country in order that, if they are not willing to do right of themselves, they may be compelled to do so by the action of the courts.

---

1 On the same subject and of the same date as the preceding letter.
2 Dorotheus.

88. Without Address, for a Tax-Collector[1]

Your Honor, more than all others, knows the difficulty of collecting gold furnished by contribution.[2] Moreover, we have no better witness of our poverty than you, who in your remarkable kindness have both sympathized with us and up to the present shown all possible indulgence, at no time having altered the gentleness of your manners because of the agitating urgency of those in high authority. Therefore, since a little of the gold is still lacking from the whole account, and this must be collected from the contribution to which we urged the whole city, we ask your Clemency to prolong the appointed time a little for us, so that those also who are outside the city may be reminded. The majority of the magistrates are in the country, as you yourself are not unaware. So, then, if the contribution could be sent incomplete by just as many pounds as, in fact, are lacking, we entreat you let this be done. The remainder will then be sent later. However, if it is absolutely necessary that the whole amount be sent in one payment to the treasury, we ask, as we did at the beginning, that the appointed time be extended.

---

1 Another letter concerning the collection of taxes in the same year as the preceding.
2 The Benedictine editors explain *chrysíon pragmateutikón* as the gold collected for the purpose of providing equipment for the troops, according to Gothofredus on *Cod. Theol.* 7.6.3. With the exception of Osroene and Isauria, all the provinces of the East contributed gold instead of actual equipment. A law by Valens on this subject specifies that the gold must be paid between September 1 and April 1. Since St. Basil is attempting to secure an extension, this letter may be dated shortly before April 1.

89. To Meletius, Bishop of Antioch[1]

The good God, in providing us with occasions for friendly greetings to your Honor, soothes the intensity of our longing. He Himself is witness of the desire which we have to see you personally and to enjoy your excellent and soul-profiting instruction. And now, through our fellow deacon, the most pious and zealous brother Dorotheus,[2] who is going to you, we beseech you in the first place to pray for us, that we may not become an obstacle to the people, nor a hindrance to your prayers of supplication to the Lord. Next, we also suggest that you deign to give directions through the brother just mentioned. Moreover, if there is any need of writing to our brethren in the West, do you yourself dictate the letter, which ought, of necessity, be carried to them by one of our men. For, since we have met Sabinus, the deacon they sent, we have written to the Illyrian bishops and to the bishops throughout Italy and Gaul, and also to some of those who wrote personally to us. Furthermore, it would be well advised for some one to be sent as from a general synod carrying a second letter; do you yourself have it written.

---

1 For Meletius, Bishop of Antioch, cf. Letters 57 and 68. This letter was written before Easter, 372.
2 Dorotheus was a deacon of the Church of Antioch and of the communion of Meletius. St. Basil had used him the year before to carry two letters to St. Athanasius, asking him to use his influence with the bishops of the West so that they would intervene and heal the schism of the Church in Antioch by uniting all under Meletius. Cf. Letters 48, 50, and 52. Toward the end of the same year, St. Basil again sent Dorotheus to St. Athanasius with letters for Pope Damasus and the Western bishops, asking for assistance in uniting the East. Cf. Letter 52. Dorotheus spent the winter in Italy but was unable to accomplish any good. He returned in 372 with letters from Pope Damasus to St. Basil and St. Athanasius which testified to their unity of faith. Cf. Letters 61, 62, and 273. St. Basil is now sending Dorotheus to Meletius requesting him to draw up more urgent letters to the bishops of the West.

Now, concerning the most revered Bishop Athanasius, we are reminding your distinguished Wisdom, although you are accurately aware of it, how impossible it is to further or to accomplish anything which should be done by letters from me alone, unless in some manner he receives Communion from you who formerly deferred it. In fact, he himself is said to be exceedingly eager for union with us and to be using all his power to bring it about, yet to be grieved because he was sent away at that time without Communion and because the promises still remain unfulfilled.[3]

How these facts are regarded in the East has most certainly not escaped the ears of your Reverence, all of which the brother mentioned above will himself relate more in detail. Be so kind as to send him out immediately after Easter, because he is waiting for the decisions from Samosata. Also commend his good will and send him forth to the appointed tasks strengthened by your prayers.

90. To the Most Holy Brothers and Bishops of the West[1]

The good God, who always joins consolations to afflictions, has even now in the midst of our many distresses let us find some degree of comfort from the letters which our most honorable father, Bishop Athanasius, received from your Rectitude and which he sent on to us. They are a testimony of sound faith and give proof of your inviolable harmony and

---

[3] Tillemont contends that it is not the great St. Athanasius that is referred to here, since Meletius would not dare refuse him Communion. However, Maran (*Vita Basilii* xxii) shows that the circumstances fit in and also that the statement of Meletius' refusal is borne out by the Letter 258.3. St. Athanasius himself was so far committed to the other side in the Antiochene dispute that he could not recognize Meletius.

union, making clear that the shepherds are following in the footsteps of the Fathers and tending the people of the Lord with understanding. All these facts have gladdened us to such an extent as to relieve our dejection and to produce in our souls a brief smile, as it were, in the gloom of affairs in which we are now situated.

Moreover, the Lord has increased our consolation through our son, the most pious fellow deacon, Sabinus, who nourished our souls by his accurate relation of your goodly condition and who, having learned by actual observation, will also clearly report to you the state of our affairs. This he will do in order, primarily, that you may aid us in our struggle by your earnest and persevering prayer to the Lord, and secondly, that you may not refuse to bring to the afflicted churches all possible consolation. Affairs here are in a distressing condition, most honorable brothers. The Church, like a boat in the midst of the sea racked by the continuous blows of the waves, has been reduced to utter exhaustion by the incessant attacks of her opponents, unless there should be some speedy visitation of the goodness of the Lord. Therefore, just as we esteem as a personal blessing your mutual agreement and union, so also we beg you to compassionate us in our dissensions, and not, because we are separated by the situation of our countries, to sever us from yourselves, but since we are united in the communion of the Spirit, to admit us to the harmonious union of one body.

Our afflictions are well known, even if we do not recount them; they have already been sounded forth through the whole world. The doctrines of the Fathers are despised; the traditions of the Apostles are set at nought; the crafty inventions of innovators are introduced in the churches; men now are skillful masters of words, and not theologians; the wisdom of the world takes first place, the glory of the cross having been thrust aside. The shepherds are driven out, and in their places fierce wolves are brought in, who tear asunder the flock of Christ. The houses of prayer are destitute of those who assembled there; the deserts, full of lamenting people. The older men grieve, comparing their former state with the present; the young are more to be pitied, being unaware of their deprivation.

These facts are sufficient to rouse the sympathy of those who have been taught the love of Christ, but, compared with the true state of affairs, my words fall far short of depicting reality. If, therefore, there is any consolation of love, any communion of the Spirit, if there are any feelings of pity, bestir yourselves to come to our relief. Employ zeal in the pursuit of piety, deliver us from this storm. And let that blessed dogma[2] of the Fathers be spoken fearlessly among us, that dogma which confounds the hateful heresy of Arius and builds up the churches on the sound doctrine in which the Son is acknowledged to be consubstantial with the Father, and the Holy Spirit is numbered with Them and adored with equal honor, in order that that fearlessness in defense of the truth which the Lord gave to you, and that glory in the confession of the divine and saving Trinity, may also through your prayers and your co-operation be bestowed upon us. But, the particulars the deacon mentioned above will announce to your Charity. Moreover, we are in agreement with everything that has been done canonically by your Honor, and heartily approve of your apostolic zeal for orthodoxy.

---

1 Newman considers this plea for help and also Letter 92 to be closely connected with Letter 70, which appears to have been addressed to Pope Damasus. It was written before Easter, 372.
2 St. Basil, contrary to the present usage, generally employs the word *kerygma* for a dogma of the Church, and calls *dógmata* the doctrines and practices privately sanctioned in the Church.

91. To Valerian, Bishop of the Illyrians[1]

Thanks be to the Lord who permitted us to see in your Purity[2] the fruit of pristine[3] love. Although separated from us in the flesh by such a great distance, you have united yourself with us by letters, and by embracing us with your spiritual and holy love you have engendered in our souls an unspeakably great affection. In fact, we have learned by experience the force of the proverb: 'As cold water to a thirsty soul, so is good tidings from a far country.'[4]

For, the famine of love among us, honorable brother, is terrible. And the cause is easily seen, 'because iniquity has abounded, the charity of the many has grown cold.'[5] For this reason your letter is very dear to us, and we are answering you through the same messenger, our most pious fellow deacon and brother, Sabinus. Through him we are making ourselves known to you, and we entreat you to be mindful of us in your prayers, that the holy God may give tranquillity and peace to our affairs and rebuke this wind and sea. Thus we shall be freed from the tossing and turmoil in which we now are, continually expecting to be completely plunged into the sea.

---

1 St. Valerian, Bishop of Aquileia, is first mentioned as being present at the Council of Rome in 371. Cf. Theodoret, *H. E.* 2.17. He presided at a council held in 381 at Aquileia against the Arian bishops, Palladius and Secundinus, at which St. Ambrose was leader of the Catholics. He was also at the Council of Rome in 382. Cf. Theodoret, *H. E.* 5.9. The date of his death is uncertain. He is commemorated on Nov. 27. Under his rule there grew up in Aquileia that group of people whom St. Jerome calls in his chronicle (378) 'a company of the blessed,' and of whom he was one. Dorotheus or Sabinus had brought letters from St. Athanasius, and Sabinus one from Valerian. St. Basil is here taking the opportunity to reply. This letter was written in 372.
2 *Katharótēti*—a title of address used only this once by St. Basil.
3 I.e., an exemplification of Christian love as taught in the early Church.
4 Cf. Prov. 25.25.
5 Cf. Matt. 24.12.

But, this favor the Lord has graciously granted us at the present—the hearing that you are in strict agreement and union with one another, and that the dogma of true religion is proclaimed among you without hindrance. For at some time (if, indeed, the time of this world is not yet ended but some days of human life still remain) there will be need for you to renew the faith in the East, and to render to it in due measure a return for those blessings which you received from it. In fact, the sound among us and those who claim the true religion of the Fathers are sufficiently wearied, since the Devil in his wiliness has violently disturbed them by the many and varied assaults of his subtleties. But, by the prayers of you who love the Lord, may the wicked heresy which misleads the people, the false doctrine of Arius, be extinguished. And may the good doctrine of our Fathers, who assembled at Nicaea, blaze forth, so that the doxology in harmony with the words of saving baptism may be accorded to the Blessed Trinity.

92. To the Bishops of Italy and Gaul[1]

To our most dearly beloved of God and most holy[2] brethren and fellow ministers in Italy and Gaul, bishops of like belief with us, we, Meletius,[3] Eusebius,[4] Basil,[5] Bassus,[6] Gregory,[7]

---

1 An appeal to the Western bishops to assist in driving out heresy and establishing peace in the Eastern Church, written in 372.
2 *Hosiōtátois*—a title of distinction applied by St. Basil only to the clergy.
3 Of Antioch.
4 Of Samosata.
5 Of Caesarea.
6 Tillemont (*Basil*, note 52) suggests Barses of Edessa.
7 The elder, of Nazianzus.

Pelagius,[8] Paul, Anthimus,[9] Theodotus,[10] Vitus,[11] Abraham,[12] Jobinus,[13] Zeno,[14] Theodoretus, Marcianus, Barachus, Abraham,[15] Libanius, Thalassius, Joseph, Boethus, Iatrius,[16] Theodotus, Eustathius,[17] Barsumas, John, Chosroes, Iosaces,[18] Narses, Maris, Gregory,[19] and Daphnus, send greetings in the Lord.

Even a groan drawn forth repeatedly from the depth of the heart brings some relief to distressed souls, and perhaps, also, a tear trickling down has dispelled the greater part of an affliction. However, the telling of our sufferings to your Charity does not offer us a relief only as a sigh or a tear do, but comforts us with a somewhat happier hope that, perhaps, if we should make known to you our sorrows, we might rouse you to come to our assistance. We have, in truth, long expected that you would bring this succor to the churches in the East, but we have not yet obtained it—no doubt, because God, who in His wisdom administers our affairs according to the inscrutable judgments of His justice, has ordained that we should suffer these trials for a still longer time. Now, surely, you have not been ignorant of the state of our affairs, most honorable brethren, since the report of it has gone forth to the uttermost parts of the world; nor are you without sympathy, as I think, toward your brethren who hold the

---

8 Of Laodicea.
9 Of Tyana.
10 Of Nicopolis.
11 Of Carrhae.
12 Of Batnae.
13 Of Perrha.
14 Of Tyre.
15 Of Urimi in Syria.
16 Maran would read Otreius of Melitine for Iatrius.
17 Of Sebasteia.
18 Maran would read Isaaces, identifying him with Isacoces of Armenia Major.
19 Probably Gregory of Nyssa, lately consecrated.

same belief with you, since you are disciples of the Apostle[20] who teaches that the fulfillment of the law is love toward one's neighbor. But, as we have said, the just judgment of God, which measures out to us for fulfillment the suffering appointed for our sins, has checked your interest. However, through your zeal for the truth and your sympathetic feelings for us, we urge you, now at least, to let yourselves be roused, when from the most pious brother, our fellow deacon, Sabinus, you have learned all, even what escaped your ears before. He will be able personally to relate to you whatever is wanting in our letter. Through him we urge you to clothe yourselves with feelings of pity, and putting aside all hesitation, to take up the labor of love and also not to consider either the length of the journey or business at home or any human concerns.

For, it is not a question of danger concerning only one church; nor are there two or three churches which have fallen in this bitter storm. In fact, the evil of heresy is spread almost from the mountains of Illyricum to the Thebaid. Its pernicious seeds were formerly sown by the detestable Arius, and, having taken deep root because of the many who in the meantime diligently cultivated the impiety, they have now produced their destructive fruit. For, the doctrines of true religion have been overthrown and the laws of the Church have been made void. A lust for power in men who do not fear the Lord infests the posts of authority, and now the first place is openly offered as the prize for impiety, so that he who has uttered the most grievous blasphemies is considered more deserving of the office of bishop of the people. Gone is the dignity of priesthood. They who tended the flock of the Lord with understanding have left, while those lusting for power waste the revenues of the poor on their personal pleasures

---

20 Cf. Rom. 13.10.

and in the distribution of gifts. Strict observance of the canons has been weakened. License to commit sin is widespread, for they who have come into power through the patronage of men return the favor of these good offices in this very manner—by affording every occasion for pleasure to sinners. Righteous judgment has perished. Each one proceeds according to the desire of his heart. Wickedness is unmeasured; the people are dead to admonition; their leaders are without freedom of speech. For, they who have obtained power for themselves through other men are the slaves of those who have bestowed the favor. And already, forsooth, the 'defense of sound doctrine' has been invented by some as a weapon in the war against one another; and, dissembling their personal hatreds, they pretend that they hate for the sake of true religion. Others, to evade dishonor for most shameful crimes, enkindle the people to strife against one another in order that they may shroud their own actions in public evils.

Therefore, this war is truceless, because they who have done the evil mistrust general peace lest it uncover their shameful secrets. At these conditions the unbelievers laugh; those of little faith waver; faith is uncertain; ignorance envelops souls, because those who maliciously corrupt the doctrine imitate the truth. The mouths of the pious are hushed, but every blasphemous tongue is loosed. Sacred things are profaned; the people who are sound in faith flee the houses of prayer as schools of impiety, and throughout the deserts they raise their hands to the Lord in heaven with groans and tears. However, that which has happened in most of the cities has assuredly been relayed even to you—that the people with their wives and children and with even their aged ones pour out before the walls of the cities and offer their prayers in the open, enduring all the inclemencies of the weather with much patience, waiting for help from the Lord.

What lamentation is adequate to describe these misfortunes? What fountains of tears will suffice to wash away such evils? Therefore, while some still seem to stand, while still a trace of our former condition is preserved, before utter shipwreck comes upon the churches, hasten to us. Hasten at once, we earnestly beg, most true[21] brothers; stretch out your hand to us who have fallen to our knees. Let your brotherly affection be stirred in our behalf; let your tears of sympathy be poured forth. Do not allow half of the world to be swallowed up by the error. Do not permit that faith to be extinguished in those among whom it first shone forth.

Now, by what means you will give help in our troubles and how you will show sympathy to the afflicted, you will certainly not need to learn from us, but from the Holy Spirit Himself who will suggest it to you. Only, there is need of haste to save those who still remain, and of the presence of more brethren so that those coming here may make up the full number of a synod, to the end that they may have the prestige to set matters right not only because of the dignity of those sending them, but also from their own number; and that they may restore the creed written in Nicaea by our Fathers, banish the heresy by proclamation, and discuss with the churches matters pertaining to peace, bringing together into harmony those who are of the same belief. For this, surely, of all things is the most deserving of pity, that even that part which appears to be sound is divided against itself, and that there surround us, as it seems, calamities like those which formerly encompassed Jerusalem during the siege of Vespasian. They were at the same time oppressed by war from without and spent by the dissension of their own people with-

---

21 *Gnēsiótatoi*—a title of distinction applied by St. Basil to the clergy.

in. And in our case, in addition to the open war of the heretics, still another that has sprung up among those who seem to be orthodox has reduced the churches to the lowest state of weakness. On this account, we especially need help from you, in order that those professing the faith of the Apostles, after putting an end to the schisms which they devised, may become subject for the future to the authority of the Church, so that the body of Christ being restored to soundness in all its members may be made perfect, and that we may not only rejoice over the blessings of others, as we now do, but may also behold our own churches regaining the ancient glory of orthodoxy. For, truly, it is deserving of the highest praise that the Lord has bestowed upon your Reverence the power to distinguish the spurious from the approved and pure, and to proclaim the faith of the Fathers with no evasion. This faith we also received and we recognized it from the apostolic qualities by which it was stamped, and we assented both to it and to all the doctrines canonically and lawfully taught in the synodical letter.[22]

---

[22] For this synodical letter, cf. Theodoret 1.8 and Socrates 1.9. The Benedictine editors are surprized that St. Basil shows agreement with this synodical letter, since it defines the Son as *tes autes hypostáseos kaì usías* (of the same essence and substance). It is, however, not in the synodical letter, but in the anathemas originally appended to the creed, that it is denied that He is of a different substance or essence. Even here it is not said positively that He is of the same substance or essence. For a discussion of these theological terms, cf. Letters 8 and 38, with notes.

93. To the Patrician Caesaria, about Communion[1]

Now, to receive Communion daily, thus to partake of the holy Body and Blood of Christ, is an excellent and advantageous practice; for Christ Himself says clearly: 'He who eats my flesh and drinks my blood has life everlasting.'[2] Who doubts that to share continually in the life is nothing else than to have a manifold life? We ourselves, of course, receive Communion four times a week, on Sundays, Wednesdays, Fridays, and Saturdays;[3] also on other days, if there is a commemoration of some saint.

As to the question concerning a person being compelled to receive Communion by his own hand in times of persecution, when there is no priest or minister present, it is superfluous to show that the act is in no way offensive, since long-continued custom has confirmed this practice because of the circumstances themselves. In fact, all the monks in the solitudes, where there is no priest, preserve Communion in their house and receive it from their own hands. In Alexandria and in Egypt, each person, even of those belonging to the laity, has Communion in his own home, and, when he wishes, he receives with his own hand. For, when the priest has once and for all completed the sacrifice and has given Communion, he who has once received it as a whole, when he partakes of it daily, ought reasonably to believe that he is partaking and

---

[1] Tillemont (*Basil*, note 34) says that Arnaud does not consider that this letter is St. Basil's, but he gives no reason for his opinion. Tillemont himself thinks that it is only a portion of a letter, but sees no reason for rejecting its authenticity. Its manuscript tradition is poor, but does not offer sufficient cause for doubting its authorship. It was probably written in 372.
[2] John 6.55.
[3] The Greek meanings are literally: Lord's Day, the Fourth, Preparation, and Sabbath.

receiving from him who has given it. Even in the church the priest gives the particle, and the recipient holds it completely in his power and so brings it into his mouth with his own hand. Accordingly, it is virtually the same whether he receives one particle from the priest or many particles at one time.[4]

94. To Elias, Governor of the Province[1]

I have been especially eager to approach your Honor myself, lest, because of my failure to appear, I should have less advantage than they who are slandering me. But, since the infirmity of my body has prevented me, afflicting me much more severely than usual, I have, of necessity, resorted to writing. Accordingly, O admirable Sir, when recently I met your Honor I was desirous of communicating with your Wisdom concerning all my temporal affairs, and I also wished to have some conversation in behalf of the churches, in order

---

[4] Cf. *Catholic Encyclopaedia,* under 'Eucharist.' In general, it is by divine and ecclesiastical right that the laity should as a rule receive Communion only from the consecrated hand of the priest. Cf. Trent. Sess. 13, cap. 8. The practice of the laity giving themselves Communion was formerly, and is today, allowed only in case of necessity. In early Christian times it was customary for the faithful to take the Blessed Sacrament to their homes and communicate privately, a custom to which St. Basil refers above. Cf. also Justin, Martyr, *Apol.* 1.85; Tertullian, *De. orat.* 19 and *Ad uxor.* 2.5; Cyprian, *De lapsis* 132; and Jerome, Letter 125. Up to the ninth century is was usual for the priest to place the Sacred Host in the right hand of the recipient, who kissed it and then placed it in his own mouth. Women from the fourth to the ninth centuries were required to have a cloth wrapped about their right hand in this ceremony.

---

[1] For Elias, Governor of Cappadocia, cf. Letters 84 and 96. St. Basil is here defending himself from the slanders directed against him by enemies because of the church and hospital which he had recently built in the suburbs of Caesarea. Cf. Greg. Naz., *Oratio* 20; Theodoret, *Eccl. Hist.* 4.19; and Sozomen, 6.34. The letter was written in 372, at the departure of Valens.

that, henceforth, no occasion might be left for slanders. But, I restrained myself, considering that it was an altogether meddlesome act and ambitious beyond measure to impose unnecessary cares upon a man already burdened with such a mass of business. And at the same time—for the truth will be told—I hesitated especially, lest we should ever be forced by disputes with each other to wound your soul, which ought in its pure piety toward God to reap a perfect reward for its religious service. For, truly, if we shall turn your attention to ourselves, we shall leave you little leisure for the public affairs, and we shall be doing very nearly the same as one who would weigh down with additional freight the pilot who is guiding a newly built ship in the midst of mighty waves. There is need, rather, to remove some of the cargo and to lighten the load as much as possible. For this reason, it seems to me, our great emperor, when he learned of our bustling activity, allowed us to govern the churches by ourselves.

Nevertheless, I wish that those annoying your honest ears be asked what harm the state suffers from us, or whether public interests either little or great have suffered loss because of our administration of the churches—unless someone might say that it brings harm to state affairs to raise up to our God a magnificently constructed house of prayer, and around it a dwelling, a stately residence reserved for the bishop and inferior quarters assigned to the servants of God according to rank. Moreover, the use of these is free to you, the officials, and to your followers. And whom do we wrong by building inns for guests, both those visiting us on their journey and those needing some treatment in their illness, and by appointing for them the necessary comforts—nurses, doctors, beasts of burden, and escorts?[2] It was necessary also for oc-

---

[2] At this time, the clergy acted as guides and escorts. Cf. Letters 98 and 243.

cupations to follow in the wake of these, both those indispensable for support, and such as were devised for a more respectable manner of living. Again, other buildings suitable for these occupations had to be erected, and all of these are an ornament to the place and a source of pride to our governor, since words of praise redound upon him. Certainly, not on this account were you forced to direct your attention to us—because you are able alone by the might of your intellect to restore works which have fallen into ruin, to people the uninhabited spaces, and, in short, to transform solitudes into cities. Therefore, was it more consistent to drive out and to insult him who is co-operating in these matters, or to honor and respect him? And do not think, most noble Sir, that our part consists only in words, for we are already engaged in the work itself, having in the meantime helped to procure the materials.

So much, then, for my defense before the governor. But the answer in reply to the censures of fault-finders, which should be given to a Christian and a friend who is concerned for our reputation, must now be left unsaid on the ground that it is both too long for the limits of a letter and, especially, that it is not safely to be entrusted to lifeless writing. But, in order that you may not, during the time before our meeting, be led on by the slanders of certain men and forced to relinquish any of your good will toward us, act as Alexander did. It is said that he, when one of his friends was being slandered, offered one ear to the slanderer, but carefully stopped the other with his hand, showing that he who intends to judge rightly must not be at once completely carried away by those coming first, but must keep half of his hearing unprejudiced for the defense of the absent one.[3]

---

3 Cf. Letter 24 for this story about Alexander.

95. To Eusebius, Bishop of Samosata[1]

Although I had long since written to your Reverence about other matters, and especially concerning our meeting with each other, I was utterly disappointed in my expectation, since the letter did not reach your Honor's hands. The blessed deacon, Theophrastus,[2] who had taken the letter at a time when we were obliged to set out on certain visits, did not send it on to your Reverence, being prevented by the illness from which he died. This accounts for my writing too late to expect that there will be any advantage from this letter, because so little time remains. For Meletius and Theodotus,[3] bishops dearly beloved of God, bade us come to visit them, considering our conference proof of our love, and desiring that some correction of matters now annoying them be effected. They also appointed for us the time for the conference, the middle of the coming month of June, and the place, Phargamos, a spot famous for the renown of its martyrs as well as for the full attendance at the synod held there each year. But, when I learned, on my return, of the death of the blessed deacon and that the letters from us were lying undelivered, it was necessary for me not to be idle, since there still remained for us only thirty-three days until that appointed time. Therefore, with all haste I am sending this letter to the most revered brother Eustathius, our fellow minister, so that through him it may be conveyed to your Dignity and the answer speedily brought back to us. For, if it is possible, or at all satisfactory for you to attend, we also shall be pres-

---
[1] Another letter to Eusebius, written in May, 372.
[2] Probably the bearer of a letter to Meletius from St. Basil in 371. Cf. Letter 57.
[3] Theodotus of Nicopolis was disturbed about St. Basil's being in communion with Eustathius. On Meletius, Bishop of Antioch, cf. Letters 57, 68, 89, 120, 129, 216, and notes.

ent; if not, we ourselves, God willing, shall pay last year's debt of a meeting with you, unless, because of our sins, some obstacle again comes in our way; in which case we shall defer the meeting of the bishops until another time.

96. To the Master Sophronius[1]

Who is as devoted to his city, honoring even as he does his parents the land which bore and nurtured him, as you yourself are, you who pray for blessings for the whole city in general and for each person individually, and not only pray, but also confirm your prayers through your personal efforts? Certainly, it is by the grace of God that you are able to do such things, and may you retain this power for a very long time indeed, since you are so very kind.

Nevertheless, our country became rich drowsing under your protection, because it had a man entrusted with its care whose like they who know the conditions existing among us from the earliest times said had never before mounted the governor's chair. But, it has been suddenly deprived of him through the malice of some men who made the man's frankness and inaccessibility to flattery an occasion for hostility toward him, and who secretly invented slanders against him for the ears of your Perfection. Therefore, all of us, the whole mass of the people, are downcast, suffering the loss of a governor, the only one able to lift up our city which has already fallen to her knees, a true guardian of justice, a man easy of access for the wronged, dreaded by the lawless, equally just to the poor and rich, and, greatest of all, one restoring Christianity to its former honor. For, the fact that he is the most incorruptible

---

[1] For Sophronius, cf. Letter 32 n. 1. Cf. also Letters 84 and 94, which St. Basil wrote to Elias. This letter was written in 372.

of all men whom we know, and that he does not bestow favors on anyone in violation of justice, we pass by, as being less important in comparison with the other virtues of the man.

We are, in truth, testifying to these things too late, like men who sing a dirge to console themselves, but do nothing useful in their troubles. Only this is not useless—that the recollection of the man be stored up in your great mind, and that you be grateful to him as to a benefactor of the country which bore you. Moreover, if anyone of those who are embittered because the just man was preferred should attack him, it is not useless to fight in his defense and to succor him, making it evident to all that you consider the man a friend of yours, regarding as sufficient grounds for friendship the excellent testimony concerning him and also the experience of his performance, which is not according to the pattern of the times, since matters which would not have been accomplished in many years by another were set right by him in a short time. It will also be an enduring favor for us and a consolation for what has happened, if you will recommend him to the emperor and refute the slanders brought against him. Believe that your whole fatherland addresses these words to you through our one voice and that it is the common prayer of all that through your Perfection justice may be done to the man.

97. *To the Senate of Tyana*[1]

The Lord who reveals the depths and makes manifest the counsels of hearts has also given to the lowly comprehension of artifices difficult, as some think, to understand. Therefore,

---

[1] The dismay and dejection of Caesarea at this time is vividly depicted by St. Basil in Letters 74, 75, and 76.

nothing has escaped us; nor is anything which has been done still hidden. Nevertheless, we ourselves neither see nor hear anything, except the peace of God and what leads to it. For, even if others are powerful and great and self-reliant, we are nothing and of no worth. Consequently, we would never attribute so much to ourselves as to think that we, single-handed, could succeed in our difficulties, knowing well that we need the help of each one of our brethren more than one hand needs the other. Then, too, the Lord has taught us the necessity of unity of action from the very construction of our bodies. For, when I reflect upon these our limbs, that not one of them is sufficient in itself for activity, how shall I consider that I alone am strong enough to combat the troubles of life? In fact, neither could one foot move safely forward unless the other helped to support it, nor could the eye see clearly if it did not have the other as its partner, and if it did not, in harmony with it, cast its glance upon the objects to be seen. The hearing is more accurate when it receives the sound through both channels; the grasp is stronger through the cooperation of the fingers. And, in general, I see that none of the actions performed either naturally or by inclination is accomplished without the agreement of kindred forces, since even prayer itself which does not come from persons praying together is much feebler, the Lord having declared that He will be in the midst if two or three call upon Him with oneness of mind.[2] The Lord even undertook the Incarnation in order that through the blood of His cross He might be a peacemaker both on earth and in heaven.

As a result, because of all these things, we pray that our remaining days may be spent in peace, and we beg that our death may be in peace. For the sake of this peace, therefore, I have determined to leave no labor whatsoever undone, to

---
2 Cf. Matt. 18.20.

omit nothing as too humble to say or to do, to take no account of the length of journeys, and to shrink from no other irksome trials, so that I may meet with the reward of the peacemaker. And if anyone follows us as we point out this way, that is excellent, and my prayer attains its end; but, if he draws away to the opposition, I shall not, in consequence, withdraw from my decision. But, each one himself on the day of retribution will recognize the fruits of his own labors.

98. To Eusebius, Bishop of Samosata[1]

Although I was exceedingly eager to go to Nicopolis, after receiving the letter from your Holiness containing your refusal to go, I gave up my desire, at the same time recalling all my infirmities. Moreover, I realized the perfunctory manner of those inviting me, giving us a cursory invitation through the most revered brother Hellenius,[2] the assessor of Nazianzus, and not deigning to send a second messenger to remind us of these same matters or to escort us on the road. At all events, since our sins have made us an object of suspicion to them, we feared lest, perhaps, we might cloud the brightness of the festival for them by our presence. Now, with your Excellency we do not hesitate to strip ourselves for great struggles, but without you we are unequal to the task of facing even trifling afflictions. Since our discussion with them was to be on ecclesiastical matters, we have, therefore, let the time

---

1 This letter was written, according to Loofs (*op. cit.* 25), at Sebaste in the middle of June, 372.
2 A surveyor of customs at Nazianzus and a confidential friend of St. Basil and St. Gregory of Nazianzus. He was an Armenian and had a brother who, like himself, had acquired a reputation for eloquence. In 371 Hellenius had conveyed a letter from St. Gregory to St. Basil; cf. St. Basil, Letter 71.

of the festival pass, and deferred the conference until a period of quiet and tranquillity. We have also resolved to go to Nicopolis to talk over the needs of the churches with Bishop Meletius,[3] dearly beloved of God, if he should refuse the journey to Samosata. But, if he should not refuse to go, we shall accompany him, if this fact is made clear to us by both of you—by him in his answer to us concerning these matters (for we have written), and by your Reverence.

We were intending to hold a meeting with the bishops from Cappadocia Secunda, but, since they had been given the name of another province,[4] they suddenly believed that they had become of a different nation and race from us. They ignored us as completely as those who have had no acquaintance with us at all, and have never come to speak with us. Likewise, a second interview with the most revered Bishop Eustathius was expected, and this we have had. For, since many were crying out against him on the ground that he was in some way perverting the faith, we held a conference with him, and we found, with the help of God, that he was prudently consistent with the true faith in its entirety. The letters of the bishops were not carried to your Honor through the fault of those very persons who ought to have transmitted ours, but the fact, being driven out of my mind by my continual worries, escaped my notice.

I wanted my brother Gregory[5] to govern a church commensurate with his natural ability. This meant the whole Church under the sun gathered into one. But, since this is impossible, let him be a bishop, not exalted by the place, but himself exalting the place. For, it is truly characteristic of

---
[3] For Meletius, cf. Letters 57, 68, 89, 120, 129, and 216.
[4] Cf. preceding letter and note.
[5] According to Tillemont, this reference is to St. Basil's own brother, St. Gregory of Nyssa. Maran, however, thinks that St. Basil is referring to St. Gregory of Nazianzus.

a great man not only to suffice for great things but also by his own power to make little things great.

Now, what must be done about Palmatius,[6] who, even after so many admonitions from the brethren, is still serving Maximus[7] in the persecutions? But, in spite of all, they do not even now hesitate to write to him; for they are not permitted to come themselves because of ill health and their own duties at home.

Yet, be assured, Father, most beloved of God, that our affairs have exceeding great need of your presence, and it is necessary for you, yet this once, to bestir your venerable age in order to sustain Cappadocia, which is already wavering and near its fall.

99. *To Count Terentius*[1]

Although I had felt the greatest eagerness to obey, at least in part, both the imperial command and your Honor's friendly letter, whose every word and every opinion, I felt confident, was laden with a right motive and a noble intention, I was not allowed to direct my zeal to the work. And the

---

6 Otherwise unknown.
7 Governor of Cappadocia and successor of Elias. Cf. Tillemont, note 58. Although here represented as a persecutor of the orthodox, in the next year, when he was removed from office and accused of embezzlement of public funds, he found no warmer advocate than St. Basil. St. Basil wrote three letters in his behalf, Letters 147, 148, and 149. The persecution here mentioned may simply have been severe exactions of tribute.

---

1 Terentius was a general and a count under Valens, and, though orthodox, held the Arian emperor's favor. St. Basil addressed the present letter to Terentius in Iberia, where he was in command of the twelve legions. Letter 214 is also addressed to Terentius, while Letter 105 is addressed to the daughters of Terentius. The present letter was written from Satala in July or August, 372. Cf. Loots, *op. cit.* 27.

cause—the first, indeed, and truest—is my sins, which everywhere come out to meet me and trip my steps; and, secondly, our estrangement from the bishop who had been assigned to co-operate with us. For, our most revered brother, Theodotus,[2] who had promised from the beginning to assist us in everything and had readily brought us down from Getasa to Nicopolis, when he saw us in the city, from I know not what impulse, was filled with such a loathing for us and such a fear of our sins that he could not endure to take us either to morning or to evening prayer. He acted justly as regards us, and in a manner befitting my life, but did not plan advantageously for the general tranquillity of the churches. And he alleged to us as the reason for this that we had willingly received into communion the most revered Bishop Eustathius. Yet what we have done is as follows.

Since we had been summoned to a synod held by our brother Theodotus, and were eager through charity to heed the invitation, in order that we might not seem to make our meeting unavailing and fruitless, we endeavored to have an interview with the brother Eustathius mentioned above. And we put before him all the charges concerning the faith which the followers of our brother Theodotus bring against him. Moreover, we demanded that, if he was a follower of the right faith, he should make it evident to us so that we might be in communion with him, but, if he was differently disposed, that he should know definitely that we also would be unfavorably disposed toward him. Accordingly, after we had

---

2 The Bishop of Nicopolis in Lesser Armenia, and an aged prelate of high character and unquestioned orthodoxy. Theodotus was greatly respected by St. Basil, but he was extremely annoyed at St. Basil's reluctance to sever relations with Eustathius of Sebaste. For this reason he refused to co-operate with St. Basil in giving bishops to Armenia, and virtually excommunicated St. Basil on his arrival at Nicopolis where he had invited him. Friendly relations were later re-established between the two. Letters 121 and 130 are addressed to Theodotus.

discussed much with each other, and all that day had been spent in the examination of these matters, finally, when evening had come, we separated from each other without having brought our discussion to any final agreement. On the following day again, having taken our stands early in the morning, we were arguing on the same points, and at this time the brother Poimenius, a presbyter of Sebasteia, came, and he zealously defended the opposing doctrine against us.[3] Little by little, then, we freed ourselves of those charges which he seemed to bring against us and led them on to such agreement regarding the points which we were investigating that, by the grace of the Lord, we were found to differ not in the slightest degree from each other. Thus, then, somewhere around the ninth hour we rose up to pray and returned thanks to the Lord who granted us the favor of believing and speaking the same doctrine. In addition to this, I ought to have secured a written admission from the man so that his agreement in doctrine might be evident to those opposed to him, and might be for the rest sufficient proof of the man's good will. But I myself wished, for the sake of greater exactness, to meet with the followers of Theodotus, to secure from them a written statement of the faith, and to offer it to Eustathius mentioned above. My purpose was twofold, that he might confess the true faith, and that they might be fully assured, having no occasion for controversy because of his admitting their propositions. But, before learning why we were meeting, or what we had accomplished by our interview, the followers of Bishop Theodotus no longer deemed it proper to call us to the synod. We turned back in the middle of our journey, being disheartened because they were making ineffectual our labors for the peace of the churches.

After this, then, when the necessity of a journey to Ar-

---

[3] 'Us' and 'we' here mean St. Basil alone, not St. Basil and Eustathius.

menia befell us, knowing the individuality of the man, and wishing to defend my actions before a trustworthy witness and to fully satisfy him, I went to Getasa, the field of Meletius, the bishop dearly beloved of God, where Theodotus, whom I mentioned before, was present with me. So, when we were accused by him there because of our connection with Eustathius, I reported the success of our conference—that I found him agreeing perfectly with us in everything. But, as he affirmed that [Eustathius] had denied this after his departure from us, and that he had declared to his own followers that he had agreed with us in no way concerning the faith, in reply to this I said (and consider, admirable Sir, if I did not give most just and incontrovertible answers to this) that I was persuaded, inferring from the constancy of the man in other respects, that he did not turn so lightly to the opposite views, and that he did not at one moment admit, and at the next deny, what he had said. I was convinced that a man who shunned deceit even in trifling matters as something terrible, to say nothing of matters of such importance and so universally noised abroad, would never choose to be opposed to the truth. But, even if that which is talked among you should happen to be true, a written statement must be offered to him, containing a complete exposition of the right faith. Certainly, then, if I find him expressing his agreement in writing, I shall remain in communion with him, but, if I detect him shrinking back, I shall withdraw from union with him. When Bishop Meletius approved my words and also brother Diodorus, our fellow presbyter (for he was present on this occasion), then the most revered brother Theodotus agreed and invited us to go to Nicopolis in order that we might inspect his church, and might take him as our fellow traveler on our journey to Satala. However, he left us in Getasa, and, when we arrived at Nicopolis, forgetful of what he had heard from me and of what he had agreed with us, he dismissed us, after having covered us with shame by those insults and those ignominies which we described a short while ago.

How, therefore, was it possible for me, most honorable Friend, to carry out any of your commands and to give bishops to Armenia, since the companion of my cares entertained such feelings toward me? Through him I was expecting to find suitable men, because there are in his diocese both pious and intelligent men who are skilled in the language and understand the other peculiar traits of the nation. Although I know their names, I shall willingly keep silence, in order that no obstacle may arise to prevent their service in Armenia at another time, at least.

And now, having arrived at Satala in such a state of health, I seem to have settled all the rest, by the grace of God. I reconciled the bishops of Armenia and gave them the proper instructions, so that they may lay aside their accustomed indifference and assume a true zeal for the churches of the Lord. Concerning transgressions indifferently committed throughout Armenia, I also gave them rules as to how they might properly deal with them. Then, too, I received proposals passed by the majority from the Church of Satala, containing a request that we give them a bishop. Next, this became an object of care to me—to investigate the slander spread abroad about our brother Cyril, Bishop of Armenia; through the grace of God we discovered that it was falsely set in motion through the prejudice of those who hate him. This they openly confessed in our presence. Moreover, we seem in some measure to have appeased the people of Satala in his regard, so that they no longer avoid communion with him. Now, if these are slight matters and worth nothing, nevertheless, there was nothing else that we could do, because of our mutual lack of harmony caused by the machinations of the Devil. I should have been silent about these matters, in order that I might not seem to be publishing the disgraceful treatment accorded me. However, since I could not otherwise defend myself to your Excellency, I was obliged to relate all the truth of what has happened.

100. To Eusebius, Bishop of Samosata[1]

In the neighboring country of Armenia I beheld the letter of your Charity as men at sea would descry a beacon shining afar off on the waters, especially if the sea should happen to be wildly agitated by the winds. For, though, indeed, a letter of your Dignity is naturally pleasing and affords much comfort, yet, at that time especially, the circumstances increased my gratification from it. Now, what these circumstances were and how they grieved us I should not say, since I have decided once and for all to forget those distressful things. Our fellow deacon, however, will relate all to your Reverence.

My body has failed me so completely that I cannot endure even the slightest movements without pain. Yet, I pray that now, at least, it may be possible for my former desire to be fulfilled through the help of your prayers, even though this journey abroad has brought me much difficulty through the long neglect of affairs in our own church. But, if God, while we are upon earth, will deem us worthy to see your Reverence in our church, we shall have for the future truly good hopes of not being altogether cut off from the gifts of God.

---

1 Another of St. Basil's letters addressed to Eusebius, Bishop of Samosata. Previous letters to him are Letters 27, 30, 31, 34, 47, 48, 95, and 98. This letter, according to Loofs, *op. cit.* 30, was written from Armenia in July or August, 372.

Therefore, we ask, if it be possible, that this visit take place at the time of the synod which we celebrate yearly on the seventh day of the month of September in memory of the blessed martyr, Eupsychius,[2] an event now approaching. For, matters deserving of attention and needing assistance from you lie before us, namely, in regard to the appointment of bishops and in reference to a consultation and consideration of the actions directed against us by Gregory of Nyssa, who is organizing synods in Ancyra and in no way is ceasing, in his simplicity,[3] to scheme against us.

101. A Letter of Consolation[1]

That this, our first letter to you, should have a more cheerful subject is a matter worthy of prayer. For, in this way, everything would have been according to our desire, because we wish that the whole life of all those who choose to live in piety should proceed prosperously toward a good end. But, these circumstances have been assuredly ordered for the benefit of our souls by our Lord who directs our lives according to His ineffable wisdom. For, through them, He has rendered

---

[2] The martyrdom of Eupsychius, according to the Roman calendar, is celebrated on April 9 (*Boll. Acta. SS. April* 9). He suffered during the reign of Julian for helping to destroy a temple to Fortune. Cf. Sozomen, *Ecc. Hist.* 5.11. The orders of Julian for the rebuilding of the temple were never fulfilled, but a church was built on the spot and dedicated to Eupsychius. St. Basil is here inviting Eusebius to a festival held annually in honor of Eupsychius, and in Letter 252 he summons the bishops of Pontus to the festival of the dedication of this church.
[3] According to the Benedictine editors, this is another occasion on which St. Gregory displays his lack of tact. For it is lack of tact and not of affection toward St. Basil that causes his opposition. Cf. also, Letter 58.

---

[1] Editions anterior to the Benedictine add to this title, 'to the wife of Arinthaeus,' but no manuscript known at present contains it. The letter was written in 372.

life painful to you and has led us, who are joined with you through the love of God, to sympathy. Now, on learning from our brethren in what troubles you were, it seemed that we ought to bring you all possible consolation. If, therefore, it had also been possible to cross over to the place in which your Nobility happens to reside, I would have considered it as of the greatest importance to do so. The feebleness, however, of our body and the numerous duties in which we are engaged, both rendering even this journey which we have undertaken a cause of great harm to our churches, have induced us to visit your Dignity by letter, reminding you that these afflictions from the Lord who watches over us do not happen to the servants of God without benefit, but for a trial of true love toward the God who created us. For, as the toils of the contests lead the athletes on to their crowns, so also the test through tribulations leads Christians on to perfection, if we receive with becoming patience and in all gratitude what is dispensed to us by the Lord.

All things are directed by the goodness of the Master. Nothing which happens to us should be received as distressful, although at present it affects our weakness. In fact, even if we are ignorant of the reasons for which each event is applied as a blessing to us from the Master, nevertheless, we ought to be convinced of this—that what happens is assuredly advantageous either for us as a reward for our patience, or for the soul which was taken up, lest, tarrying too long in this life, it should be filled with the evil which exists in this world. For, if the hope of Christians were limited to this life, with reason would the premature separation from the body be considered difficult, but, if the beginning of true life for those living in God is the release of the soul from these corporeal chains, why do we grieve, even as those who have no hope?² Therefore, be encouraged. Do not succumb to your afflictions, but show that you are superior and have risen above them.

102. To the Citizens of Satala[1]

Constrained by your own appeals and those of the whole people, I took upon myself the care of your church and I promised you before God to leave undone nothing that should come within my power. Therefore, as it is written, I was compelled to touch, as it were, the apple of my eye.[2] Thus, my extraordinary esteem for you permitted me to remember nothing, neither relationship nor my intimacy with the man from childhood, in preference to your demands. On the contrary, I was forgetful of all that existed personally between us as friends. I took no account of the many lamentations uttered by my people when deprived of his leadership, nor of the tears of all his relatives. I did not take to heart the affliction of his mother, already aged and depending upon his assistance alone. I paid no regard to all these things, so important and at the same time so numerous. I had but one purpose—to adorn your church with the leadership of such a man and to bring it aid, since it had already fallen to its knees because of its long-continued lack of leadership, and needed much able guidance for its restoration.[3]

---

2 Cf. 1 Thess. 4.12.

---

1 The Benedictines give the year 372 as the date of this letter, but Loofs, *op. cit.* 20f, places it in 373.
2 Cf. Zach. 2.8.
3 The person of whom St. Basil is thinking is Poemenius. Cf. Letter 122.

So much, then, for our part. And we ask that your response may not appear less than our expectation and the assurance which we gave to the man that we have sent him out to friends most dear to us, but that each of you may strive to surpass the other in your esteem and love for him. See to it, therefore, that you show this noble rivalry, and by your extraordinary attention console his heart, so as to make him forget his country, forget his relatives, and forget the people who were as dependent upon his leadership as a new-born babe upon the breasts of its mother.

We have sent Nicias[4] ahead to make known to your Honorable Selves what has been done, in order that, on receiving the news, you may celebrate and give thanks to the Lord who has deigned through us to fulfill your prayer.

103. To the People of Satala[1]

The Lord has answered the prayers of His people, and through our Lowliness has given to them a shepherd worthy of the name, and not one who makes traffic of the title as many do. He is a man capable of pleasing you exceedingly in the name of the Lord who has filled him with His spiritual gifts, since you love the true doctrine and have accepted a life in accordance with the commands of the Lord.

---
4 Otherwise unknown.

---
1 On the same subject and of the same date as the preceding letter.

104. To the Prefect Modestus[1]

The very act of writing to so great a man, even if no other pretext were added, is to be esteemed a special honor in the eyes of the discerning, because association with men who preeminently surpass all others confers the highest distinction on those deemed worthy of it. But, as for me, who am in distress for my entire country, the petition to your Lordship is a necessity, and I beseech you to bear it kindly and as you are wont to do, and to stretch out your hand to our country which has already fallen to its knees. And this is the matter for which we are making our petition.

Our ministers, consecrated to God, both presbyters and deacons, were left free of taxation by the former census. But our present registrars, on the ground that they have received no order from your exalted Highness,[2] have enrolled them, except, perchance, some who were otherwise exempt on account of age. Therefore, we ask that this record of your kindness be left us to preserve for all future time a goodly memory of you, and that the clergy be exempt from taxation according to the former law. Moreover, we ask that the exemption should not be made to the persons of those now receiving it (for thus the favor will pass on to their successors, who do not always happen to be worthy of being priests). But some

---

[1] Modestus was Prefect of the Praetorium and under Valens a persecutor of the Catholics. By command of Valens he had given St. Basil the choice between deposition and communion with the Arians. Shortly after this he became ill, which he attributed to the divine vengeance because of his treatment of St. Basil. He summoned St. Basil, asked his pardon, and begged for prayers. On his recovery, which he attributed to the prayers of St. Basil, he regarded him with the greatest respect, and used his influence in his favor. Six of St. Basil's letters to Modestus are extant: Letters 104, 110, 111, 279, 280, and 281. The present letter was written in 372.

[2] *Exousias*—a title of address used by St. Basil for laymen only.

general concession should be made for the clergy according to the draft in the open register,³ so that exemption may be given by the administrators of the churches each time to those who are actually engaged in the divine service.

This will both render immortal your Excellency's reputation for good deeds, and will procure many intercessors with God for the imperial family. It will provide much benefit for the state, too, since we offer the relief which comes from tax exemption not altogether to the clergy, but to those as well who are at any time suffering afflictions. Now, this is what we do in our state of freedom, as can be ascertained by anyone who wishes to know.

105. To the Deaconesses, the Daughters of Count Terentius[1]

I expected, in truth, to meet your Modesties when I stopped at Samosata; when I failed to do so, I did not bear the disappointment easily, wondering when it would be either possible for me to approach your neighborhood again or pleasing to you to visit our country. But, let those decisions remain with the will of the Lord.

As to the present, however, when I found that my son Sophronius[2] was setting out in your direction, I gladly entrusted him with this letter which carries a greeting to you and reveals our disposition of mind—that, by the grace of God, we do not cease to remember you and to give thanks for you to the Lord that you are the noble offspring of a

---

3 Probably the public census list.

---

1 For Count Terentius, cf. Letter 99. This letter was written in the autumn of 372.
2 Perhaps the disciple of Eustathius mentioned in Letter 119.

noble root, fruitful in good works, and truly like lilies among thorns.[3] For, the fact of your not yielding to their deceits when you were surrounded by the great perverseness of men who corrupt the doctrine of truth, and of your not abandoning the apostolic pronunciation of the faith, turning to the innovations prevalent at the present time—is not that deserving of great thanksgiving to God, and does it not most justly win for you great commendation? You have believed in the Father and the Son and the Holy Spirit. Do not betray this trust: Father, the beginning of all things; only-begotten Son, begotten of Him, true God, Perfection from Perfection, living Image, wholly showing in Himself the Father; Holy Spirit, having His subsistence from God, Fount of Holiness, life-giving Power, perfecting Grace, through which man is adopted and the mortal is made immortal, in all respects united with the Father and the Son in glory and eternity, in power and kingdom, in sovereignty and divinity, as the tradition of the saving baptism testifies.

But, they who say that either the Son or the Spirit is a creature, or who in general reduce the Spirit to the ministering or servile order, are far from the truth. We should flee communion with them and avoid their conversation, as being poisonous to the soul. But, if at some future time the Lord shall grant us the favor of seeing you, we shall explain in fuller detail our words concerning the faith, so that from Scriptural proofs you may be able to recognize the strength of the truth and the weakness of heresy.

---

3 Cf. Cant. 2.2. St. Basil is fond of borrowing expressions and phrases from the Bible.

106. To a Soldier[1]

Although we must thank the Lord for many things of which he has considered us worthy in our travels, we judge that the acquaintance with your Honor which was granted to us by our good Master is our greatest blessing. For, we have come to know a man who makes clear that it is possible even in the military life to maintain a perfect love toward God, and that it behooves the Christian to be distinguished not by the style of his dress, but by the disposition of his soul.

Even at that time, therefore, we were most desirous of meeting you, and now, as often as we call you to mind, we enjoy the happiest thoughts. Accordingly, act the man, and be strong, and always strive to nourish and augment your love of God, in order that the abundance of His blessings to you may continue to increase. Moreover, we need no other proof that you remember us, since we have the testimony of your deeds.

107. To the Widow Julitta[1]

I was exceedingly distressed on reading in the letter from your Nobility that the same difficulties again beset you. What really should be done in regard to men who show such an unstable disposition, saying at one time one thing and at another another, and not abiding by their personal agree-

---

1 This letter was written in 372.

1 St. Basil wrote this letter to a widow of Cappadocia who was being troubled by the guardians of her heirs. The two following letters are also written in her behalf. Tillemont, though without sufficient evidence, wishes to identify her with the other widows to whom St. Basil has letters addressed. The date of this letter is 372.

ments? If, after the promises made before me and before the ex-prefect, the man now, as if he had said nothing, shortens to such an extent the appointed time, he seems to be absolutely beyond shame before us.

Nevertheless, I have written to him, reprehending him, and reminding him of his promises. I also wrote to Helladius,[2] servitor of the prefect, in order that through him the prefect might be informed of your difficulties. For, I did not think that it was appropriate for me, as I had never written to him about any private business, to be so overbold myself with so important an official, and I suspected that I would receive some censure, since, as you know, great men easily become provoked at such things. However, if there is to be any help, it will be through Helladius, a man both honest and well disposed toward us, and one who fears God and enjoys untold freedom of speech with the prefect. Yet, the Holy One can free you of all affliction, if only with a true and sincere heart we place our hope in Him.

108. To the Guardian of the Heirs of Julitta[1]

I was amazed when I heard that, forgetful of your former kind promises, so becoming to your Liberality,[2] you were now bringing a most severe and rigid claim against this sister of ours. What I should infer from the reports I do not know. For, I am not only conscious of your great generosity, acknowledged by those who have had experience of it, but

---

2 Helladius, to whom also Letter 109 is written, is otherwise unknown.

1 This letter is of the same date and on the same subject as the preceding.
2 *Eleutheria*—Sophocles (Greek Lexicon) questions whether St. Basil is using this at a title. No other instance of its use as such is found.

I also remember your promises which you made before me and this man.³ You said that you were specifying in writing a rather short time, but would grant more, because you were willing to accomodate yourself to the exigencies of the affair and to show leniency to the widow who was compelled to deliver so much money all at one time from her property.

What, then, the cause is for such a great change taking place I cannot understand. Only, whatever it is, I urge you, being mindful of your generosity and looking to the Lord who requites your good will, to grant the time of grace which you formerly promised, in order that they may be able to pay the debt by the sale of some of their possessions. I clearly remember, also, your promising, if you should receive the stipulated amount of gold, to hand over to the widow just mentioned all the papers agreed upon, both those negotiated before the prefects and those privately drawn up.

I beseech you, then, bestow this honor upon us and obtain from the Lord great glory for yourself, calling to mind your promises and realizing that you are a man and that you yourself must expect occasions when you will need help from God. Do not exclude yourself from this help by your present harshness, but win for yourself the compassion of God by showing to the afflicted all kindness and fairness.

109. To Count Helladius¹

I apologize exceedingly for being troublesome to your Excellency, lest I should seem to make use beyond measure of

---
3 I.e., the ex-prefect.

1 On the same subject and written at the same time as the two preceding letters.

your friendship because of your great authority. Nevertheless, I am not permitted by the stress of circumstances to be silent. Therefore, when I saw this sister, a relative of ours, suffering the affliction of widowhood and burdened with the care of the estate of her orphan son, now being oppressed beyond her strength by insupportable hardships, sick at heart I pitied her. I hastened to appeal to you, in order that, if it is at all possible, you may deign to co-operate with the man sent by her, so as to deliver her from further abuse, since she has already paid that which she promised in my presence. For, she was promised that the interest would be cancelled if she paid the principal.

Now, however, those who have the care of her heirs, after having received the principal, are attempting to collect the interest. Therefore, as one who knows that the Lord makes His own the affairs of widows and orphans, be zealous about using your efforts in this matter, in the hope of a recompense from God Himself. For, I think that, when his Clemency, our admirable prefect, has learned that the principal has been paid, he will sympathize with this now pitiable and afflicted house which is fallen to its knees and is no longer equal to the abuses inflicted on it from without. Therefore, I beg (and pardon the necessity because of which I have troubled you), co-operate in this matter, also, according to the power which Christ has given you, since you are kind and honest in your disposition and use for a good end whatever you have received.

110. To the Prefect Modestus[1]

In the same measure as you have granted us honor and

---
[1] For Modestus, cf. Letter 104. This letter was written in 372.

freedom of speech, being content in the gentleness of your disposition to descend to our level, in that measure and still more do we pray that our good Master will bestow on you an increase of dignity during your whole life. Although I had long ago set my heart on writing and enjoying the honor, yet, respect for authority restrained me, for I was careful lest I should ever seem to be using that freedom to excess.

But, I now am forced to take courage from the fact that your incomparable Excellency has authorized us to write, as well as from the need of those who are being afflicted. Therefore, if among the mighty supplications from the lowly have any weight, let me entreat you, admirable Sir, by your kind assent graciously to give security to the pitiful country people, and to order that the tax on iron be made endurable for the inhabitants of the iron-producing country of Taurus, so that they may not be wiped out once and for all, but that their service to the public treasury may be lasting. We are convinced that this of all things is especially an object of concern to your admirable Benevolence.[2]

111. To the Prefect Modestus[1]

I would not have had the courage in other circumstances to trouble your Excellency, since I know how to estimate myself and how to recognize the powers of others. But, when I saw this man, a friend of mine, acutely disturbed because he had been summoned, I dared to give him this letter, so that,

---
2 *Philanthropia*—a title of address used by St. Basil for laymen.

---
1 For Modestus, cf. Letter 104. This letter is of the same date as the preceding one.

by offering it in lieu of an olive branch,[2] he might meet with some kindness. Assuredly, even if we ourselves are of no account, our very moderation is sufficient to supplicate the kindest of prefects, and to obtain pardon for us, in order that, if no wrong has been done by the man, he can be saved through truth itself, and, even if he has erred, that he may be forgiven because of our intercession.

But, as to the condition of our affairs here, who knows better than you, who observe the weak spots in each one and with wonderful foresight keep everything under control?

112. To the Leader Andronicus[1]

If I had such health as to be able easily to endure journeys and to bear the hardships of winter, I would not be writing. On the contrary, for two reasons I should be going in person to visit your Magnanimity. The first is that I might pay the long-standing debt of my promise (for I know that I agreed to go to Sebasteia, there to enjoy the company of your Perfection; and I did go, but I missed the meeting, since I arrived a short time after the departure of your Honor). And the second is that I might personally perform a mission which I had for a long time hesitated to commit to writing, since I judged that I was too insignificant to obtain such a great favor. At the same time I did not think that anyone, when interceding for another, would persuade either an official or a private individual as readily by letter as if he himself were present, dismissing some of the charges, pleading excuse for

---
2 An olive branch held in the hand of a suppliant as a symbol of his condition and claim.

---
1 Both Andronicus and Domitian are otherwise unknown. This letter was written in the year 372.

others, and asking pardon for the rest, none of which could be easily accomplished through a letter. Now, because I had one advantage—your own godlike person—to offset all these disadvantages, and because it will be sufficient to unfold to you the opinion which we have about the matter, you yourself adding the rest, I did not shrink from the undertaking.

But you see how I am going around in a circle, hesitating and shrinking from revealing the cause for which I am writing these words. This Domitian has been a friend of ours, as were our parents, so that he differs in no way at all from a brother. Why should one not speak the truth? Accordingly, having learned the reason for which he was suffering, we said that he deserved to suffer thus. Indeed, let there be no one who shall escape vengeance if he has shown negligence, little or much, toward your Excellency.[2] Yet, when we saw him living in fear and in dishonor, and his safety depending upon your decision, we believed that he had had sufficient punishment; so we humbly beg you to be both generously and kindly disposed toward him. For, to subject one's opponents to his power is truly the mark of a strong man and a ruler, but to be kind and gentle to those who have fallen is characteristic of one who surpasses all men in greatness of mind and clemency. Thus it will be possible for you, if you desire, to show your greatness of soul to one and the same person, either, as you would wish, in punishing or in saving. But, the fear of the penalties expected and which he knows he deserves to suffer is a sufficient measure of punishment for Domitian. We beg you to add no further penalty to this. In fact, consider that there have already been many persons with power over wrong-doers in former times, and of these no word has been handed down to posterity; but those who excelled the many in wisdom and put away their wrath, the

---

2 *Aretén*—here used as a title of address by St. Basil.

memory of these is handed down immortal for all time. Let this also be added to the reports about you. Grant us who desire to celebrate your praises to be able to excel the songs of kindly deeds sung in previous times. Thus, even Croesus[3] is said to have restrained his wrath against the slayer of his son, who handed himself over for punishment; and Cyrus the Great, after conquering him, is said to have become a friend to this same Croesus.[4] We shall include you among these men; with all our strength we shall publicly proclaim these facts, unless we should be considered an altogether too insignificant herald of such a great man.

Among other things we must mention this, that we punish those who have done any wrong whatsoever, not for what has already happened (for what means would there be to undo that which is already done?), but that they themselves may become better in the future, or that they may be an example for others to learn self-control. However, in the present case, one might say that neither of these results is lacking, for he himself will remember this even after death, and I think that the rest, looking at him, are frightened to death. Therefore, if anything should be added to his punishment, it would seem to be for the satisfaction of personal wrath. This, I would say, is far from being true in your case, and I would not have been induced to speak any of these words if I had not observed that the reward is greater for him who gives than for those who receive. For, to not a few will the magnanimity of your disposition be evident. In fact, all the Cappadocians are looking to the future, and I would pray them to reckon this magnanimity among the other virtues belonging to you.

I hesitate to stop writing, believing that what I have omitted will be a loss to me. At least I will add this much, that, al-

---
3 Cf. Herodotus 1.45.
4 Cf. Herodotus 1.88.

though he had letters from many interceding for him, he held this one from us more precious than all, having understood, I know not how, that a word of ours is of influence with your Perfection. Therefore, in order that he may not be deceived in the hopes which he has in us, and that we may be mentioned with reverence among our own people, let me urge you, my unsurpassed Master, to consent to our request. Certainly, you have observed human affairs no less than the philosophers of the past, and you know how fair is the treasure which is reserved for all those who render service to the needy.

113. To the Presbyters at Tarsus[1]

On meeting this man, I felt great gratitude toward the holy God, because by the presence of such a one He gave me comfort from my many afflictions, and through him clearly showed your love. From the principles of this one man I have learned, I might say, the zeal which all of you have for the truth. Now, what we discussed in private with each other he himself will inform you. But, what is proper for me to make known to your Charities is this.

The present time shows a great inclination toward the destruction of the churches, and it is quite a long time since we first observed this. Further, as to the building up of the Church, the correction of errors, compassion toward the weak among the brethren, and protection for those who are sound—not one of these things exists. Yet, neither is there assistance or remedy for this disease that has seized upon us, nor any protection against that which may be expected. And, actually, the condition of the Church now (to use a clear

---

1 This letter was written in 372.

illustration, even though it may seem to be rather commonplace) is like that of an old garment easily rent by any trifling strain, and incapable of being restored to its original strength. Therefore, there is need of great zeal and great care in such a time, so that the churches may receive some benefit. And it is a benefit for those hitherto separated to be united. Moreover, there would be union, if we would be willing to accommodate ourselves to the weaker in whatever matters do no harm to souls.

Therefore, since many mouths are opened against the Holy Spirit, and many tongues are spurred on to blasphemy against Him, we ask you to reduce the group of blasphemers to as small a number as lies in your power. We also ask you to receive in communion those who do not say that the Holy Spirit is a creature, in order that blasphemers may be left alone, and that either being ashamed they may return to the truth, or continuing in their sin may be held unworthy of credit because of their small number. Therefore, let us seek for nothing more, but hold out to the brethren who wish to be united with us the Creed of Nicaea; and, if they agree with it, let us require further that they must not say that the Holy Spirit is a creature, nor be in commuion with those who say it. But, I think that we should demand nothing beyond this. In fact, I am convinced that by a longer association and an experience together without strife, even if it should be necessary to add more for the purpose of explanation, the Lord who makes all things work together unto good for those who love Him will grant it.[2]

---

[2] Cf. Rom. 8.28.

114. To Cyriacus and His Followers in Tarsus[1]

Why should we proclaim among men who are sons of peace how great is the blessing of peace? Since, therefore, this blessing, great and wondrous and eagerly desired by all those who love the Lord, now runs the risk of being reduced to a bare name, 'because iniquity has abounded, the charity of many having now grown cold,'[2] I think that those who serve the Lord sincerely and truly ought to have this one ambition —to bring back to unity the churches which have been severed from each other at 'sundry times and in divers manners.'[3] And, certainly, if I myself should attempt to do this, I should not justly be charged with being a busybody. For, nothing belongs so peculiarly to a Christian as being a peacemaker,[4] and therefore the Lord has promised us the greatest reward for it. Accordingly, when I had met the brethren, and beheld their brotherly love and their affection toward you, and their still much greater love of Christ, as well as their exactness and strength in the faith, and when I also saw that they were showing great zeal for two things—not to be separated from your love, and not to betray the sound faith—I approved their good course of action. Further, I am writing to your Dignity, urging with all love that you regard them as truly united and as sharers of all your solicitude for the Church. And I have attested before them to your correctness of faith, and to the fact that you yourself, by the grace of God, with zeal for the truth are ready for everything which you may have to suffer for the true doctrine.

---

1 Cyriacus is unknown. This letter is on the same subject as the preceding and was written at about the same time.
2 Cf. Matt. 24.12.
3 Cf. Heb. 1.1. The translation of the Greek *polymerōs* is, literally, 'in many portions.'
4 Cf. Matt. 5.9.

242   SAINT BASIL

Now the following conditions, I am convinced, are not objectionable to you, and are sufficient assurance in themselves for the brethren mentioned above—namely, that you profess the faith as set forth by our Fathers once assembled in Nicaea and deny not a single one of the statements there, but realize that the three hundred and eighteen, coming together without contention, did not speak without the operation of the Holy Spirit; and that you add to that Creed also that one must not say that the Holy Spirit is a creature, nor, moreover, be in communion with those who say it, that thus the Church of God may be pure, having no admixture of weeds. If this certainty is offered to them by your Mercifulness, they are also ready to exhibit a like submission to you. I pledge myself on the part of the brethren that they will in no way oppose, but will show to you all good behavior in the highest degree, if this one thing sought by them is readily offered by your Perfection.

115. To the Heretic Simplicia[1]

Ill-advisedly do men heap abominations upon their betters and indulge their inferiors. Therefore, I myself now restrain my tongue, stifling by silence any rebuke for the insolence

---

[1] The tone of this letter (written in 372 or 373) is entirely different from that of St. Basil's other letters, but there seems no reason for questioning its authenticity. The circumstances referred to in the letter can be understood from Letter 38 of St. Gregory of Nazianzus. It appears that a certain church in Cappadocia elected as its bishop the slave of a very wealthy woman called Simplicia, who was very generous but of suspected orthodoxy. St. Basil and St. Gregory unwisely ordained the man before receiving the permission of his owner, who in her anger threatened St. Basil with the vengeance of her slaves aṅd eunuchs. In this letter St. Basil answers her threats. After the death of St. Basil she directed her efforts to St. Gregory in order to compel him to annul the ordination. Cf. Maran, *Vita Basilii*, xxv. The Migne edition states

directed against me. I shall wait for the Judge above who knows how to finally avenge every evil. For, even though a person should pour out money more plentifully than sand, he injures his soul if he tramples upon justice. Now, God always demands a sacrifice, not, I mean, as if needing it, yet accepting a pious and righteous mind as a precious sacrifice. But, when anyone treads on his own soul by transgressing, God considers his prayers profane.

Therefore, be mindful of the last day, and do not, if you please, argue with us. We have more knowledge than you, and we are not so choked within with thorns, nor do we mix tenfold evil with a few virtues. You have roused up against us lizards and toads,[2] creatures of spring, forsooth, but unclean ones. However, a bird will come from above to devour them. For, the account I must render is not according to what you think, but as God knows how to judge. And, if there is also need of witnesses, slaves will not take the stand, nor the ignominious and utterly abandoned race of eunuchs—this they certainly are, neither man nor woman, lustful, envious, venal, quick-tempered, effeminate, gluttonous, avaricious, rough, querulous about their dinner, unstable, niggardly, acquisitive, insatiable, mad, and jealous. And what further is it possible to say? Condemned to the knife at their very birth, how can their minds really be straight, whose very feet are twisted? They are chaste without reward—as a result of the

---
that the Codex Caesareus 67 contains the following prefatory note for this letter: 'Letter of the same to Simplicia, about her eunuchs. She was a heretic. Now, when Basil was ill, and was entering a bath to wash, the same Simplicia ordered her eunuchs and maids to throw his towels outside; and straightway the just judgment of God destroyed some of them. And the same Simplicia sent money to the same blessed Basil to make amends for her insult, but he would not receive them and wrote this to her.' The writer of this comment was evidently unacquainted with the letter of St. Gregory of Nazianzus quoted above.

2 Apparently, the slaves and eunuchs.

knife. They are mad with passion without fruition—because of their own turpitude. These will not stand as witnesses at the Judgment, but the eyes of the just and the countenances of virile men, who then will see with their eyes what they are looking toward with their understanding.

116. To Firminus[1]

Your letters are both rare and brief, either because of your reluctance to write, or for some other reasons—because you are planning to escape the satiety arising from voluminous correspondence, or even because you are accustoming yourself to brevity in speech. For us, certainly, they are not at all sufficient. However, even if their number should be excessive, they are less than we desire, because we wish to learn every detail about you—how your health is; how your practices of asceticism progress; whether you are persevering in the resolutions formerly determined upon, or have made some change, altering your decision according to circumstances.

Now, if you had persevered, we would not have been asking for a large number of letters, but this much would suffice for us: 'So-and-so to So-and-so: be assured that we are well, and farewell.' Yet, since we hear what we are ashamed even to say, that, having left the ranks of your blessed forefathers, you are going over to the side of your paternal grandfather and are striving to become Brettanius instead of Firminus, we are eager to hear the facts themselves and to learn the reasons inducing you to change to this profession. But, since

---

[1] Firminus, as well as his father, Firminus, and grandfather, Brettanius, are unknown except through this letter. Firminus seems to have abandoned the ascetic life which he had first embraced in order to join the army. St. Basil wrote this letter about 372.

you yourself have been silently ashamed of your resolution, we urge you not to make plans deserving of shame, and, if any such thing has crept into your mind, drive this out of your thoughts and become master of yourself again and, saying a long farewell to army and weapons and to the hardships of camp, return to your fatherland. There, consider it sufficient for security of life and for all renown to rule over the city like your forefathers. Observing your fitness by nature and the absence of rivals, we feel confident that this honor will come to you without trouble. Therefore, if this decision was not made from the beginning, or after having been made was again rejected, inform us at once, but if—and may it not be so—your plans remain the same, let the misfortune come to us self-announced. Truly, we do not want letters.

117. Without Address, on the Practice of Asceticism[1]

I own that I am already indebted to your Honor; besides, this present solicitude in which we are involved necessarily makes us dependent on assistance in such troubles, even if those advising are chance persons, to say nothing of you, who are joined to us by many other lawful claims. And, so, it is not necessary to review the past, since we might say that we are responsible for our own disorders, because we were obstinately eager to depart from that blessed life of asceticism which alone leads to salvation. Perhaps, on this account also we were given over to this confusion of temptation. But, those things are past, and they were considered worthy of mention

---

1 This is evidently an answer from Firminus to the preceding letter, and there does not appear to be any reason for doubting its authenticity. This and all other unaddressed letters are lacking in the MSS of the Aa family, but this is probably because they were unknown. Cf. Bessières 156, 159, 160. This letter was written about 372.

only lest we fall a second time into a similar perplexity. As to the future, I most earnestly wish your Reverence to be fully satisfied that, God willing, it will go very easily with us, since the matter is both lawful and holds no difficulty, and since our many friends at court are ready to show us favors. Therefore, our petition will be drawn up to correspond to the form given to the Vicar,[2] and, according to it, if there is no delay, we shall be dismissed immediately on presenting the permission given in the writ.[3] But, I am convinced that in such matters our deliberate choice is more powerful than the royal commands, and if we show it inflexible and steadfast as regards a life of perfection, the keeping of our virginity will, with the help of God, be unassailable and inviolate for us.

We were glad to see the brother whom you entrusted to us, and we hold him among our friends, praying that he may be worthy of God and of your testimony.

---

2 The Empire was divided into thirteen civil dioceses, of which the first was subject to the court of the East. Egypt was governed by an Augustal perfect, and the remaining eleven dioceses by vicars or vice-prefects.

3 Letter 123 of St. Gregory of Nazianzus makes it evident that a written discharge was necessary for soldiers. He says to a certain Ellelichus: 'Mamanta, the slave Reader, whose father was a soldier, was consecrated to God because of his noble character. Give him to God and to us, but do not let him be numbered among vagabond soldiers. Give him his freedom in writing, so that he may not be threatened by others.' Cf. *P. G.* 32.534 n. 99.

118. To Jovinus, Bishop of Perrha[1]

I hold you a debtor of a goodly debt. For, I made you a loan of love which I should receive again with interest, since even our Lord does not reject such a form of interest. Therefore, pay it, my dear Friend, by coming to visit our country. Now, that, certainly, is the capital. But, what is the interest? The fact of your being present, a man as far superior to us, as fathers are better than their sons.

119. To Eustathius, Bishop of Sebaste[1]

Through my most revered and most pious brother Peter[2] I salute your Charity, urging you now, as on every other occasion, to pray for me that, turning from these detestable and harmful habits of mine, I may at length become worthy

---

[1] The MSS vary between Jovinus and Jobinus. Furthermore, all do not agree that Jovinus was Bishop of Perrha. Some read *Kérrēs* and others *Pérgēs*. Tillemont and Maran, however, prefer the reading *Pérrhēs* of six of the MSS. Perrha was in Syria and not far from the seat of Eusebius of Samosata. The letter is an excellent example of the spirit of the Second Sophistic period of Greek rhetoric. The whole is a rather far-fetched metaphor. St. Basil has visited Jovinus and compares his visit to a loan out at interest. We learn from Letter 127 that Jovinus repaid the visit. This letter was written near the end of 372 or at the beginning of 373.

---

[1] St. Basil here writes concerning the untrustworthiness of a certain Basil and Sophronius whom Eustathius had recommended to him. He was unwilling to break with Eustathius because of their mutual interest in asceticism, and for a long time seemed blind to his heretical tendencies and his duplicity. This letter records the first of a series of events which finally brought about the break between the two. Cf. Letter 79 and, for persistence in heresy, Letters 130, 223, and 244. The end of the year 372 or the beginning of 373 is given as the date of this letter.
[2] Letter 203, as well as this letter, was carried by a Peter whom St. Basil calls his brother. It is uncertain whether this is St. Basil's own brother or a spiritual brother.

of the name of Christ. Now, assuredly, even if I do not speak, you and he will converse with each other about our concerns, and he will give you an exact account of what has happened, so that you will not accept without examination the base suspicions against us which in all likelihood those will invent who have been treating us insolently in disregard of the fear of God and of the opinion of men. In fact, what sort of charges the noble Basil, whom I welcomed from your Reverence as the guardian of my life, made against us I am truly ashamed to say, but you will learn all the details from the explanations of our brother. And I say this, not to take vengeance on him (for I pray that it may not be reckoned against him by the Lord), but to make sure that your love for us remains steadfast. For, I fear lest they may cause it to waver by extravagant slanders, which they have probably prepared as a defense for their fault. Whatever charge they may make against us, let them be questioned about it by your Intelligence[3]—whether they have brought a formal accusation against us, or have sought the correction of the fault of which they now accuse us, or have made their grievance against us really clear. But, now they have revealed through their ignoble flight that, under a cheerful face and pretended words of love, they were concealing in their souls an inexpressible depth, as it were, of deceit and bitterness. How much sorrow they caused us in this, and how much occasion for laughter they gave those in this wretched city who always loathe the life of piety, and who affirm that a pretence of chastity is practiced as a means of winning confidence and as a form of deceit, is certainly known to your Intelligence even if we do not recount it. As a result, there is no practice so suspected of wickedness by the citizens here as the profession of the ascetical life.

---

3 *Anchinoéas*—a title of address used by St. Basil only for clergy.

How these things are to be remedied should be the care of your Intelligence to consider. For, the charges fabricated against us by Sophronius are not a prelude of blessings, but a beginning of division and separation, and a striving to cool the charity in us. And we urge that he be restrained by your Mercifulness from this harmful attack, and that your Charity attempt rather to bind together the parts which are disunited and not to intensify the separation of those who are eager for a division.

120. To Meletius, Bishop of Antioch[1]

I received a letter from Bishop Eusebius, dearly beloved of God, enjoining us to write again to the Western bishops concerning certain ecclesiastical affairs, and he wanted us to write the letter to be signed by all who are in communion. But, since I did not see how I could write about the matters which he commanded, I have sent the memorandum to your Reverence, so that you yourself, after reading it and being attentive to the reports from the most beloved brother Sanctissimus,[2] our fellow presbyter, may deign to write about these affairs as seems best to you. We are ready to subscribe

---

1 For the identity of Meletius, cf. Letter 66 n. 6. Previous letters addressed to Meletius are Letters 57, 68, and 89. This letter was probably written in 372. Letters 120, 121, 122, 129, and 130 are all related in the matter of chronology. Tillemont and the Benedictine editors agree as to the dating, but disagree in the identity of certain of the persons. Loofs, *op. cit.* 29, disagrees with the dating, but his arguments do not substantiate his claims.

2 Tillemont thinks that Sanctissimus was a priest from the West because of his Latin name. The Benedictines, however, consider him a presbyter of Antioch, since Roman names were common there. The interest in Eastern affairs displayed by Sanctissimus, and the fact that St. Basil calls him his 'fellow presbyter' and sends him on several important missions, would indicate that he was an Eastern presbyter.

to this and to have it quickly carried around to those in communion, so that he who is to go to the bishops of the West may set out with all the signatures. Give orders that we be informed immediately of what your Holiness has in mind, so that we may not be ignorant of your decisions.

Now, concerning the charges which are being concocted or even are already fabricated against us in Antioch, the same brother will report to your Honor, if a previous account of the happenings has not already made the circumstances clearly known to you. For, in truth, the hope of terminating the threats is near at hand. But, I want your Reverence to know that our brother Anthimus[3] has made Faustus,[4] who is with the pope,[5] a bishop, without his having received the votes, and has appointed him in the place of our most revered brother Cyril. As a result, he has filled Armenia with dissensions. Accordingly, that they may not make false reports concerning us, and, also that we ourselves may not be blamed for the confusion of these acts, I have given your Dignity this information. Without doubt, you yourself will deign to make this known to the rest, for I think that many will be distressed at this disorder.

---

3 In 371, Anthimus, a contentious and ambitious prelate, claimed to be Metropolitan of Cappadocia Secunda with his diocese Tyana as a metropolitan see. He was joined by those prelates who opposed St. Basil's election to the see of Caesarea.

4 All information about Faustus is procured from Letters 120, 121, and 122.

5 The title 'pope' was originally employed with great latitude. In the East it has always been used to designate simple priests. In the West, however, it seems always to have been restricted to bishops. It was probably in the fourth century that it became a distinctive title of the Roman Pontiff, and this was finally prescribed by Gregory VII. It is not known to whom St. Basil is referring.

121. To Theodotus, Bishop of Nicopolis[1]

The winter is bitter and prolonged, so that we do not readily have the consolation of letters. For this reason, I realize, I have seldom written to your Reverence or received letters from you. But since the most beloved brother Sanctissimus, our fellow presbyter, has undertaken a journey to you, through him I salute your Modesty and urge you to pray for me and to lend your ear to the brother just mentioned, so that you may learn from him the condition of affairs in the churches and may bring all possible zeal to the tasks lying before you.

I want you to know that Faustus came to us with a letter from a pope, asking that he be made a bishop. When we demanded a testimonial from your Reverence and from the other bishops, he disregarded us and went to Anthimus, and, after having received the appointment from him, without any mention being made of us, he returned.

---

[1] On the same subject and of the same date as the preceding letter, and one of the two (cf. Letter 130) extant letters of St. Basil to Theodotus. Theodotus, Bishop of Nicopolis and Metropolitan of Lesser Armenia, was an aged prelate of noble character and unquestioned soundness of faith, and was highly esteemed by St. Basil. Theodotus, however, suspected Eustathius of Sebaste of heresy, and, when St. Basil showed himself unwilling to believe the suspicions and manifested an evident friendship for him, Theodotus turned his suspicions on St. Basil and refused to co-operate with him in the appointment of bishops to Lesser Armenia.

122. To Poemenius, Bishop of Satala[1]

No doubt, you asked the Armenians for a letter when they returned through your city, and you learned my reason for not giving them one. Now, if they spoke with a love of the truth, you pardoned us at once; but, in case they concealed it, which I do not think probable, at least hear it from us.

Anthimus, a most notable man, who long ago made peace with us, later finding an opportune time to satisfy his vanity and to cause us some distress, consecrated Faustus by his own authority and with his own hand, waiting for the vote of none of you and ridiculing us as being too exact in such matters. Since, therefore, he violated a time-honored custom and, furthermore, showed contempt for you from whom I was waiting to receive the testimonial, and performed an act not pleasing to God, as I think, being grieved against the Armenians, I gave no letter to any of them, not even to your Reverence. But I have not admitted Faustus to communion, openly protesting that, if he does not bring me your letters, I shall hold myself for all time estranged from him and shall dispose my like-minded brethren to do the same.

If, then, the situation can be remedied, do you yourself both make haste to write, bearing witness for him, if you see that the life of the man is good, and to persuade the others to write. But, if it is incurable, make this also clear to me, so that I may no longer pay any attention at all to them, al-

---

[1] Poemenius, Bishop of Satala in Armenia, was a relative of St. Basil and had been brought up in close intimacy with him. When St. Basil had been ordered by Valens in 372 to appoint bishops for the churches in Armenia, at the earnest request of the people and magistrates he had made Poemenius Bishop of Satala. Cf. Letter 102. in which St. Basil commends Poemenius to his new flock. St. Basil is now writing him about the uncanonical appointment of Faustus which has been the subject of the two preceding letters. This letter was written at the end of the year 372 or at the beginning of 373.

though, as they have shown, they have already started to transfer their communion to Anthimus, disdaining us and this church as being too old-fashioned for friendship.

123. To the Monk Urbicius[1]

You were going to visit us (and the blessing was near at hand) to refresh us at least with the tip of your finger when we were burning up in the midst of our trials. What then? Our sins stood in the way and prevented your setting out, that we might suffer without relief. For, just as among the waves one sinks and another rises up, while still another grows black with violent agitation, so also with our evils—some have ceased, others come on, while still others are expected. The one relief from our troubles, generally, is to yield in the crises and avoid the persecutors.

But, do indeed visit us, either to comfort or to give us advice or even to encourage us, and, especially, to make us better by the very sight of you. And—what is more important—pray, and pray earnestly, that our reason may not be submerged under the flood of evils, but that we may keep ourselves acceptable in all respects to God, lest we be counted among the wicked servants, giving thanks to Him when He bestows His benefits, and not submitting when He teaches by the opposite means. But, let us derive profit even from our very difficulties, trusting the more in Him when we have more need of Him.

---

[1] Urbicius is a monk about whom nothing is known except for this letter and Letter 242. This period, from 372 to 374, was a time of great personal suffering for St. Basil. He and St. Gregory of Nazianzus, his lifelong friend, had become estranged; Theodotus, whom he esteemed highly, suspected him of heresy and refused to co-operate with him; he at last realized the treachery and ingratitude of Eustathius of Sebaste and was forced to break with him; and, finally, his friend, Eusebius of Samosata, had been exiled to Thrace by the Emperor Valens. The year 373 is assigned as the date of this letter.

124. To Theodorus[1]

Some say that, if those held captive by the passion of love are drawn away from those loved by some unusually urgent necessity, whenever they look at a likeness of the beloved one they relieve the vehemence of the passion through the pleasure derived from the sight. Now, whether this is true or not, I cannot say, but what has happened to me with regard to your Goodness[2] is not very different from this. For, since I have, so to say, a certain loving affection for your holy and guileless soul, but the enjoyment of my friends, as also of any other good, is for us not easy of attainment because of the opposition of our sins, I thought that I had perceived a very distinct image of your Goodness in the presence of our most pious brothers. And, if I had happened to meet your Nobility[3] apart from them, I would have considered that I had seen them also in you, because, I mean, the measure of love in each of you is such that there appears equally in the case of each an eagerness to excel. I gave thanks to the holy God for this, and I pray that, if any span of life is still left to me, it may become through you a pleasant life. At the present time, however, I consider this existence a wretched and detestable thing, since I am separated from the company of those nearest and dearest to me. For there is nothing, in my opinion, in which anyone may take delight, if he is separated from those who truly love him.

---

1 The identity of Theodorus is unknown. This letter was written in 373.
2 *Hagiótēta*—a title of address used by St. Basil in addressing clergy.
3 *Gnēsiótēti*—a title of address used by St. Basil for the clergy.

125. A Transcript of Faith Dictated by the Most Holy Basil, Which Eustathius, Bishop of Sebaste, Signed[1]

Those who have either previously accepted another pro-

---

[1] This letter represents but one step in St. Basil's gradual disillusionment as to the character of Eustathius of Sebaste. On Eustathius, cf. Letters 79 and 119, with notes. The series of incidents leading up to St. Basil's break with Eustathius may be described briefly as follows. Theodotus, Bishop of Nicopolis, had invited St. Basil to attend a synodical meeting at Nicopolis. St. Basil, on his way there, interviewed Eustathius, which at once barred him from attending the synod. Grieved and humiliated at this treatment from Theodotus, St. Basil returned home and sought counsel from Eusebius of Samosata. This occurred in May, 372. In the following June or July he again returned to Armenia, not only to confer with Meletius, but also to comply with an order from the emperor to place bishops in the vacant sees of that province. Because of the coolness between himself and Theodotus, St. Basil went first to Getasa, the home of Meletius, and there, in the presence of reliable witnesses, he justified his conduct with Eustathius and refuted the accusations of Theodotus. The latter, who was present, maintained that Eustathius had denied any agreement with St. Basil's propositions. Accordingly, to satisfy Theodotus, St. Basil offered to make Eustathius sign a profession of faith containing all the articles of the Nicene Creed. Theodotus accepted the plan, and promised to assist St. Basil in appointing bishops in Armenia. However, upon his arrival in Nicopolis, Theodotus forgot all that had passed and virtually excommunicated St. Basil. Under these circumstances, St. Basil was prevented from making the appointments. Fatigued, disappointed, and grieved over the turn of affairs, he returned home only to find sadly neglected conditions in his own diocese. St. Basil made a third visit to Armenia in the year 373, probably in connection with the ordination of Faustus. It was on this trip that the people of Armenia demanded an assurance of the orthodoxy of Eustathius. St. Basil willingly offered to go in person to Eustathius and have him sign a profession of faith. The present letter was accordingly drafted. Some think it is written by St. Basil together with Theodotus, while others believe that it has the tone of a synodical decree. At any rate, a meeting was arranged and the transcript signed in the presence of witnesses. For St. Basil's own account of the signing, cf. Letter 244, sec. 2. But, St. Basil's suspicions, once aroused, were not easily allayed. He accordingly proposed another meeting so that the prelates of Caesarea and Sebaste might be united with one another and their communion for the future be sincere. Both the place and the date were decided upon, but Eustathius and his colleagues failed to keep the appointment. In spite of all efforts on the part of Eusebius of Samosata to effect a reconciliation and finally win Eustathius to the Nicene faith, Eustathius, shortly after signing the present letter, renounced communion with St. Basil

fession of faith and wish to transfer to unity with the orthodox, or even those who now for the first time wish to be instructed in the doctrine of truth, must be taught the Creed written by the blessed Fathers in the synod assembled formerly at Nicaea. And the same thing would be useful also for those suspected of being opposed to sound doctrine and who obscure the meaning of their false teaching by their specious subterfuges. For these, also the Creed inserted here is sufficient. For, either they will correct their hidden disease or, if they hide it completely in the depths [of their hearts], they will themselves bear the condemnation for their deceit, but will prepare for us an easy defense in the Day of Judgment, when the Lord will reveal 'the things hidden in darkness and make manifest the counsels of hearts.'[2] Therefore, it is proper to receive them if they profess that they believe according to the words set down by our Fathers at Nicaea and according to the clearly expressed meaning of these words.

Now, there are some who are corrupting the doctrine of truth in this Creed and are twisting the sense of the words in it according to their own will. In fact, even Marcellus,[3]

---

and openly attacked him on the ground of Apollinarianism. Although pained at the duplicity of his former friend, and distressed over his false charges, St. Basil for about three years maintained a discreet silence. He, then, for the first time, openly defended himself against the slanders of Eustathius. Cf. Letter 223.

2 1 Cor. 4.5.

3 Marcellus of Ancyra was one of the bishops present at the Councils of Ancyra and Nicaea. He was a strong opponent of Arianism, but in his zeal to combat Arius adopted the opposite extreme of modified Sabellianism. He was several times condemned, and died, deprived of his see, in 374. Marcellus confused the Personality of God, declaring that God was originally only one Personality, but at the creation of the universe the Word or Logos went out from the Father and was God's activity in the world. This Logos became incarnate in Christ and was thus constituted Son of God. The Holy Spirit likewise went forth as the third Divine Personality from the Father and from Christ according to St. John 20.22. At the consummation of all things, however, Christ and the Holy Spirit will return to the Father, and the Godhead will be again an absolute unity. Cf. *Cath. Encyclopedia,* under Marcellus of Ancyra. Cf. also Jerome, *De vir. ill.* 86.

when speaking impiously against the person[4] of our Lord
Jesus Christ and explaining Him as mere 'Word,' dared to
allege by way of excuse that he took his principles from the
Creed, giving a wrong explanation of the meaning of 'consubstantial.' And some from the impious sect of the Libyan
Sabellius,[5] interpreting 'person' and 'substance' as the same,
take as the starting point for the fabrication of their blasphemies the fact that it is written in the Creed that, 'if anyone says that the Son is from another substance of person,
the Catholic and Apostolic Church excommunicates him.'
Now, it is not said in this latter statement that substance and
person are the same thing. For, if the words expressed one
and the same idea, what was the need of both of them? But,
it is evident that, since some deny that the Son is of the substance of the Father, and others say that He is not, indeed,
of the substance but that He is of some other person, they
thus have rejected both views as foreign to the mind of the
Church. Now, when [the Fathers] declared their opinion,
they said that the Son was of the substance of the Father,
not adding further, 'of the person.' Thus, that former statement is laid down as a rejection of the evil opinion, but this
latter contains a declaration of the doctrine of salvation.
Accordingly, it is necessary to confess that the Son is con-

---

4 For a definition of the theological terms used in this letter, cf. Letter 8.
5 Sabellius affirmed that there exists in God only a single person, and
 that this unity or monad constitutes the absolute being of God. When
 the Divine Essence departed from its quiet and inactivity, manifesting
 itself and acting, it was called the Word. It is the Word which created
 the world, and, again, it is the Word which undertook the salvation
 of humanity. For this work it took three successive modes of existence:
 three aspects (*prósōpa*), three denominations (*onómata*), corresponding to the three economies which succeed each other in the order of
 salvation: Father, Son, and Holy Spirit. But, these three modes of existence are transitory and accidental. Each of them is to cease at the
 same time as the object which necessitates each.

substantial with the Father, as it is written, and to confess the Father in His own Person, the Son in His own, and the Holy Spirit in His own, just as [the Fathers] themselves have clearly explained. For, they proved sufficiently and clearly by saying 'Light from Light' that the One is the Light which begot, and the Other the Light which was begotten, truly Light and Light; so that the meaning of substance [in regard to the Father and to the Son] is one and the same. At this point, let us insert also the very Creed which was written at Nicaea.

We believe in one God, the Father Almighty, maker of all things visible and invisible; and in one Lord Jesus Christ, the Only-begotten Son of God, begotten of the Father, that is, of the substance of the Father; God of God, Light of Light, true God of true God; begotten, not made; consubstantial with the Father, by whom all things were made both in heaven and on earth. Who for us men and our salvation came down; and was incarnate and was made man; suffered, and rose again on the third day; He ascended into heaven, and is coming to judge the living and the dead; and in the Holy Spirit. But as for those who say 'There was once a time when He was not,' and 'Before He was begotten He was not,' and that 'He was made from what was not,' or affirm that the Son of God is of another person or substance, or that He is capable of change or variation, such persons the Catholic and Apostolic Church excommunicates.

Whereas, then, the other doctrines are here fully and accurately defined, some for the correction of what has already been perverted, others for a protection against what may be expected to arise, nevertheless the doctrine concerning the Holy Spirit is laid down very briefly as requiring no discussion, because at that time this question had not yet been stirred up, but the concept of it remained unchallenged in the souls of the faithful. Little by little, however, the wicked seeds of impiety increased. These were formerly thrown down by Arius, the author of heresy, and later they were fostered by his evil successors, to the detriment of the churches, and the consequent impiety suddenly burst into blasphemy against the Spirit. So, before those who have no consideration for themselves and do not take thought of the inevitable threat which our Lord held out for those who blaspheme against the Holy Spirit it is necessary to set forth this statement: that we must excommunicate those who say that the Holy Spirit is a creature; also, those who think so; and those who do not confess that He is holy by nature, as the Father is holy by nature and the Son holy by nature, but exclude Him from the divine and blessed nature. And, a proof of orthodox opinion is not to separate Him from the Father and the Son (for we must be baptized as we have received the words; and we must believe as we are baptized; and we must give glory as we have believed, to the Father, and to the Son, and to the Holy Spirit), but to withdraw from the communion of those who call Him a creature, on the ground that they are clearly blasphemers. Since this has been agreed upon (for the comment is necessary because of the slanderers), that we do not say that the Holy Spirit is either unbegotten—for we know one Unbegotten and one Beginning of things in existence, the Father of our Lord Jesus Christ—nor begotten—for we are taught in the tradition of faith that there is one Only-begotten—then, having been taught that the Spirit of Truth proceeds from the Father, we confess that He is from God without being created. And we must also excommunicate those who say that the Holy Spirit is of the ministering order, on the ground that by this word they reduce Him to the rank of a creature. For the Scripture has handed down to us the ministering spirits as creatures, saying: 'All are ministering spirits, sent for service.'⁶ Now, because of those who mix up everything and do not preserve the teaching in the Gospels, we must add this further principle: that it is necessary to shun those, also, as being openly in opposition to piety, who change the sequence which the Lord handed down to us, placing the Son before the Father, and putting the Holy Spirit before the Son. In fact, we must preserve unaltered and inviolable the sequence which we received from the very words of the Lord, who said: 'Go, therefore, and make disciples of all nations, baptizing them in the name of the Father, and of the Son, and of the Holy Spirit.'⁷

Signature of Eustathius, Bishop

I, Bishop Eustathius, having read this aloud to you, Basil, have understood and have agreed with what is written above. Moreover, I have signed it in the presence of my brothers, our Fronto,⁸ and the suffragan bishop Severus,⁹ and some other members of the clergy as well.

---

6 Cf. Heb. 1.14. St. Basil does not give the full quotation.
7 Matt. 28.19.
8 Fronto was a priest under the jurisdiction of Theodotus, Bishop of Nicopolis, to whose see he was elevated after the latter's death. However, he did not possess Theodotus' firmness of character, for he fell into heresy.
9 Known only from this passage.

126. To Atarbius[1]

We came to Nicopolis in the hope of correcting the disorders which had been stirred up and of applying a possible remedy to what had been done irregularly and contrary to ecclesiastical law. And we were exceedingly disappointed when we did not find your Excellency on our arrival, but learned that you had gone out in all haste, even though the synod which you were holding was scarcely half finished. On this account we have been compelled to write a letter, through which we suggest that you meet us in order that you may personally relieve our grief, by which we are distressed even to the point of death. For, we have heard that in the midst of the Church you have dared actions which have never before this day come to our hearing. And, even though these things are both painful and grievous, they are still endurable because they have been done against a man who, having entrusted to God the vengeance for what he has suffered, is wholly desirous of peace and of having nothing harmful happen through his own fault to the people of God.

But, some of the brethren who are held in honor and worthy of all trust have reported to us that you have made some innovations concerning the faith and have talked in a manner contrary to sound doctrine. They have been aroused the more on this account and exceedingly distressed, lest in addition to these countless wounds with which the Church has

---
1 For Atarbius, Bishop of Neo-Caesarea, cf. Letter 65. Although related to St. Basil, he was the leader of the Neo-Caesareans in their revolt against St. Basil. Cf. Letter 207. This letter is a good example of St. Basil's firm and tactful manner of dealing with those who had failed against the orthodoxy of the faith or had wronged him. It was written in 373.

been afflicted by those who have erred against the truth of the Gospel, still another evil should rise up by the renewal of the old heresy of Sabellius,[2] the enemy of the Church (for the brothers have announced to us that the statements made are of the same nature as this). For this reason we have written, in order that you may not hesitate to bestir yourself for this short journey and to come to us, and, by giving satisfaction regarding these matters, both to assuage our pain and to console the churches of God, which are now grieved unbearably and harshly at what has been done and what has been reported to have been said by you.

127. To Eusebius, Bishop of Samosata[1]

Our loving God, who adds consolations commensurate with our afflictions and comforts the downcast that they may not be overwhelmed unawares by their excessive grief, has afforded us a consolation equal to the disorders which assailed us at Nicopolis. For, He has brought in at an opportune moment Jovinus, a bishop dearly beloved of God. And how very opportune for us was his appearance let him tell per-

---

2 Cf. Letter 125 n. 5.

---

1 All the information which we have of Eusebius of Samosata has been gathered from the letters of St. Basil and St. Gregory of Nazianzus. He was instrumental in the consecration of Meletius as Bishop of Antioch, and was his staunch supporter during the long years of schism and exile. It was through his efforts, likewise, that St. Basil was elevated to the see of Caesarea. This was the beginning of a mutual and unbroken friendship. After Easter, 374, Eusebius was exiled to Thrace. He was recalled in 378, and on his return to Samosata was martyred. Previous letters addressed to him are Letters 27, 30, 31, 34, 47, 48, 95, 98, and 100. Shortly after St. Basil's return from Nicopolis, whither he had gone to investigate the trouble caused by the uncanonical consecration of Faustus, Jovinus paid him a visit and rallied to his support. Jovinus himself is apparently the bearer of this letter, telling the good news to Eusebius. This letter was written about 373.

sonally. We shall be silent that we may be sparing in the length of our letter, and also that we may not seem, by the mention of their fault, to hold up to public scorn, as it were, those who by a change of heart have become dear to us.

But, may the holy God grant that you will come to our district so that I may embrace your Grace and recount everything in detail. For, it is natural somehow for things which have grieved us when we experienced them to afford some gratification when we relate them. But, for those matters concerning which the bishop, dearly beloved of God, was stirred to action most successfully as far as regards his love toward us, but primarily and also unyieldingly as far as regards the strict observance of the canons, praise him; and give thanks to the Lord, that everywhere your disciples show the characteristics of your Dignity.

128. To Eusebius, Bishop of Samosata[1]

I have not yet been able worthily to give practical proof of my zeal for reconciling the churches of the Lord. But I protest that I have in my heart so great a desire that I would even gladly deliver up my own life to extinguish the flame of hatred kindled by the Evil One. And, if I wished to approach the regions of Colonia[2] not through the desire for peace, may my life not be spent in peace. The peace I seek, of course, is the true peace left to us by the Lord Himself; and what I asked to be given to me as an assurance[3] is what one would

---

1 For Eusebius, see preceding letter. This letter is in reply to Eusebius, who was attempting to effect a reconciliation between St. Basil and Eustathius of Sebaste. On Eustathius of Sebaste, cf. Letter 19 n. 1.
2 Letters 227 and 228 are addressed to the clergy and magistrates of Colonia in Armenia. This was probably the place in which Eustathius of Sebaste was to subscribe to the Creed as defined in Letter 125.
3 I.e., of the orthodoxy of Eustathius of Sebaste.

ask who desires nothing else than the true peace, even though some persons[4] perverting the truth interpret otherwise. Let those, therefore, use their tongues for whatever they wish; at some time, assuredly, they will repent of these words.

But, I urge your Holiness to remember the questions proposed from the beginning, and not to be misled into accepting answers for other questions, nor to sanction the sophisms of those who most terribly of all men are falsifying the truth, without the ability to speak from their mere opinion alone. For I have put forward propositions that are simple, clear, and easy to remember: whether we reject for communion those who do not accept the Nicene Creed, and whether we refuse to have any part with those who dare to say that the Holy Spirit is a creature. Yet, instead of answering the questions to the point, he repeated to us by heart those statements which you had written to us; and he did not do this through any simplicity of mind, as one might think, nor through inability to be aware of the consequences. Now, he supposes that, by denying our proposition, he will make his position evident to the people; but, if he agrees with us, he will withdraw from the middle course, than which up to the present time nothing has been more precious to him. Therefore, let him not lead us astray by sophisms nor deceive your Wisdom along with the rest, but let him send to us a concise answer to the question, either confessing communion with the enemies of the faith, or denying it. If you will persuade him to do this, and send me answers which are correct and such as I pray for, I am the one who has been completely wrong in the past. I take all the blame upon my-

---

4 These are probably the two monks, Basil and Sophronius, who had been recommended to St. Basil by Eustathius, and who had been spreading calumnies against St. Basil. Cf. Letter 119.

self. Then demand of me a proof of humility. But, as long as none of these things is done, pardon me, Father, dearly beloved of God, for not being able to stand at the altar of God with hypocrisy. For, if I did not fear this hypocrisy, why did I separate myself from Euippius,[5] a man of such great learning, so advanced in age, and possessing so many just claims of friendship with us? And if we then acted nobly and properly in behalf of the truth, it would surely be absurd to seem to be in union with those who make the same declarations as he did through the mediation of these clever and charming men.

Yet, it does not seem best to me to alienate ourselves altogether from those who do not accept the faith, but to show some concern for these men according to the ancient laws of charity, and to write to them with one accord, setting forth every exhortation with compassion, and holding out the faith of the Fathers to invite them to unity. And, if we convince them, we should be united with them in communion, but, if we fail, we should be content with one another and banish the uncertainty from our spirit, taking up the evangelical and guileless life in which they live who from the beginning yielded themselves to the Word. For, He said: 'The believers were of one heart and one soul.'[6] If, therefore, they heed you, that is best. But, if not, be assured that they are warmongers, and stop writing to us for the future about reconciliations.

---

5 Euippius was a bishop with tendencies to Arianism, from whom St. Basil had left himself obliged to separate altogether. Cf. Letter 56. Eustathius of Sebaste, in 360, violently denounced Euippius as not worthy to be a bishop, but in 376 Eustathius united with him and recognized the bishops and presbyters he had ordained. Cf. Letters 226, 239, 244, and 251.
6 Cf. Acts 4.32.

129. To Meletius, Bishop of Antioch[1]

I knew that the present charge brought against Apollinaris,[2] who is so prone to say anything, would astonish the ears of your Perfection. In fact, I myself, until now, was not conscious that he had been accused. At present, however, the citizens of Sebasteia, after making investigations in some place or other, have produced these statements and are carrying a document, through which they are also trying to condemn us especially, on the ground that we hold the same opinions. It contains such expressions as these: 'Therefore, it is necessary to conceive the first identity always conjointly, or, rather, in union with the difference; saying that the second and the third are the same. For, what the Father is first, this the Son is secondly, and the Spirit thirdly. But again, what the Spirit is first, this the Son is secondly, in as far as the Lord is also the Spirit; and the Father thirdly, in as far as the Spirit is God.' And, to interpret this horrible saying more forcefully: 'that the Father is paternally the

---

1 St. Meletius, Bishop of Antioch, was born in Melitene in Lesser Armenia, and died at Antioch in 381. He apparently believed that truth lay in delicate distinctions, but his formula was so indefinite that it is difficult even today to grasp it clearly. He was neither a thorough Nicene nor a decided Arian, and he passed alternately as an Anomean, a Homoiousian, a Homoian, or a Neo-Nicene, seeking always to remain outside any inflexible classification. After his death his name long remained for the Eastern faithful a rallying sign and a synonym of orthodoxy. It is in this letter that St. Basil, in refuting the charge of teaching heresy, names Apollinaris as the author of the document which is being attributed to himself. The Benedictines assign this letter to the year 373. Loofs presents rather unconvincing evidence to prove that this and the following one were written in the summer of 375.
2 Apollinaris the Younger, Bishop of Laodicea, flourished during the last half of the fourth century. He was at first highly esteemed by St. Basil and St. Athanasius for his classical culture, piety, and steadfastness to the Nicene Creed. Later, he taught that Christ had a human body and a human sensitive soul, but no rational mind, the Divine Logos taking the place of the last.

Son, and the Son is filially the Father, and in like manner as regards the Spirit, in so far as the Trinity is one God.'

These are the expressions that are being bruited about. I can never believe that they are the inventions of those circulating them, although from their slanders against us I think that there is nothing they have not dared. In fact, when they wrote to some of their own followers, after adding the slander against us they introduced these statements, specifying that they were the words of heretics but not revealing the author of the document, in order that we might be considered by many to be the writer. However, their inventiveness would not have gone so far as to compose these words, I am convinced. Therefore, in order to disclaim the charge of blasphemy which was current against us, and to manifest to all that there is nothing in common between us and those who make these statements, we have been compelled to mention that man[3] as one who is approaching the impiety of Sabellius.[4] So much, then, for this matter.

However, there has come from the court a messenger announcing that, after the first resolution of the emperor, to which those who were pouring out slanders against us had roused him, a second thought had occurred to him, so that, as a result, we were not given over to the accusers nor were we surrendered to their will, as had been determined at first; at least, up to the present, there has been some delay. Now, whether matters remain the same, or whether something more lenient is decided, we shall make known to your Reverence. And, if the former measure prevails, this also will not be hidden from you.

No doubt, the brother Sanctissimus has been with you for a long time, and what he is seeking has been made known to

---
3 I. e., Apollinaris.
4 For Sabellius, cf. Letter 125 n. 5.

your Perfection. If, then, the letter to the Western bishops seems to contain anything urgent, be so kind as to draft it and send it on to us, so that we may get it signed by those who are of like mind with us, and may have ready the subscription drawn up on a separate sheet. This we can fasten to it when it is being carried around by the brother, our fellow presbyter. For, since I found nothing important in the memorandum, I did not have anything to write to those in the West. In fact, the necessary points have been taken up before, and to write superfluities is absolutely foolish. And would it not be ridiculous to be a nuisance about the same matters?

This, however, seemed to me to be some untouched material, as it were, and to offer grounds for a letter—to urge them not to receive without investigation the communion of those coming from the East, but, having once chosen one part, to receive the rest on the testimony of those who are already in communion and not to associate themselves with everyone who writes the Creed on a pretense, indeed, of orthodoxy. For, thus they will find themselves in communion with those who are at odds with each other, who frequently put forward the same statements of doctrine, but fight with one another as violently as those who are most widely at variance. In order, then, that the heresy may not be further enkindled when those who are in disagreement with each other bring forward their opposing formulae, the bishops of the West must be urged to make a distinction as regards their communion with chance-comers and communion established by written document according to the regulation of the Church.[5]

---

[5] From this passage and Letter 224 the Benedictine editors perceive two kinds of communion: the first, personal, in the Eucharist and prayer; the second, by letter.

130. To Theodotus, Bishop of Nicopolis[1]

Deservedly and fittingly have you reproached us, our truly most honorable and beloved brother, because from the time that we departed from your Reverence carrying those propositions concerning the faith to Eustathius,[2] we have let you know nothing either little or great about his affairs. However, I did not overlook the matter on the ground that the acts which he committed against us were negligible, but because the report had been published abroad to all men already, and there was no need of any explanation from us to learn the intention of the man. For, he even contrived this himself, as if fearing lest he might have few witnesses of his views, sending the letters which he had written against us to every farthest corner of the world. At all events, he has cut himself off from communion with us, since he refused to meet us at the appointed place and did not bring his disciples as he had promised, but, together with the Cilician Theophilus,[3] even denounced us in the general synods, saying with plain and undisguised slander that we were sowing in the souls of the people doctrines which were foreign to his teachings.

---

1 Theodotus, Bishop of Nicopolis, a staunch friend of St. Basil, died in 375. He is mentioned in Letters 92, 95, 99, 121, 229, and 237. For the date of this letter, see Letter 129 n. 1.
2 Eustathius of Sebaste (300-377). He was Bishop of Sebaste in 356 and was one of the founders of monasticism. He had studied under Arius and was all his life inclined toward Semi-Arianism. St. Basil had been a close friend of his until about 372 or 373, when he learned the real character of the man. Eustathius had once signed the Nicene Creed, for he had gone with Theophilus and Silvanus on a mission to Rome in 365-366, and they had acknowledged their adherence to the Nicene Creed before Pope Liberius. Cf. Letter 245. However, he seems to have been a vacillating character and to have signed practically all the creeds of his age.
3 Theophilus was Bishop of Castabala or Hieropolis on the River Pyramis in Cilicia, where he had been transferred from Eleutheropolis. Cf. Letters 244 and 245. He was on friendly terms with St. Basil at one time, and was sent to Rome on an embassy. See note above.

Now, this was, in truth, sufficient to dissolve all our connection with him. Furthermore, when he had come into Cilicia where he met a certain Gelasius,[4] he offered him a creed which could have been written by an Arius only or some true disciple of his; then we were even more firmly fixed in our separation. For, we considered that neither will the Ethiopian ever change his skin, nor the leopard his spots,[5] nor can he who has been nourished with perverse doctrines get rid of the evil of heresy.

Moreover, in addition to this he has committed further outrages by writing against us, or, rather, by composing long treatises full of every abuse and slander. Up to this time we have made no answer concerning them because we have been taught by the Apostle[6] not to avenge ourselves but to give place to the wrath. At the same time, too, reflecting on the depths of the hypocrisy which always marked his dealings with us, we were seized with a sort of speechlessness in our consternation.

But, even if there had been none of those abuses, in whom would this recent bold act which he dared have not inspired absolute horror and aversion for the man? He has even, as I hear (at least, if the report is true and is not a fiction based on slander), had the effrontery to reordain some men, a thing which until today no one of the heretics appears to have done. How, then, is it possible for us to endure such acts calmly, and to think that the errors of the man can be remedied? Do not, therefore, be misled by his lying words, and do not trust the suspicions of men who easily accept everything in a bad sense, as, for insance, that we regard such matters as indifferent. For, be assured, most beloved and honorable

---
4 This Gelasius is otherwise unknown.
5 Cf. Jer. 13.23.
6 Cf. Rom. 12.19.

friend, that I am not aware that I have ever, at any time, suffered such sorrow in my soul as now, when I have heard of the violation of the ecclesiastical laws. Only pray that the Lord may grant us the grace to do nothing through anger, but to have charity which is not ambitious, is not puffed up.[7] For, see how those who did not have it have been lifted up beyond human limits, and are ambitious in their lives, daring bold deeds of which the past holds no such examples.[8]

131. To Olympius[1]

Truly, hearing of unexpected events is enough to make the two ears of a man ring. And this has now happened to me. For, although the news of those writings being circulated against us fell on my ears already inured to it, because I myself had formerly received the letter, which befits my sins but is certainly not what I had ever expected to be written by those who sent it, nevertheless, the second reports appeared to us to have such excessive bitterness in them as to overshadow the previous ones entirely. How was it possible that I was not almost out of my mind on reading the letter to the most pious brother Dazinas,[2] full of countless insults and un-

---

7 Cf. 1 Cor. 13.4.5.
8 The Benedictine editors remark that St. Basil is incorrect in maintaining that there was no heretical precedent for such actions. The Arians are accused of it in the Book of the Prayers of Faustus and Marcellinus, *Bib. Pat.* V 655. Cf., also, Constantius' letter to the Ethiopians against Frumentius; Athan., *Apol. ad Const.* 31.

---

1 A wealthy layman of Neo-Caesarea, and an intimate friend of St. Basil. The subject matter is the same as that of the preceding letters. The date of this letter is about the year 373. Other letters written to Olympius are Letters 4, 12, 13, and 211.
2 In this letter Eustathius accused St. Basil of bad faith and of Apollinarian errors.

bearable charges and attacks against us, as if we had been found engaged in most hurtful plots against the Church? For instance, even proofs that the slanders against me are true were brought forward from a document written by I know not whom. Now, parts, in truth, I admit I recognized had been written by Apollinaris[3] of Laodicea, not because I had ever read them in his book, but because I heard others mention them. But, I found some other things included which I neither read at any time nor heard another speak of —and there is a faithful Witness of these statements in heaven. How it can be, then, that men who turn away from falsehood, who have been taught that love is the fulfillment of the law, who profess that they bear the infirmities of the powerless, have allowed themselves to bring these slanders against us and to condemn us from the writings of others, is a thing for which, although I have pondered much, I am not able to conceive the reason, except that, as I said from the beginning, I have decided that the pain from these worries is a part of the chastisement due to me because of my sins.

Now, at first I grieved in my soul because truths were held of so little account by the sons of men. But then, also, I feared concerning myself, lest ever, in addition to my other sins, I should be disposed to a hatred of mankind, considering that there is nothing trustworthy in any man, if, indeed, those trusted by me in the most important matters showed themselves so unfaithful toward me and so unfaithful in regard to truth itself. Be assured, therefore, brother, and everyone who is a friend of the truth, that the writings are not mine, nor do I approve of them, since they have not been drawn up according to my views. Even if I did write formerly many years ago to Apollinaris or to anyone else, I ought not to be blamed. For, I myself do not bring any charge

---

3 For Apollinaris, cf. Letter 129 n. 2.

if anyone is cut off for heresy from any brotherhood (and you certainly know the men, even if I do not mention them by name), because each one will die by his own sin.

Now, I have given this answer to the document that was sent, in order that you yourself may know the truth and make it clear to those who do not wish to withhold the truth unjustly. And, if it is necessary to speak more at length in defense of each of the charges brought against us, we shall, with God's help, do that, also. We, Brother Olympius, neither say that there are three gods, nor are we in communion with Apollinaris.[4]

132. To Abramius, Bishop of Batnae[1]

Since late autumn I have not known where your Reverence was living. In fact, I was getting varied reports, since some were announcing that your Reverence was tarrying in Samosata, and others in the country; still others were affirming that they had seen you around Batnae itself. Therefore, I did not continue to write. But, now, since I have learned that you are staying at Antioch, in the home of the most revered Count Saturninus,[2] I have readily given this letter to the most beloved and most pious brother Sanctissimus, our fellow presbyter. Through him I greet your Charity, urging you,

---

4 Cf. Letter 125; also, Greg. Naz., *Orat.* 1 and 29.

1 Abramius or Abram was Bishop of Batnae in Osrhoene, near the Euphrates. His name appears with those of Meletius, Eusebius, St. Basil, and others in the letter written by the bishops of the East to those of Italy and Gaul. Cf. Letter 92. He was also present at the Council of Constantinople in 381. The Benedictines place this letter as of the year 373. Loofs, *op. cit.* 28ff and 46ff, prefers the spring of 375 as the date of its composition.

2 This Saturninus is otherwise unknown.

wherever you may be, to be mindful first of all of God, and then of us, whom from the beginning you chose to love and to hold numbered among your most intimate friends.

133. To Peter, Bishop of Alexandria[1]

Eyes are the promoters of sensuous friendship, and the intimacy engendered through a long stretch of time strengthens it. But, the gift of the Spirit brings about true love, joining together things separated by long distances and making known the beloved ones to each other not through physical characteristics but through the peculiar qualities of the soul. This, indeed, the grace of the Lord has accomplished in our case, allowing us to see you with the eyes of our soul and to embrace you with true charity, and, as it were, to be joined with you and to come into one union through the communion of our faith. For, we are convinced that you, being the disciple of such a man[2] and having enjoyed long association with him, walk in the same spirit and agree with the same doctrines of piety.

Therefore, we salute your Honor and we exhort you to succeed the great man in his affection for us among other things, to write regularly to us news of yourself, and to give heed to the brotherhood everywhere with the same kindness and the same zeal which that most blessed one employed toward all those who in truth loved God.

---

1 This Peter, at the request of St. Athanasius, succeeded him on his death in May, 373. This letter was written in that same year.
2 St. Athanasius.

134. To the Presbyter Paeonius[1]

You can undoubtedly imagine from what you wrote how much your letter delighted us, so clearly apparent from the contents was the purity of heart from which those words came forth. For, as the stream reveals its own source, so the nature of the speech reveals the character of the heart which has brought it forth. Therefore, I confess that I have experienced something extraordinary and far different from what seemed likely. I am always eager to receive news from your Perfection, but, when I took your letter into my hands and read it, I was not more pleased with what you had written than I was grieved at considering how great a loss had befallen me during your period of silence.

But, since you have begun to write, do not cease doing so, for you give more delight than do those who send much money to the lovers of wealth. But, there has not been a scribe near me—neither a calligraphist nor a shorthand writer. For, of those whom I happen to have trained, some have returned to their former manner of life and others, being afflicted with chronic ailments, have given up the work.

---

[1] Paeonius is unknown except through this letter. St. Basil here refers to the calligraphists and tachygraphists whom he has trained. Letters 134, 135, 223, 333, and 334 have been quoted in some studies of stenography. A. Schramm ('Korrespondenzblatt.' *Amtliche Zeitschr. des k. Stenographischen Instituts zu Dresden* 48 (1903) 221 and 241ff.) would conclude from the present letter that St. Basil himself was a master of tachygraphy, and did not scorn to give instructions in it. F. Maier (*idem*, 49 (1904) 42ff.) rightly objects to this conclusion. In any case, St. Basil employed tachygraphy and had his difficulties with it. Cf. the present letter and Letter 135. This letter was written in 373.

135. To Diodorus, Presbyter of Antioch[1]

I have read the books sent by your Honor. And I have really enjoyed the second one very much, not only because of its brevity, as would one who is lazily disposed toward everything and at present without health, but because it is at one and the same time close-packed with ideas and explicit as to the objections of opponents and answers to them. Moreover, the simplicity of the style and the absence of elaboration seemed to me to be proper to the purpose of a Christian, who writes more for the general good than for show. But the first one, which has the same importance of subject matter but which is polished off with more extravagant style, varied figures of speech, and charming dialogue, seemed to me to require not only a long time for the reading but also much mental labor for gathering the ideas and keeping them in memory. Indeed, although the charges of our opponents and also the convincing evidence of our side inserted in the work seem to introduce some dialectic charms in the treatise, nevertheless, by causing a pause and a waste of time, they break up the continuity of the thought and weaken the force of the argumentative speech.

For, assuredly, your Intelligence is aware of this—that those of the heathen philosophers who wrote dialogues, Aristotle and Theophrastus, for instance, immediately attacked the

---
1 Diodorus was a pupil of Silvanus, Bishop of Tarsus. Cf. Theodoret, *Hist. Eccl.* 4.24. In Letter 16, Theodoret speaks of his obligations to him as a teacher. Diodorus became Bishop of Tarsus in 378. Only a few fragments of his works are extant; the greater part is said to have been destroyed by the Arians. Cf., also, St. Basil's Letter 160. This letter contains St. Basil's ideas on the rhetoric of his day. They are similar to what a person of good taste would hold today, although they probably did not correspond with those of his contemporaries. Certainly, St. Basil's own works show that his practice was consistent with his views. This letter was written in 373.

arguments themselves, because they realized their lack of the literary graces of Plato. But, Plato with his power of eloquence both assails the opinions and at the same time satirizes incidentally the persons, attacking the rashness and recklessness of Thrasymachus, the levity of mind and frivolity of Hippias, and the boastfulness and pompousness of Protagoras.[2] But, when he introduces indefinite characters into his dialogues, he uses the speakers in order to clarify his points, and he brings nothing else from the characters into the arguments. This is particularly what he did in the *Laws*.

Therefore, since we set out to write, not for love of honor, but because we wish to leave behind for the brethren some counsels on useful subjects, if we bring in any person who is well known by all for his surly disposition, we also must weave into our speech some of the natural qualities of the person, if it actually is our duty to censure men who neglect their obligations. But, if the matter of the dialogue is indefinite, the digressions against persons disrupt the unity and tend to no useful end.

I have said all this in order that it may be shown that you have not sent your works to the hands of a flatterer, but have shared your toils with a most sincere brother. And I have not spoken for the correction of what has already been written, but for a precaution in regard to what shall be written. For, certainly, he who employs such skill and zeal in writing will not hesitate to write, since those who supply the subject matter do not cease doing so. Moreover, for us it will suffice to read your works, but we fall as far short of being able to write anything as, I may almost say, of being healthy, or even of enjoying some reasonable leisure from our occupations.

I have at present sent back the first and larger book by

---

[2] I.e., in the *Republic,* the *Hippias,* and the *Protagoras,* respectively.

my reader, since I have gone through it as far as I was able. But the second one I have retained, as I wish to copy it and I do not have available for a while my fast copyist. To this state of poverty have the once envied fortunes of the Cappadocians come!

136. To Eusebius, Bishop of Samosata[1]

In what condition the excellent Isaac[2] found us, he, better than I, will describe to you in person, even though he does not have a tongue able to report in tragic manner the excesiveness of my sufferings; such was the gravity of my illness. But, in all probability, this is known to everyone who is acquainted with me ever so little. For, if, when in apparent good health, I have always been weaker than those whose lives are despaired of, it is possible to realize in what a state I was during my illness. Yet (now pardon one who is talking nonsense in his fever), since sickness has been natural to me, I should now be enjoying in my present change of condition the best of good health. But, since it is the scourge of the Lord which augments our sufferings by additional trials according to our deserts, I have acquired one infirmity after another. The consequence of this is evident even to a child —that this bodily shell of ours must certainly go hence, unless, perhaps, the loving kindness of God, granting us in His forbearance time for repentance, would also now, as frequently before, bring about some release and a way of escape from inconceivable sufferings. At all events, these matters will be as is pleasing to Him and beneficial to us.

As to how the affairs of the churches have been ruined

---
1 For Eusebius, Bishop of Samosata, cf. Letter 27 n. 1.
2 Otherwise unknown.

and heedlessly sacrificed while we neglect for the sake of our security the affairs of our neighbors, and are not even able to perceive this—that private interests also perish in a public disaster—what need I say? And, above all, to you, a man who, foreseeing everything from afar, both protested and made proclamations beforehand, and not only were yourself the first to rise up but also helped to rouse others, writing them letters, making personal visits, omitting no act, leaving unuttered no word! These things we remember as each event occurs, but we are no longer benefitted by them. Even now, if my sins had not stood in my way—in the first place, the most pious and beloved brother Eustathius,[3] our fellow deacon, falling into a serious illness, delayed me for two whole months while I waited day after day for his return to health; and then all my companions became ill, the remaining details of which the brother Isaac will recount; and, finally, I myself was tied down by this sickness—I would have been with your Honor long ago, not offering any help for the common interests, but getting great profit for myself from my intercourse with you. For, I had determined to be out of reach of the ecclesiastical darts because of my lack of protection against the intrigues of our adversaries. May the mighty hand of God preserve you for all mankind, the noble guardian of the faith, the watchful protector of the churches, and may He consider us worthy before our death of an interview with you for the advantage of our soul.

---

[3] This deacon enjoyed St. Basil's confidence, and once before conveyed a letter for him to Eusebius of Samosata. Cf. Letter 47.

137. To Antipater[1]

At present, I seem to be especially sensible of the loss which I suffer by my illness, when during the administration of our country by such a great man I myself am compelled to be absent because of the care I must give my body. For a whole month already I have been taking the treatments of the natural hot springs in the hope of receiving some benefit from them. But, I seem to labor in vain in the solitude, or even to appear to most people to be deserving of ridicule, as one who does not understand the proverb which says: 'Hot springs are of no use to the dead.'

Now, even though I am in such a state, I desire, disregarding everything else, to come to visit your Grace, so as to enjoy your noble qualities, and through your integrity to settle in a proper manner the affairs of my house. For, the home of our most revered[2] mother Palladia is my own, since not only family relationship joins her to us but also the kindliness of her character has caused her to take the place of a mother to us. Therefore, since some commotion has been stirred up about her house, we ask your Lordship to defer the examination for a little while and to await our arrival, not so that justice may be thwarted (for I would prefer to die ten thousand times rather than ask such a favor from a judge who is devoted to the laws and to justice), but that you may know from me by word of mouth those matters which it is not proper for me to write. In fact, in this way you yourself will not go astray from the truth nor will we suffer anything contrary to our will. I ask, then, as the per-

---

[1] Antipater is the Governor of Cappadocia to whom St. Basil is recommending the protection of his old friend and relative, Palladia. Cf. Letters 186 and 187. Palladia is otherwise unknown. This letter was written in 373.
[2] *Semnotátēs*—a title of distinction used by St. Basil.

son is in safe custody and is held by the soldiers, to grant us this favor, a favor free from offense and from reproach.

138. To Eusebius, Bishop of Samosata[1]

How do you think I felt when I received the letter from your Reverence? Considering the spirit of your message, I immediately wanted to fly straight to Syria, but, looking at the weakness of my body, which fettered me, I perceived that I was incapable not only of flying but even of turning over in bed. For, that day on which the beloved and zealous brother, our fellow deacon Elpidius,[2] came to us was the fiftieth day of my illness. I was much exhausted by the fever which, because of lack of material to nourish it, concentrated itself in this dry flesh as in a burnt wick and brought on a decline and a long-continued weakness. Then, immediately, my former plague, this liver complaint, succeeding, turned me away from food, chased away sleep from my eyes, and held me on the border line between life and death, permitting me to live only so much as to be sensible of the hardships of life. And, so, I have not only made use of the hot springs but have also received some treatments from doctors. But, this mighty evil has got the best of all these. Another, indeed, might bear it if he were accustomed to it, but, when it makes an unexpected assault, no one is so invincible as to stand it.

Although I have been troubled by this disease for a long time, I was never so distressed as now, when I am hindered

---
1 On Eusebius, Bishop of Samosata, cf. Letters 27, 30, 31, 34, 47, etc. This letter was written in 373.
2 Elpidius is the deacon at whose hands St. Basil received the present letter from Eusebius and by whom he sent a letter of consolation to the Egyptian bishops who were in exile for the Faith in Palestine (Letter 265).

by it from meeting your true Charity. For, of what pleasure we have been deprived I myself know, even though with but the tip of my finger I took a taste of the very sweet honey of your church a year ago.

I also wanted to confer with your Reverence with regard to some other urgent affairs, and both to communicate and to learn many things. For, it is not even possible here to meet with true charity. Moreover, when I find a person who shows very great love, he is not one who is able to give us advice concerning the business before us with anything like the perfect wisdom and the experience which you have gathered from your many toils for the churches.

Now, there are other matters which I cannot put in writing; but those which, at all events, it is safe to set forth are as follows. The presbyter Evagrius,[3] the son of Pompeianus[4] of Antioch, who formerly accompanied the blessed Eusebius[5] to

---

3 Evagrius of Antioch, as he is known. The dates of his birth and death are unknown. He was consecrated bishop over one of the parties at Antioch in 388-389. He went to Italy with Eusebius, Bishop of Vercelli, and at the death of that prelate returned to Antioch in company with St. Jerome. He was probably the ascetic who trained St. John Chrysostom in monastic discipline. He belonged to the Eustathian division of the Orthodox Church at Antioch. After nine or ten years spent in aiding Pope Damasus against his rival Ursinus, he returned to the East, stopping at Caesarea to visit St. Basil (373). Later, from Antioch, Evagrius wrote St. Basil a harsh letter, accusing him of love of strife and controversy. St. Basil's reply is a model of courteous sarcasm. Evagrius afterwards became the instrument for prolonging the schism. Cf. Theodoret, *Ecc. Hist.* 5.23, and St. Basil, Letter 156.

4 Pompeianus, the father of Evagrius, was, according to St. Jerome, a descendant of the officer of that name who accompanied Aurelian against Zenobia of Palmyra in 273.

5 St. Eusebius, Bishop of Vercelli, 283-371. According to St. Ambrose, he was the first bishop of the West to unite the monastic with the clerical life; cf. St. Ambrose, Letter 63, *Ad Vercellenses*. Being entirely orthodox, he refused at the synod of Milan in 355 to sign the document condemning St. Athanasius. In 363, on his return to Vercelli from exile, he became one of the chief opponents of the Arian bishop Amentius of Milan. The Church honors him as a martyr on December 16.

the West, has now returned from Rome asking us for a letter containing the same things word for word which they have written (moreover, he brought back to us our own letter, as it was not acceptable to the very strict brethren there). He also asks that a sort of embassy of important men be hastily summoned, so that they may have a fair pretext for visiting us.

Those at Sebaste who hold our opinions, having laid bare the festering wound of Eustathius' heterodoxy,[6] are asking us for some ecclesiastical care.

Iconium is a city of Pisidia, formerly the second city in importance, and now the capital of a part, composed of different sections, which has received the administration of its own government. This city is inviting us for a visit so that we may give it a bishop, for Faustinus is dead.

Therefore, whether I should not refuse to perform ordinations beyond our boundaries, and what sort of an answer I should give the Sebastenes, and how I should be disposed toward the proposals of Evagrius I wanted to learn through a personal interview with your Honor. But, of all of this I have been deprived through my present illness. If, then, it is possible for you to secure someone who is soon coming to us, be so kind as to write me the answers to everything; if not, pray that that which is pleasing to the Lord may come to my mind. Moreover, order a remembrance to be made for us in the synod and do you yourself pray for us and invite the people also to pray, so that for the remaining days and hours of our sojourning it may be granted us to serve in a manner well pleasing to the Lord.

---

6 For Eustathius of Sebaste. cf. Letters 79 n. 1 and 119 n. 1.

139. To the Alexandrians[1]

The report of the persecutions which have been taking place throughout Alexandria and the rest of Egypt reached me long ago, and it has deeply affected my soul, as was to be expected. For, we thought of the artifice of the Devil's warfare, who, when he saw that by the persecutions of our enemies the Church was increasing and thriving the more, changed his plan. He no longer makes war openly, but places hidden snares for us, concealing his treachery by means of the name which his followers bear, in order that we may endure the same sufferings as our fathers, and yet not seem to suffer for Christ, since our persecutors have the name of Christians. We sat for a long time considering these things, amazed at the tidings of what had happened. In truth, both of our ears rang on learning of the shameless and inhuman heresy of those who persecuted you; that they had no regard for age, nor for the labors of a life well spent, nor for the affection of the people. On the contrary, they tortured and dishonored bodies, handed them over to exile, and plundered whatever property they were able to find, not fearing the censure of men nor foreseeing the fearful requital of the just Judge. These things have dazed us and almost put us out of our mind. But, along with these considerations, there came this thought also: The Lord has not entirely abandoned His churches, has He? And this is not the last hour, is it, and apostasy is finding an entrance through them, in order that now the impious one may be revealed, 'the son of perdition,

---

[1] The persecution here referred to is the one caused by Valens, who tortured the Eastern Catholics from 369 to the end of his reign. This letter was written in 373.

who opposes and is exalted above all that is called God, or that is worshipped'?[2]

But, if the trial is transitory, bear it, noble champions of Christ; or even, if all things are given over to complete destruction, let us not be careless with regard to the present, but let us await the revelation from heaven and the manifestation of our great God and Saviour, Jesus Christ. For, if all creation is destroyed and the scheme of this world is altered, what wonder is it that we, also, being a part of creation, suffer the common evils and are given over to afflictions? These the just Judge lays upon us in proportion to our strength, 'not permitting us to be tempted beyond our strength, but with the temptation also giving us a way out that we may be able to bear it.'[3]

The crowns of martyrs await you, brothers; the choirs of confessors are ready to reach out to you their hands and to receive you into their own number. Remember the saints of old, that no one of those living luxuriously nor open to flattery was considered worthy of the crown of patient endurance, but all being tried by the fire of great tribulations gave proof of themselves. For, some 'had experience of mockery and stripes,' others 'were sawed asunder,' and others 'were put to death by the sword.'[4] These are the glories of the saints. Blessed is he who is deemed worthy of suffering for the sake of Christ! But, more blessed is he who has abounded in sufferings, because 'the sufferings of the present time are not worthy to be compared with the glory to come that will be revealed in us.'[5]

Certainly, if it had been possible for me to come in per-

---

2 Cf. 2 Thess. 2.4.
3 Cf. 1 Cor. 10.13.
4 Cf. Heb. 11.36-37.
5 Rom. 8.18.

son, I would have desired nothing more than a meeting with
you, so that I might both see and embrace the athletes of
Christ and have part in your prayers and spiritual graces.
But, since my body is now wasted by a long sickness, so that
I am not even able to leave my bed, and since there are many
lying in wait for us, like ravenous wolves, watching for an opportunity when they may be able to plunder the sheep of
Christ, I have been compelled to visit you by letter. I urge
you, in the first place, to make earnest entreaties for me in
order that I may be deemed worthy, at least for the remaining days or hours, to serve the Lord according to the Gospel
of His Kingdom, and, in the second place, to pardon my
absence and the tardiness of this letter. For, it was with difficulty that I found a man who was able to comply with our
desire. We mean our son, Eugenius, the monk, through whom
I urge you to pray for us and for the whole Church and to
write back to us about your affairs, so that, when we have
some information, we may feel more cheerful.

140. To the Church at Antioch[1]

'Who will give me wings like a dove? And I will fly' to you
'and be at rest'[2] from my longing desire for a conference with
your Charity. At present, however, I am in want not only
of wings, but of a body itself, since mine has for some time past
been laboring under a long-continued weakness, and now
has been completely crushed by uninterrupted afflictions. For,
who is so hard of heart, who so absolutely without sympathy
and kindliness that, when he hears the groans which strike
upon our ears from all sides as if from some sorrowful choir

---
1 This letter was written in 373.
2 Cf. Ps. 54.7.

sounding forth in harmony a sort of universal dirge, he is not afflicted in spirit and bowed down to the earth and wholly prostrated by these desperate troubles? But, the holy God is able to give some release from these difficulties, and to bestow upon us some respite from the prolonged sufferings. Therefore, I pray you to have the same consolation and, rejoicing in the hope of solace, to endure the present pain of your afflictions. For, if we are paying the penalty of our sins, our scourgings are sufficient to turn aside hereafter the wrath which God directs against us, or, if we are called upon to struggle in behalf of religion by these trials, the Judge is just, so that He will not permit us to be tempted beyond what we are able to bear,[3] but He will give to us, for what we have previously suffered, the crown of our patient endurance and of our hope in Him. Let us, then, not grow weary of contending in the struggles for religion, and let us not abandon in despair the fruits of our labors. For, not one act of courage nor one brief labor proves the staunchness of the soul, but He who makes trial of our hearts wishes us through a long and protracted test to be shown forth as victors of righteousness.

Only, let our spirit be kept unyielding, let the foundation of our faith in Christ be maintained unshaken, and He who will be our Helper will come speedily. He will come and will not delay. In fact, expect tribulation upon tribulation, hope upon hope, for yet a little while, yet a little while. Thus the Holy Spirit knows how to attract His disciples by the promise of the future. At any rate, after the tribulations comes hope, and near at hand is that for which we have hoped. For, even if one would speak of the whole life of man, very short is the span from first to last in comparison with that endless age which lies beyond in our hopes.

---
3 Cf. 1 Cor. 10.13.

Now, as to a creed, we neither receive a more recent one written for us by others nor do we ourselves dare to hand over the fruits of our own mind, lest we make the words of religion mere human words, but, whatever we have been taught by the holy Fathers, that do we announce to those who ask us. Therefore, there has been introduced in our church from the times of the Fathers the Creed written by the holy Fathers assembled at Nicaea. And we think that this is also in use among you. However, we do not refuse, lest we take upon ourselves the charge of indolence, to reproduce the words themselves in our letter. Here they are:

We believe in one God, the Father Almighty, Maker of all things visible and invisible; and in one Lord, Jesus Christ, the Only-begotten Son of God, begotten of the Father, that is, of the substance of the Father; Light of Light; true God of true God; begotten, not made; consubstantial with the Father, by whom all things were made both in heaven and on earth; who for us men and for our salvation came down; and was incarnate and was made man; suffered, and rose again on the third day; He ascended into heaven, and is coming to judge the living and the dead; and in the Holy Spirit. But as for those who say, 'There was once a time when He was not,' and 'Before He was begotten He was not,' and that 'He was made from what was not,' or affirm that the Son of God is of another person or substance, or that He is capable of change or variation, the Catholic and Apostolic Church excommunicates them.[4]

---

[4] The Benedictine editors tell us that St. Leontius, who was present at the Council, brought the Nicene Creed to Caesarea, and both he and his successor Hermogenes bravely defended it, as can be seen in Letter 81. However, Dianius, who succeeded Hermogenes, did not follow in their footsteps but signed several Arian formulae. Still, he supported the Nicene Creed, as is testified in Letter 51.

We believe these truths. But, since the doctrine concerning the Holy Spirit was undefined, as at that time the Pneumatomachi[5] had not yet appeared, they[6] were silent as to the necessity of anathematizing those who say that the Holy Spirit is of a created and servile nature. For, absolutely nothing of the Divine and Blessed Trinity is created.

141. To Eusebius, Bishop of Samosata[1]

I have already received two letters from your inspired and most perfect Wisdom. One of them vividly described to us how we had been expected by the people under the jurisdiction of your Holiness, and how much grief we had caused by being absent from the most holy synod. And the other, the earlier one, as I judge from the contents, but which was delivered to us later, contained instructions such as are worthy of you and necessary for us—that we should not be negligent of the churches of God nor little by little yield the

---

5 The Pneumatomachi flourished in the countries adjacent to the Hellespont. They denied the divinity of the Holy Spirit and so received their name. Macedonius, their founder, was intruded into the see of Constantinople by the Arians in 342 and enthroned by Constantius, who had for a second time expelled Paul, the Catholic bishop. They are sometimes called Macedonians after the name of their founder.
6 I.e., the Fathers of Nicaea.

1 St. Eusebius, Bishop of Samosata (Commagene), died in 379. His feast is celebrated on June 22 by the Greeks, and on June 21 by the Latins. The dissensions and unrest of the Eastern Church between the years 361 and 379 are reflected in his life more than in that of any other. Eusebius was a moderate supporter of the Creed of Nicaea, was threatened by Constantius, and was compelled under Valens to travel in disguise through his diocese. He was finally banished by Valens and only returned to his diocese in 376 after the death of Valens. Later, he was killed with a stone by an Arian woman. Cf. Tillemont, note 64. This letter was written in 373.

control of affairs to our opponents, since in this way their influence will increase and ours will diminish. I think that I have answered both letters; nevertheless, since it is not evident whether those entrusted with the duty brought our answers safely, I am at present also offering a defense on the same subjects. As regards my absence I am writing a very true excuse, the report of which I think has reached even to your Holiness—that I was detained by an illness which led me down to the very gates of death. And, even now, when writing concerning these matters, I write while still enduring the after-effects of my weakness. And these are of such a nature that in another they would suffice to be grievous disorders.

But, in reference to this, that it was not by our negligence that the interests of the Church were handed over to our opponents, I wish your Reverence to know that the bishops who pretend to be in communion with us, because of reluctance, or because of their still being suspicious toward us and insincere, or because of the opposition engendered by the Devil against good works, are unwilling to help us. But, though the majority of us are joined with each other, forsooth, in appearance, and even the worthy Bosporius[2] is united with us, yet they actually take part with us in none of the most pressing matters. As a result, I am retarded in my recovery for the most part by this despondency of mine, since, as a result of excessive grief, my infirmities continuously recur.

And what can I do alone, since the Canons,[3] as you your-

---

[2] Bosporius, an intimate friend of St. Basil, was Bishop of Colonia in Cappadocia Secunda. Cf. Letter 51.

[3] These Canons, falsely ascribed to the Apostles, are sometimes cited by St. Basil among the canonical epistles. He seems here to refer to the twenty-seventh, where it is ordained that in each province the bishops should not initiate anything of an important character without the opinion or consent of him who is of highest rank among them, and that each should be content with his own province; but he should not do anything without the good will of all. St. Basil observed this canon very scrupulously. Cf. the note of the Benedictine editors.

self know, do not grant administrative power of such a kind to one man? Yet, what remedy have I not employed? Of what decision have I not reminded them, now through letters, and again through personal conferences? They even came as far as the city at the report of my death. But, since it was pleasing to God that they should find us alive, we spoke to them as was proper. In my presence they are respectful and make all reasonable promises, but, after they have left, they again return to their own opinions. In these matters we, too, have the benefit of the general state of affairs, since clearly the Lord has abandoned us whose charity has grown cold because of the increase of wickedness. But, against all these things let your great and powerful petition to God suffice for us. For, perhaps, we may either become somewhat useful in the circumstances, or, if we fail in the object of our desires, we may escape condemnation.

142. To the Accountant of the Prefects[1]

At the synod of the blessed martyr Eupsychius[2] I brought together all our brothers, the suffragan bishops,[3] to make them known to your Honor. But, since you were absent, they must be introduced to your Perfection by letter. I would like you, therefore, to know this brother, who is worthy of being trusted by your Wisdom because of his fear of the Lord. And in whatever matters he may have recourse to your good will as regards the poor, do not refuse to trust him as one who is telling the truth, and to furnish your powerful assistance for the oppressed. Without doubt, you will also deign to visit the

---
1 There were two *numerarii*, or accountants of the prefect, in every province. This letter was written in 373.
2 For the martyr Eupsychius, cf. Letter 100 n. 2.
3 For suffragan bishops, cf. Letter 53 n. 1.

almshouse of the district which is subject to him and to exempt it entirely from the tax. For, it has already pleased your colleague to free from taxation the petty possessions of the poor.

143. To the Second Accountant[1]

If it had been possible for me to visit your Honor, I would certainly have appealed in person for what I wanted, and I would have taken my stand as defender of the oppressed. But, since weakness of body and business affairs hold me back, I am recommending to you, in my place, this brother, the suffragan bishop,[2] so that, giving heed to him in all sincerity, you may use him for a counselor. For, he is a man able to advise you truthfully and prudently concerning our affairs. Now, when you will deign to visit the almshouse he established (for you will see it, I well know, and will not pass it by, since you are not inexperienced in the work; moreover, as a certain person has reported to me, you maintain one in Amasea[3] from the possessions which the Lord has given you), so, then, when you see this one, you will grant him all that he requests. For, your colleague[4] has already promised me some concession as regards the almshouses. I say this, not that

---

1 Cf. the preceding letter. This letter was written in 373.
2 Cf. Letter 53 n. 1.
3 A city in Pontus, situated on the Iris.
4 By the word 'colleague' here is not meant the other accountant to whom the preceding letter is addressed, because in that letter also St. Basil remarks that he has been promised help for the poor by the addressee's colleague. Since there were but two accountants, this probably refers to another officer who had similar duties. The Benedictine editors conjecture him to be the prefects' officer, to whom the next letter is addressed and who is asked to fulfill certain promises he has made. However, it may be that St. Basil, to gain his end, is telling each of the two what the other has promised.

you yourself may imitate another (indeed, it is right for you to be the leader of others in noble deeds), but that you may know that others also have shown respect to us in these matters.

144. To the Prefects' Administrator[1]

Surely you know this man through your interview in the city. Nevertheless, I am presenting and recommending him to you also by letter, because, in view of his ability to suggest intelligently and prudently what should be done, he will be useful to you for many of the works toward which you are directing your efforts. And there is now an opportunity to give practical proof of what you told me in private, when the afore-mentioned brother explains the condition of the poor.

145. To Eusebius, Bishop of Samosata[1]

I know the countless labors which you have endured in defense of the churches of God, and I am not ignorant of the numerous occupations in which you are engaged, since you do not carry on your administration carelessly but according to the will of God. I also bear in mind that man[2] who, close at hand, lies in wait for you, because of whom each of you, like birds cowering under cover beneath the eagle, must not stray far from the shelter. None of these facts has escaped me. Yet, yearning is irresistible both in hoping for the unattainable and in undertaking the impossible. Rather,

---
1 Similar to the preceding letter and written at about the same time.
---
1 For Eusebius, cf. Letter 141 n. 1. This letter was written in 373.
2 I.e., Valens.

my hope in the Lord is the strongest of all. For, not with unreasoning desire, but in the strength of faith I even expect that a way will appear in the midst of the desperate situation, and that you will easily overcome all obstacles so that you may see the church which is most dear to you, and also, of course, that you may be seen. This is the most precious of all its blessings—to look upon your countenance and to hear your voice. Do not, therefore, render its hopes fruitless. For, when I returned a year ago from Syria bringing that promise which I had received, how hopefully elated do you think I caused all to become? Do not, therefore, defer your visit until another time, admirable Sir. Even if a visit should be possible at some future time, that will not be when we also are present, since disease is pressing us to depart soon from this wretched life.

146. To Antiochus[1]

I am not able to charge you with idleness because you were silent when an opportunity of writing a letter offered itself. For, the salutation which you sent me by your honored hand I prize more highly than many letters. Therefore, in return, I greet you and I urge you to give earnest care to the safety of your soul, training all carnal passions according to reason and keeping the thought of God continually fixed in your soul, as in a most holy temple. In every deed and every speech place before your eyes the judgment of Christ, so that all your actions when brought together for that strict and fearful scrutiny may bring you glory in the day of retribution when before every creature you are adjudged worthy of praise. But,

---

[1] Antiochus was the nephew of Eusebius, Bishop of Samosata. This letter was written in 373. Letters 157, 158, and 168 are also addressed to him.

if that great man[2] should permit himself a journey to us, it will be no small profit for us to see you with him in our land.

147. To Aburgius[1]

Formerly, I used to think that the tales of Homer were a fable whenever I read the second part of the poem in which he narrates the sufferings of Odysseus. But, the sudden disaster befalling Maximus, a most excellent man in all respects, has taught us to consider as entirely probable those things until now regarded as fabulous and incredible. For, he was governor over no very insignificant people, just as Odysseus was leader of the Cephallenians. Now, Odysseus, although he took with him much money, returned stripped of all. Misfortune has also reduced this man to such a state that he runs the risk of appearing at home in borrowed garments. And he has endured these sufferings because, perhaps, he provoked against himself Laestrygones, or encountered Scylla, who, under the form of a woman, possessed the inhumanity and savagery of a dog. Since, then, he has scarcely been able to swim through this inescapable flood of troubles, through us he makes his supplication to you. He begs you to respect our common nature, and with compassion for his undeserved calamities not to conceal in silence his misfortunes but to make them known to those in power, so that he will, above all, have some assistance against the calumny that has been fabricated.

---

2 I.e., Eusebius of Samosata.

---

1 This appeal to Aburgius is in behalf of Maximus, the former Governor of Cappadocia, who had been unjustly accused of embezzlement, stripped of his office, and forced to flee to Caesarea. Aburgius was a wealthy layman whose intercession St. Basil often asked in behalf of unfortunate acquaintances and friends. Other letters to Aburgius are Letters 33, 75, 178, 196, and 304. On Maximus, cf. Letter 98. This letter was written in 373.

But, if that is not possible, he asks you at least to make public the intentions of the man treating him so outrageously. For, the disclosure of the wickedness of those plotting against him will be a satisfying consolation for a man who has been wronged.

148. To Trajan[1]

It brings much consolation to the afflicted even to be able to lament their misfortunes bitterly, and, especially, when they find men who are able, because of the nobility of their character, to sympathize with them in their grievances. Now, the most revered brother Maximus, he who ruled our country, has endured such sufferings as no other man has yet endured, and has been stripped of all his belongings, both such as he inherited from his father and such as he had amassed by his former labors. Moreover, having suffered bodily evils without number by his wanderings to and fro, and not even having preserved intact his rights of citizenship, for the sake of which free men are accustomed to endure anything, he has loudly bewailed his misfortunes in our presence. Furthermore, he has asked that through us the Iliad of evils encompassing him should be briefly made known to you. And, since I was not otherwise able to relieve him of his dire troubles, I readily granted him his favor -to notify your Modesty of a few of the many things which I had heard from him, since he himself seemed to me to blush at relating openly his misfortunes.

For, even if what has happened does not prove the perpetrator of the injustice to be a wicked man, still it shows

---

[1] Cf. preceding letter. This Trajan may be, although it is not certain, the commander-in-chief of the army under Valens. This letter was written in 373.

that the victim has a most pitiable lot, since the very fact of his having fallen into evils sent by God seems somehow to furnish a proof that he has been handed over to afflictions. But, it is a sufficient consolation for him in his troubles for you to look upon him with kindly eye and to extend to him that very helpful favor, which, although many enjoy, they are not able to exhaust—I mean the favor of your clemency. And we are also all positively convinced that in the courts your support will be a great means toward victory for him. Moreover, this man, who has requested our letter on the ground that it will be of some use to him, is himself the most righteous of all men. May we see him among the rest praising your Dignity with all the strength of his voice.

149. To Trajan[1]

You yourself have seen with your own eyes the misery of the formerly renowned but now most pitiable Maximus, who was governor of our country. Would that he had not been! For, I think that the government of the peoples will be shunned by many, if governorships are likely to come to such an end. So, why should we report separately each thing which we have seen and which we have heard to a man who is able by the keenness of his intellect to infer from a few incidents what has been omitted? But, at least in saying this, I shall perhaps not appear to you to speak overmuch—that, although there were many horrible outrages committed against him before your arrival, those perpetrated after that were of such a nature as to cause the former ones to be considered kindly deeds. Such excessive insolence and loss of goods and bodily

---

[1] The MSS. assign this letter to the Trajan of the preceding letter. It also was written in 373.

sufferings did those acts entail which were later devised against him by the vicar! And, now, he has come under guard to complete the rest of his penalties here, unless you will be willing to hold your mighty hand in protection over the afflicted man. Assuredly, I know that I am performing a superfluous act in urging your Excellency to kindliness. Only, since I wish to be of service to the man, I beseech your Grace for our sake to add something to your natural zeal for good, so that the benefit of our intercession for him may be evident to the man.

150. To Amphilochius, in the Name of Heracleidas[1]

I recall the conversations which we once had with one another, and I have not forgotten either what I myself said nor what I heard from your Nobility. And, now, public life does not hold me back. Although I am the same in heart and have not yet put off the old man, except, indeed, in appearance and in having removed myself far from the affairs of life, I seem now, as it were, to have entered upon the path of life exemplified by Christ. And I sit by myself like those about to put out to sea, looking steadily to the future. For, the sailors have need of winds for a fair voyage, but we of someone to lead us by the hand and bring us safely through the bitter waters of life. Now, I consider that I need, first of

---

[1] Amphilochius, later Bishop of Iconium, had abandoned his practice of law and was living in retirement at Ozizala, not far from Nazianzus where Gregory, his uncle, was bishop. Other letters addressed to him by St. Basil are: 161, 176, 190, 200, 201, 202, 218, 231, 232, 233, 234, 235, 236, and 238, besides those dealing with the canons. Heracleidas, a friend of Amphilochius and also a retired lawyer, was living at St. Basil's famous hospital at the time that this letter was written. St. Basil wrote this letter for Heracleidas to let Amphilochius know why Heracleidas had not joined him in his retreat, to explain what Heracleidas was doing at Caesarea, and to attempt to persuade Amphilochius to come to St. Basil. It was written in 373.

all, a curb against my youth, and, then, spurs for the race of piety. And the provider of these, without doubt, is reason, now moderating our disorderly conduct, now arousing the sluggishness of our soul. Again, I need other remedies so as to purify the sordidness of my manners. For, you know that we who for a long time have been accustomed to the forum are unsparing of our words and are not on our guard against the imaginations, which are aroused in our mind by the Evil One. Moreover, we are overcome by honor and we do not easily lay aside the habit of thinking somewhat highly of ourselves. Against these things I realize that I need a great and an experienced teacher. Then, in truth, the cleansing of the soul's eye, so that it may be able to fix its gaze on the beauty of the glory of God when all darkness of ignorance, like some rheum, has been removed, I consider no little task nor one that brings profit only for a short time.

I know full well that your Eloquence is aware of this and desires that there should be someone to give this assistance. Moreover, if ever God grants me to meet your Modesty, I shall, without doubt, learn more concerning the matters to which I must give heed. For, now, by reason of my great ignorance I am not able even to understand in how great need I am, but at least I have not repented of my first attempt, nor does my soul sink down at the prospect of a life according to God. About this you rightly and in a manner befitting yourself felt anxiety in my case, lest, ever turning back, I should become a 'statue of salt,'[2] a thing which, as I hear, happened to a certain woman. Yet, truly, the powers from without still hinder me, like magistrates searching out some deserter. But, especially, my own heart holds me back, testifying to itself to all those things which I have said.

But, when you recalled our agreements and announced

---
2 Cf. Gen. 19.26.

that you would bring charges, you made me laugh even in the midst of this dejection of mine, because you are still an advocate and are not giving up your cleverness.[3] For, I think thus—that, unless like an unlearned person I am straying from the truth altogether, there is one road which leads to the Lord, and all those going to Him travel in company with one another and proceed according to one rule of life. Therefore, where can I go and be separated from you and not live with you and with you serve God, to whom we have by common consent fled for refuge? For, our bodies may be separated by material space, but certainly the eye of God looks upon us both together, if my life is really worthy of being viewed by the eyes of God, for I have read somewhere in the Psalms that 'the eyes of the Lord are upon the just.'[4] And I do indeed pray to be bodily present both with you and with everyone who makes a choice similar to yours, and also every night and day to bend my knees to our Father in heaven with you and with any other who is worthily calling upon God. I know that union in prayers brings much gain. Yet, if the charge of falsehood will assuredly follow me as often as I shall happen to complain when cast aside in a different little corner, I cannot contradict the word. But, I already condemn myself as a liar if I have made any statement in my former condition of indifference which makes me liable to the charge of a falsehood.[5]

After I had come near enough to Caesarea to become acquainted with the state of affairs, since I was not willing to

---
[3] Apparently, Amphilochius and Heracleidas had made an agreement with each other to abstain from public life. As Heracleidas had broken the agreement, Amphilochius threatens to bring action against him.
[4] Ps. 33.16.
[5] Amphilochius had evidently found fault with Heracleidas in consequence of a complaint he had made, and had accused him of repenting of having entered upon the ascetic life.

enter the city itself, I took refuge in the nearby almshouse in order to learn there what I wished. Then, when the bishop dearly beloved of God came to visit according to his custom, I referred to him what your Eloquence had commanded us. And, though we could not keep in memory what he answered, and it exceeded the length of a letter, yet to sum up, concerning poverty he said that this was the measure—that each should limit his possessions to the last tunic. And he offered us proofs from the Gospel—one from John the Baptist who said: 'Let him who has two tunics share with him who has none';[6] and another from our Lord who forbade His disciples to have two tunics.[7] And he added to these, also, the statement: 'If thou wilt be perfect, go, sell what thou hast, and give to the poor.'[8] And he also said that the parable of the pearl refers to this, because the merchant who found the precious pearl, going away, sold all his possessions and bought it. Again, he added to this that a person ought not to leave the distribution of his substance to himself, but to him who has been entrusted with the management of the affairs of the poor. And he proved this from the Acts,[9] that they would sell what belonged to them and, bringing [the price], 'lay it at the feet of the apostles, and by them distribution was made to each according as anyone had need.' For, he said that the power of distinguishing him who is truly in need from him who is asking through avarice required experience. And he who gives to the afflicted has given to the Lord and from Him will receive the reward, but he who provides for every wanderer has cast it to a dog, troublesome because of his shamelessness, but not to be pitied on account of indigence.

Now, concerning the matter of how we ought to live day

---

6 Luke 3.11.
7 A reference to our Lord's statement in Matt. 19.9-10.
8 Matt. 19.21.
9 Cf. Acts 4.34-35.

by day, he had time to say but little, considering the importance of the subject, but I would prefer for you to have learned this from the man himself. For, it is not reasonable for me to mar the exactness of his teachings. But, I have prayed to visit him some day with you, in order that you, while preserving accurately in your memory what is said, may also by your own intelligence find out what is left unsaid. For, from the many things I heard I remember this—that instruction on how the Christian should live is not so much in need of speech as of daily example. And I know that, if the bond of responsibility for your aged father did not hold you back, you yourself would have preferred nothing to a conference with the bishop, nor would you have advised me to leave him and wander into the solitude. For, the caves and the rocks await us, but the advantages accruing to us from men are not always at hand. Therefore, if you would permit me to advise you, you would impress upon your father that he should allow you to depart from him for a little while and to meet the man who knows much both from the experience of others and from his own intelligence, and is able to offer it to those who come to him.

151. To Eustathius, the Physician[1]

If there is any benefit from our letters, do not for any length of time cease writing to us and rousing us to write, for we ourselves are certainly made happier by reading the letters of intelligent men who love the Lord. And, whether you yourself really find something deserving of esteem in our letters, it is for you who read them to know. By all means, if we

---
[1] Letter 189 is also addressed to this Eustathius. This letter was written in 373.

were not drawn away by the press of business engagements, we would not refrain from the pleasure of writing continuously. But you, whose cares are less, charm us as often as it may be possible with your letters. For, they say that wells become better by being used. But, your counsels drawn from the art of medicine are apparently beside the point, since we are not employing the knife, but they who have become corrupted are falling upon one another.² Now, there is a Stoic saying: 'When,' it is said, 'matters do not happen as we wish, we wish them as they happen.' But, on my part, I cannot conform my will to the matter in hand; yet, I do not condemn men who perform a necessary act against their will. For, you physicians do not wish to cauterize the sick or otherwise cause them to suffer; nevertheless, you permit it frequently in consequence of the seriousness of the condition. Neither do those who go to sea willingly throw out their cargo,³ but, in order to escape shipwreck, they submit to the jettisoning, preferring a life of poverty to death. And, so, believe that we also endure with pain and with countless lamentations the separation from those who withdraw; nevertheless, we bear it, since nothing is more precious to the lovers of truth than God and our hope in Him.

---

2 Eustathius the bishop and his followers are using the knife upon each other.
3 According to the Benedictine editors, the cargo thrown overboard represents the loss of unity suffered by the Sebastenes when they left the communion of Eustathius. Cf. Letter 237.

152. To Victor, a Commander[1]

If I should not write to some other person, I would, perhaps, justly incur the charge of negligence or forgetfulness. But, how is it possible to forget you, whose name is spoken among all men? And, how possible to neglect you, who have excelled almost all on earth in the loftiness of your honors? However, the cause of our silence is evident—we hesitate to become troublesome to so great a man. But, if in addition to your other virtues, you possess this one, also—that you not only accept the letters sent by us but also miss those which were left unsent—behold, we are now writing with confidence and we shall continually write, praying to the holy God that recompense be given to you for the honor which you pay us. You have anticipated our requests for the Church, having done everything which we would have asked. And you act not to please men, but God, who has honored you and who has given you some blessings in the present life and will give others in the life to come, because you have walked His road with truth and have kept your heart unswerving in rightness of faith from beginning to end.

153. To Victor, the Ex-Consul[1]

As often as we chance to read the letters from your Modesty,

---

[1] Victor was a distinguished general under Valens, a man of high character, and an orthodox Christian. He had been consul in 369. Cf. Gregory of Nazianzus, Letters 133 and 134. In 378, he united with Trajan, Arintheus, and other generals in remonstrating with Valens on his Arianism. Cf. Theod. *H.E.* 4.30; and Amm. Marc. 31.7. This letter was written in 373.

---

[1] In all probability, this is the same Victor as is addressed in the preceding letter. The date is about the same as that of the preceding letter.

we return thanks to God because you continue to be mindful of us, and do not because of any slander lessen the love which formerly, either by a wise judgment or a kindly practice, you consented to entertain for us. Therefore, we pray to the holy God both that you may persevere in the same disposition toward us and that we may be worthy of the honor which you bestowed on us through your letter.

154. To Ascholius, Bishop of Thessalonica[1]

You have acted rightly and according to the law of spiritual charity in having begun the correspondence between us and stirred us to a like zeal by your good example. For, the friendship of the world needs the eyes and a personal meeting to initiate an acquaintance therefrom. But, those who know how to love spiritually do not use the flesh as the promoter of friendship; on the contrary, they are led to the spiritual union through the fellowship of the faith. Therefore, thanks be to the Lord, who has consoled our hearts by showing that not among all has charity grown cold, but that there are somewhere in the world men who reveal the stamp of Christ's teaching. Accordingly, your office seemed to me to be like that of the stars, which in their nightly concourse give light, some to one part of the heavens and others to another; whose splendor is most beautiful, and more beautiful, perhaps, because of their unexpectedness. And such are you, the lights of the churches, very few and easily numbered in this gloomy

---

[1] Ascholius baptized Theodosius at Thessalonica in 380 and was present at the Council of Constantinople in 381. Cf. Letters 164 and 165; also Socrates, *Ecc. Hist.* 5.6,8. Letter 15 of St. Ambrose was written at the death of Ascholius. In it St. Ambrose says of Ascholius: '*Ad summum sacerdotium a Macedonicis obsecratus populis, electus a sacerdotibus.*' This letter was written in 373.

state of affairs, shining, as it were, in the moonless night, and, besides possessing the charm of virtue, being yet more dearly beloved because of the infrequency with which you are found.

Your letter revealed sufficiently your disposition toward us. Even if it was brief in the number of its syllables, at least in the correctness of thought it gave adequate proof to us of your principles. Now, the fact that you have been concerned about the most blessed Athanasius is the clearest evidence that you are sound in the most important matters. In return, therefore, for the pleasure derived from your letter we express our great gratitude to our most honorable son Euphemius,[2] for whom I, on my part, pray that there may be every assistance from the Holy One. I urge you also to pray with us, in order that we may quickly receive him back with his most modest[3] wife, our daughter in the Lord. And let me urge you, too, not to stay our happiness at its beginning, but to write on every occasion that is offered and by the frequency of your communication to increase your love toward us. Tell us also about the churches there, whether they are in accord, and pray for us here, so that there may be a great calm among us, too, after our Lord has rebuked the wind and the sea.

---

2 The bearer of the letter from Ascholius to St. Basil.
3 *Kosmiótatēs*—a title of distinction applied by St. Basil to laymen.

155. Without Address, in the Case of a Trainer[1]

Against the many charges which were written in the first and only letter that your Nobility deigned to send us, I am at a loss as to how I should defend myself, not because of the want of a just reason, but because from among a great number of accusations the choice of the more relevant is a difficult matter, as is also the choice of the point to which we must first direct our attention. Or, perhaps, by making use of the very order in which they are written, we should meet them one by one.

We did not know until today those who are setting out from here for Scythia; moreover, those of your house did not even mention the fact to us, so that we might greet you through them, although we are ready with much eagerness to salute your Honor at every opportunity. It is impossible to forget you in our prayers, unless we first forget our task to which the Lord assigned us. For, since, by the grace of God, you are faithful, you certainly remember the appointed liturgy of the Church—that we pray for our brethren on their journeys abroad. Moreover, for those who are numbered in the military service, for those who speak openly in defense of the name of the Lord, and for those who show forth the fruits of the Spirit, we offer our prayers in the holy Church. And we think that your Honor is certainly included in the

---

[1] According to the Benedictine editors, the person to whom the letter is written is Julius Soranus, a relative of St. Basil and a duke of Scythia. It applies to Soranus, since he was a 'trainer' and encourager of martyrs. In Letter 164, St. Basil calls Ascholius 'trainer' of the martyr Sabas. On the present letter and Letters 155, 164, and 165, which have to do with transferring the remains of the Gothic martyr Sabas (died April 372) to Caesarea in Cappadocia, cf. G. Pfeilschefter, *Ein neues Werk des Wulfila, Veroffentlichungen aus dem Kirchenhistor* (Seminar, München 1907) 192-224. This letter, written in 373, is one of the earliest references to the preservation of the relics of martyrs.

majority or even in all of these prayers. And, how could we personally forget you, since so many things move us to a remembrance—such a sister, such nephews, kinsmen so noble, so devoted to us, such a home, domestics, and friends, because of whom, even if we did not wish it, we are compelled to recall your good will?

Now, concerning this present matter, the brother reported nothing serious to us, nor was any decision delivered by us that was at all injurious to him. Therefore, turn your grievance against those who have been telling you falsehoods, and free both the suffragan bishop and me from all blame. If that pedant prepares some lawsuit, he has the public courts and the laws. Therefore, I ask you to make no further complaint on these points.

Now, whatever good deeds you do personally you store up as a treasure for yourself; whatever relief you offer to those who suffer persecution for the name of the Lord, this you prepare for yourself on the day of recompense. And you will do well if you send the relics of the martyrs to your native country, since, as you wrote to us, the persecution there is even now making martyrs to the Lord.

156. To Evagrius, a Presbyter[1]

So far was I from being displeased at the length of your message that the letter, because of the pleasure I derived from reading it, even seemed to me to be short. For, what is more

---

[1] Evagrius is commonly known as of Antioch, to distinguish him from others of the same name, especially Evagrius the historian. The dates of his birth and death are uncertain, but he is known to have been consecrated by Paulinus in 388. It was this act which prolonged the Meletian schism at Antioch. He lived at least until 392; cf. Letter 138. This letter was written in the late autumn of 373; cf. Loofs, *op. cit.* 31 n. 3.

pleasing to hear than the name of peace? Or what is more befitting the sacred office and more gratifying to the Lord than planning for such things? Therefore, may the Lord bestow the reward of peace-making on you, who choose so well and are so zealously engaged in a most blessed task. But believe, honored Friend, that of those foremost in zeal we yield to none, as far as regards the desire and prayer to see at some time the day on which all who are not separated from one another in opinion will gather in the same assembly. We should, in truth, be the most monstrous of all men if we exulted over the schisms and divisions of the churches, and did not esteem the union of the members of Christ's body as the greatest of blessings. Yet, realize that we fall as far short in power as we superabound in desire. For, your perfect Wisdom is not ignorant of the fact that evils strengthened by time need, first of all, time for correction, and, then, a strong and rather energetic guidance, if one proposes to reach the very depths so as to pull out by the roots the disorders of the ailing. But, you know what I mean, and, if I must speak more clearly, there is no cause for fear.

Self-love, which through long habit has taken root in souls, one man cannot destroy, nor can one letter, nor a brief period of time. The suspicions and frictions arising from controversy cannot be entirely removed unless some trustworthy person acts as mediator in the interests of peace. And if all the strength of grace flowed upon us and we were able by word and deed and the gifts of the Spirit to move our opponents, we should be obliged to attempt such a task. But, perhaps, you would not even then have advised us to start alone to make the correction, since, by the grace of God, the bishop[2] is the one to whom chiefly appertains the care of the churches; and he himself is not able to come to us, nor

---
2 Meletius of Antioch.

is it easy for us, in the meantime, to travel on account of the winter. Rather, it is absolutely impossible, not only because my body is exhausted by the long-continued illness, but also because the passages of the Armenian mountains become, a little later, difficult to cross, even for those who are in the full vigor of youth. But, I shall not refuse to make these things known to him in writing. However, I do not expect anything worthy of mention to result from letters, judging from the exactness of the man and the very nature of written words, because the transmitted message is obviously unable to persuade. For, it is necessary to say many things and in turn to listen to many things, to solve the questions arising, and to explain those points which are not evident. And the discussion in letters, spread out inert and lifeles over the paper, is incapable of this.

However, as I have said, I shall not hesitate to write. Yet, be assured, our most truly pious and much beloved Brother, that, by the grace of God, I have no personal quarrel with anyone. For, I am not aware of having been curious about the charges for which each is liable or is said to be liable. Thus, therefore, it is fitting for you to pay attention to our opinion, since we are incapable of acting through partiality, nor have we been prejudiced by slander against any. May it be the will of the Lord that all be done in the manner of the Church, and with proper order!

Our most desired son, the fellow deacon Dorotheus, caused us grief when he announced concerning your Reverence that you refused to participate with him in the religious service. Yet, such were not the matters discussed by us, if I remember anything at all. Moreover, it is absolutely impossible for me to send a representative to the West, since I have no one suitable for such a service. If any of the brothers with you wishes to undertake the task for the sake of the churches, he knows, of course, to whom he will set out, for what object, by whom he will be supplied with letters, and what sort these will be. For, truly, when I look around me, I see no one at all with me. And I pray to be numbered with the seven thousand who did not bend their knee to Baal. But, they who are laying their hands upon all seek our soul, also. Not for this, however, will we neglect any of the zeal we owe to the churches of God.

157. To Antiochus[1]

You can imagine how disappointed I was at having failed to meet you during the summer. Even our meeting of other years was not such as to completely satisfy us. However, to see, at least in a dream, the objects of their desire brings some comfort to lovers. But, you do not even write, you are so lazy; so, your absence can be ascribed to no other cause than that you are disinclined to long journeys for charity's sake. However, let us cease this. Pray for us and entreat the Lord not to abandon us, but, as He delivered us from those trials which have come upon us, so, also, for the glory of His name in which we have placed our hope, to free us from those which are threatening.

158. To Antiochus[1]

Since my sins stand against me so that I have not been able

---

[1] Other letters addressed to Antiochus, the nephew of Eusebius, are Letters 146, 158, and 168. The Benedictine editors are inclined to think that, in spite of its title, this letter was written to Eusebius. St. Basil's complaints befit Eusebius rather than Antiochus, who could not travel without his uncle's permission. This letter was written in 373.

[1] For Antiochus, cf. note 1 of preceding letter. This letter was also written in 373.

to accomplish the desire which I have long had of meeting you, I am at least consoling myself for the failure by means of letters. And we urge you not to cease remembering us in your prayers, in order that, if we live, we may be considered worthy of enjoying your company; if not, that through the assistance of your prayers we may depart from this world with great hope. We recommend to you the brother who is in charge of the camels.

159. To Eupaterius and His Daughter[1]

How much pleasure the letter of your Modesty afforded me you surely can imagine from the very contents. For, to a man who makes it his prayer that he may always associate with those who fear God and receive some advantage from them, what could be sweeter than such a letter through which knowledge of God is sought? For, if 'to us to live is Christ,'[2] it follows that our speech ought to be about Christ, and our every thought and act should depend upon His commands, and our soul should be formed to His image. Accordingly, I rejoice at being asked about such matters and I congratulate those asking. In one word, then, we honor the Creed of the Fathers assembled at Nicaea before all those that were formulated later. In it the Son is confessed to be consubstantial with the Father and of the same nature as He who has begotten Him. For, as Light of Light, and God of God, and Good of Good, and all such identities, He has been confessed by those holy Fathers and is now attested by us also who pray to walk in their footsteps.

---
1 Eupaterius and his daughter are otherwise unknown. This letter was written in 373.
2 Cf. Phil. 1.21.

Since the question which has at present arisen among those who are always attempting to make innovations, but which had been passed over in silence by the men of earlier times because the doctrine was not contradicted, has been left unexplained (I mean, of course, that concerning the Holy Spirit), we are adding the explanation of it in conformity with the meaning of the Scriptures—that as we are baptized, so, also, do we believe; as we believe, so, also, do we give glory. Therefore, since baptism has been given to us by the Saviour in the name of the Father and of the Son and of the Holy Spirit, we offer a confession of faith consistent with our baptism, and also the doxology consistent with our faith, glorifying the Holy Spirit with the Father and the Son in the conviction that He is not separated from the divine nature. For, that which is different according to its nature would not share the same honors. And we pity those who say that the Holy Spirit is a creature on the ground that by such a statement they have fallen into the unpardonable sin of blasphemy against Him. Now, the fact that a creature is distinct from the Divinity needs no further explanation to those who are even a little familiar with the Scriptures. For, the creature is subject, but the Spirit sets free;[3] the creature is in need of life, 'it is the Spirit that gives life';[4] the creature also needs teaching, the Spirit is the Teacher;[5] the creature is sanctified, the Spirit is the Sanctifier.[6] Even if you would mean angels, or archangels, or all the heavenly powers, it is through the Spirit that they receive their holiness. For, the Spirit of Himself has a natural sanctity not received through grace but joined essentially to Him, whence also He has gained in a special manner the name of 'Holy.' Accordingly, what is holy by nature, as the Father is

---

3 Cf. Rom. 8.2.
4 John 6.64.
5 Cf. John 14.26.
6 Cf. Rom. 15.16.

holy by nature, and the Son holy by nature, we ourselves do not dare to separate and sever from the Divine and Blessed Trinity, and we do not approve those who carelessly reckon Him among creatures.

Let these words, briefly set forth, suffice for your Reverence. For, from scant seeds you will produce the more fruit of piety, if the Holy Spirit is working with you. 'Give an occasion to a wise man, and wisdom shall be added to him.'[7] But, we shall hold over a more complete explanation until we meet, when it will be possible to confute the objections, to furnish more detailed testimony from the Scriptures, and to confirm every sound rule of faith. For the present, however, pardon my brevity. For, to begin with, I would not have written at all if I had not thought that to refuse the request altogether would be greater harm than to fulfill it inadequately.

160. To Diodorus[1]

A letter has reached us which bears the name of Diodorus, but which seems in all that follows to belong to anyone else rather than to Diodorus. In fact, it appears to me that some clever fellow, masquerading in your person, wished in this way to make himself seem trustworthy to his hearers. When asked by someone if it was allowable for him to marry the sister of his dead wife, he did not shudder in horror at the question, but even listened calmly, and very nobly and gloriously supported the wanton desire. Now, if I had the letter at hand I would have sent it, and you would have been able to defend both yourself and the truth. But, he who showed the

---

7 Prov. 9.9.

1 For Diodorus, cf. Letter 135 n. 1. This letter was written in 373 or 374.

letter took it away again, and carried it around like some trophy against us, since we had forbidden the act from the beginning; moreover, he declared that he had the permission in writing. Therefore, I have now written to you so that we may attack with twofold force that spurious document and leave it no power to harm easily those who read it.

First of all, then—a point which is of the utmost importance in such matters—there is the custom among us which we can bring forward and which has the force of law because of the fact that the regulations were handed down to us by holy men. This custom is as follows: If anyone being overcome at any time by the vice of impurity falls into an unlawful union with two sisters, this is neither considered marriage, nor, in short, are they admitted to the membership of the Church before they have separated from each other. Consequently, even if it were possible to say nothing else, the custom would suffice to safeguard what is right. But, since he who wrote the letter has attempted by misleading argumentation to bring such an evil into men's lives, we must not forego the assistance of reasoning, although in matters which are perfectly obvious the instinctive conviction of each is mightier than the argument.

It has been written in Leviticus,[2] he says: 'Thou shalt not take thy wife's sister for a harlot, to rival her, neither shalt thou discover her nakedness, while she is yet living.' He says that it is evident, therefore, from these words that it is permitted to take her when his wife is dead. Now, in answer to this I shall say, first of all, that whatever the law says, it says to those who are within the law; otherwise, we shall be subject to circumcision, to the observance of the sabbath, and to abstinence from meats. For, if we find something that agrees with our pleasure, we certainly shall not place ourselves under the yoke of servitude to the law, but, if some custom seems dif-

---
2 Lev. 18.18.

ficult, then have recourse to the freedom in Christ. We have been asked if it is written that he may take a woman as wife after her sister. We said what is in our opinion sound and true, that it is not written. But, to deduce by the application of inference a point which was passed over in silence is the right of him who frames the laws, not his who recites the laws, since in the latter case anyone who wishes can dare to take the sister even while his wife is still living. Now, this same sophism he also adapts to the following. For it is written, he says: 'Thou shalt not take they wife's sister for a harlot, to rival her,' so that the law did not forbid to take her except as a matter of rivalry. Of course, he who is advocate for the vice will declare that the distinctive trait of sisters is freedom from envy. Therefore, since the cause is removed for which the law forbade the cohabitation with both, what will prevent him from taking the sisters? But, this is not written, we shall say. Yet, neither was the former point defined. The sense of the deduction, however, gives permission for taking both sisters. Now, we must free ourselves from the difficulty by turning back a little to matters preceding the legislation.

The legislator, in fact, does not seem to embrace every type of sin, but to be forbidding particularly those of the Egyptians, from whom Israel had departed, and those of the Chanaanites, to whom Israel was migrating. The words are as follows: 'You shall not do according to the custom of the land of Egypt, in which you dwelt; neither shall you act according to the manner of the country of Chanaan, into which I will bring you, nor shall you walk in their ordinances.'[3] Consequently, it is very probable that this form of sin had not at that time been introduced among the Gentiles, and on this account the legislator did not need to guard against it, but was satisfied with the accepted custom for withstanding

---
3 Cf. Lev. 18.3.

the pollution. How, then, was it that, when he had forbidden the greater, he passed over the lesser sin in silence? It was because it seemed that the example of the Patriarch[4] was harmful to many carnal men, so that they cohabited with sisters still living.

But, what must we do? Say what is written, or work out for ourselves what has been passed over in silence? For example, it is not written in these laws that a father and son should not have one concubine, but it was thought to be deserving of a most serious charge by the Prophet.[5] 'For,' he says, 'the son and the father have gone to the same young woman.' How many other forms of the unclean vices has the school of the demons discovered, yet Holy Scripture has passed them over in silence, not wishing to defile its holiness with the names of these disgraceful acts, but has condemned impurities in general terms! Thus, the Apostle Paul says: 'But immorality and every uncleanness . . . let it not even be named among you, as becomes saints,'[6] embracing in the name of 'uncleanness' the unmentionable practices of both men and women. Therefore, silence assuredly does not bring permission to the lovers of pleasure.

But, I do not say that this class of sin was passed over in silence; rather, the legislator forbade it very emphatically. For the command, 'Thou shalt not approach to her that is near of kin to uncover her nakedness,'[7] embraces also this form of relationship. For, what could be more closely related to a man than his wife, rather than his own flesh? For 'they are no longer two, but one flesh.'[8] Therefore, through the wife the sister enters into relationship with the husband. In fact,

---

4 Probably Jacob; cf. Gen. 29ff.
5 Amos 2.7.
6 Eph. 5.3.
7 Cf. Lev. 18.6.
8 Matt. 19.6.

as he will not take the mother of his wife, nor the daughter of his wife, because he will not take his own mother nor his own daughter, so neither will he take his wife's sister, because he will not take his own sister. And, contrariwise, it will not be possible for the wife to cohabit with relatives of the husband, for the lawful claims of relationship are common to both. And I solemnly affirm to everyone who is deliberating about marriage that 'this world as we see it is passing away,'[9] and 'the time is short, . . . that those who have wives be as if they had none.'[10] And, if he reads for me in a wrong sense the words, 'Increase and multiply,'[11] I laugh at him for not discerning the times of the legislation. A second marriage is a remedy against fornication, not a means for licentiousness. 'If they do not have self-control, let them marry,'[12] it is said; but, even if they marry, let them not transgress the law.

But, those who are blinded in soul by the disgraceful passion do not even regard nature, which long ago distinguished the titles of kinship. Now, of what kinship will such call their children? Will they call them brothers of each other or cousins? For, both names will fit them as a result of the confusion. Do not, O Sir, make the aunt the stepmother of your little ones, and do not arm with cruel jealousy her who ought to cherish them in the place of a mother. For, it is only the race of stepmothers that carries its hatred even after death. Rather, others who were hostile to the dead become reconciled, but stepmothers begin their hatred after death.[13]

---

9 1 Cor. 7.31.
10 Cf. 1 Cor. 7.29.
11 Gen. 1.28.
12 1 Cor. 7.9.
13 Cf. Herodotus 4.154 and Euripides, *Alcestis* 309. In antiquity, the unkindness of stepmothers was proverbial.

Now, to summarize these words: If a man is eager for marriage according to the law, all the world lies open, but, if his desire is under the influence of passion, on that account let him be restricted the more, that he may learn 'how to possess his vessel in holiness and honor, not in the passion of lust.'[14] Although I had desired to say more, the length of my letter prevents me. I pray that either our advice may prove stronger than the passion, or that this pollution may not come to reside in our country, but may remain in those regions in which it has been attempted.

161. To Amphilochius, on His Consecration as Bishop[1]

Blessed be God, who chooses in each generation those pleasing to Him, making known His chosen vessels[2] and using them for the ministry of the saints. He even now has ensnared you with the inescapable nets of His grace, when you were fleeing, as you say, not us, but the summons expected through us; and He has led you into the midst of Pisidia, so that you may take men captive to the Lord and may, according to His will, draw out from the depths into light those who have been made captive by the Devil. Therefore, say also yourself the words uttered by the blessed David: 'Whither shall I go from thy spirit, or whither shall I flee from thy face?'[3] For such wonders does our loving Lord work! 'Asses are lost'[4] in order that a king may be found for Israel. But, that man, who was

---

14 1 Thess. 4.4-5.

1 For Amphilochius, cf. Letter 150 n. 1. This letter was written in 374. Cf. Loofs, *op. cit.* 46 n. 5.
2 Cf. Acts 9.15.
3 Ps. 138.7.
4 Cf. 1 Kings 9.3.

an Israelite, was given to Israel; yet, the country which nurtured you and brought you to such a height of virtue does not have you; on the contrary, she sees her neighbor embellished with her own ornament. Since, however, all those who have hoped in Christ are one people and those who are Christ's are now one Church, even though He is called upon from different regions, the country both rejoices and is gladdened by the dispensations of the Lord and does not think that one man has been lost but that through one man whole churches have been acquired. Only, may the Lord grant that we, when we are present, may see, and, when absent, may hear of your progress in the Gospel and of the good order of your churches.

Be a man, therefore, and be strong and go before the people whom the Most High has entrusted to your right hand. And, as a skillful pilot, become mightier in resolve than every tempest stirred up by the heretical blasts, keep your ship unsubmerged by the briny and bitter waves of false doctrine, awaiting the calm which the Lord will make when a voice has been found worthy of rousing Him to rebuke the winds and the sea. But, if you wish to visit us now hastening to the inevitable end under our long-continued illness, do not await a favorable time nor a sign from us, knowing that to our paternal love every time is an opportune one to embrace a beloved child, and that the affection of the soul is a more excellent summons than all speech.

But, do not lament a burden which surpasses your strength. For, if you were the one destined to bear this responsibility alone, it would not be merely heavy but utterly unendurable. But, if the Lord is the One who helps you bear it, 'Cast thy care upon the Lord,'[5] and He Himself will bear it. Only, let me urge you in all things to guard against this—that you be not borne along with others by wicked customs, but that

---
5 Cf. Ps. 55.23; also, 1 Peter 5.7.

through the wisdom given to you by God you change the formerly adopted evil practices into something good. For, Christ has sent you, not to follow others, but that you yourself may guide those who are being saved. And we beg you to pray for us, in order that, if we are still in this life, we may be considered worthy to see you with your church, but, if we are ordered to depart soon, that we may see all of you there with the Lord, your church flourishing like a good vine in good deeds, and you, as a wise husbandman and a good servant, giving in due season the measure of grain to your fellow servants, storing up for yourself the reward of a faithful and prudent steward.

All with us greet your Reverence. May you be well and cheerful in the Lord; may you be preserved in high esteem for the gifts of the Spirit and of wisdom.

162. To Eusebius, Bishop of Samosata[1]

The following reflection seems to me both to cause hesitation in writing and to indicate its very necessity. For, when I contemplate my obligation of remaining at home and at the same time take into account the benefit of a meeting, I am inclined to despise letters exceedingly, since they are not able to accomplish a shadow's worth in comparison with the real visit. Again, when I consider that my only consolation, deprived as I am of what is greatest and most important, is to address such a great man and, as is our custom, to supplicate him not to forget us in his prayers, I am inclined to decide that letters are not a trifling matter. I myself do not wish to banish from my mind the hope of a visit, nor to give up the

---

[1] Another letter to Eusebius, written after Easter of the year 374; cf. Loofs, *op. cit.* 46 n. 5.

idea of seeing your Reverence. For, I am ashamed that I should not seem to have so much confidence in your prayers as to expect to become a young man in place of an old one, if there should be need of that, and not merely to become a little stronger instead of remaining weak and wholly powerless, as I now am.

It is not easy to put into words my reasons for not being with you already, not only because I am hindered by my present illness, but also because I have never had such power of speech as to be able to describe clearly my manifold and varied diseases. But, I can say that from Easter day until now fevers and diarrhea and disturbances of my bowels, overwhelming me like waves, did not permit me to emerge. Now, the kind and the character of these present attacks our brother Barachus can tell, even if not in a manner in keeping with the truth, at least sufficiently to testify to the cause of my postponement. I am entirely convinced that, if you would truly pray with us, we should easily be freed from all these troubles.

163. To Count Jovinus[1]

I saw your soul in your letter. For, truly, no painter can so accurately portray the lineaments of a body as speech can image the secrets of the soul. In fact, the words of your letter aptly represented to us the stability of your character, the genuineness of your worth, and the purity of your mind in all respects; for this reason it also afforded us great consolation for your absence. Therefore, do not fail to use every pre-

---

[1] Count Jovinus seems from this letter to have been on intimate terms with St. Basil; nothing more is known of him. This letter was written after Easter of 374. Cf. Loofs, *op. cit.* 46 n. 5.

text which falls in your way to write and to grant us the favor of conversing with you from a distance, since the weakness of our body now causes us to despair of a personal meeting. How great that weakness is Bishop Amphilochius,[2] dearly beloved of God, will tell you, for he knows it through being with us much and is able to describe what he has beheld. Now, I wish my difficulties to be known for no other reason than to obtain pardon for the future, so that we may not suffer the condemnation of laziness if we should fail to pay you a visit. Yet, for this loss we need not so much a defense as consolation. For, if it were possible for us to be with your Dignity, I would consider this opportunity much more precious to me than those things for which others eagerly strive.

164. To Ascholius, Bishop of Thessalonica[1]

The greatness of the joy with which the letter of your Holiness filled us we cannot easily describe, for speech is but a weak tool for vivid portrayal, but you yourself ought to infer it, basing your judgment on the beauty of what you have written. For, what did your letter not contain? Did it not contain love for the Lord? Admiration for the martyrs, describing so clearly the manner of the combat that it brings their deeds before our very eyes? Honor and affection toward us? Did it not have whatever qualities one might mention as

---

[2] The visit of Amphilochius in 374 was probably the first of a series of frequent visits. St. Basil was his spiritual father. Amphilochius preferred to make his visits to St. Basil in the autumn, because the anniversary of St. Basil's hospital was celebrated at that time. This hospital had a special interest for him, because it was here that he and Heracleidas had passed a solemn crisis in their lives. Cf. Letter 150.

[1] For this Ascholius, cf. Letter 154. The following letter is also addressed to him. This letter was written in 374.

most noble? Consequently, when we took your letter into our hands and read it over and over and perceived the grace of the Spirit abounding in it, we thought that we were living in the olden times when the churches of God flourished, rooted in the faith, made one in love, since there existed a union of various members as in one body; when the persecutors were apparent and also those persecuted; when the people, though warred upon, became more numerous, and the blood of martyrs watering the churches raised up many more champions of religion, those coming after stripping themselves for the combat in emulation of the former. At that time, we Christians had peace with one another, that peace which the Lord left us, of which now there is no longer a trace remaining, so cruelly have we driven it from one another. But, our souls have returned to that pristine happiness since your letter came from afar blossoming with the beauty of love. Furthermore, a martyr has come to us from the barbarians beyond the Ister,[2] proclaiming through himself the exactness of the faith practiced there. Who could describe the joy of our souls at this? What power of speech could be devised capable of clearly expressing the feelings in the innermost depths of our heart? Truly, when we saw the athlete we congratulated his trainer,[3] who will also receive for himself the crown of justice at the hand of the most just Judge, because he has strengthened many for the contest in defense of religion.

Since you have brought to us the remembrance of the blessed man Eutyches,[4] and have exalted our fatherland as one which has supplied the seeds of piety, you have gladdened

---

2 St. Basil regularly calls the Danube by the name of Ister; cf. Letter 40.
3 St. Basil calls Ascholius the trainer of the martyr Sabas; cf. the title of Letter 155.
4 A Christian of Cappadocia who was taken prisoner by the Goths in 260, and who later with some of his fellow captives became a martyr, but only after he had sowed the seeds of the faith in the land of his captivity. Cf. Philost., *H.E.* 2.5.

us by the recollection of former times, but you have saddened us by the account of what is now seen. For, no one of us resembles Eutyches in virtue, we who are so far from taming the barbarians by the power of the Spirit and by the action of His graces, that we have even, by the greatness of our sins, made savage those who were gentle. In fact, we ascribe to ourselves and our sins the blame for such extensive spreading of the power of the heretics. For, almost no part of the world has escaped the conflagration of heresy. Now, this is your report—contests of the athletes,[5] bodies torn in shreds in defense of religion, the wrath of the barbarian despised by those undaunted in heart, the various tortures of the persecutors, the constancy of the wrestlers through it all, the beam, the water,[6] the instruments that completed the martyrdom. But, what are our conditions? Charity has grown cold. The doctrine of the Fathers is being destroyed; shipwreck in the faith is frequent; the mouths of the pious are silent; people, driven from the houses of prayer, out in the open fields lift up their hands to the Lord in heaven. Truly, the afflictions are heavy, but nowhere is there martyrdom, because those who inflict the evils upon us have the same name as we do. For these reasons do you yourself beseech the Lord and join with you in prayer in behalf of the churches all the noble athletes of Christ, in order that, if some time still remains for the existence of the world, and all things are not being driven

---

5 I.e., the gladiatorial contests in which the Christians were made to fight.
6 The following words from the Benedictine note illustrating this mode of martyrdom are from a letter of the Gothic Church, which was supposed to have been sent to the Church of Caesarea along with the body of the martyr Sabas: 'Then they bring him down to the water as he gives thanks and glorifies God, . . . and having thrown him down and placed a beam of wood upon his neck, they cast him into the deep. And, so, having met his end by beam and water, he kept the symbol of salvation undefiled at the age of thirty-eight years.' St. Sabas suffered martyrdom under Athanaricus, King of the Goths, toward the end of the fourth century.

together in the opposite direction,[7] God, being reconciled to His churches, may lead them back again to the ancient peace.

165. To Ascholius, Bishop of Thessalonica[1]

The holy God has fulfilled our long-enduring prayer, having deemed us worthy to receive a letter from your true Reverence. Now, the greatest privilege and one deserving of the highest esteem is to see you personally and to be seen by you, and in ourselves to enjoy the graces of the Spirit in you. But, since both the distance of your country and also the circumstances detaining each of us respectively prevent this, it is worthy of a second prayer that our soul be nourished by frequent letters from your Charity in Christ. And this, as a matter of fact, happened to us when we took into our hands your Intelligence's letter. For, we have been more than doubly delighted with what was written, since it was really possible to behold even your very soul, as it were, shining through a sort of mirror of words. Our pleasure was made manifold not only by the fact that you are such a man as the testimony of all shows, but also because your virtues are the source of pride to our fatherland. For, like a thriving branch sprung from a noble root, you have filled the country beyond our frontier with spiritual fruits. Therefore, our fatherland rightly glories in its own offspring, and, when you struggled through the contests for the sake of the faith, it extolled God, hearing that

---

7 I.e., to destruction.

1 Cf. Letters 154 and 155, with notes. According to the Benedictine editors, this letter is undoubtedly addressed to Soranus, Duke of Scythia, and not to Ascholius. In Letter 155, St. Basil asks his relative, Julius Soranus, to send him the relics of the Gothic martyrs. The present letter is an answer to Soranus for promptly complying with his request and sending the relics of St. Sabas. The letter was written in 374.

in you the goodly inheritance of the Fathers was carefully guarded.

But, further, what are your present deeds? With the body of a martyr who lately finished his struggle in the barbarous neighboring land, you have honored the country which bore you, like a grateful farmer sending back the first fruits to those who supplied the seeds. The gifts are truly becoming to an athlete of Christ—a martyr of the truth, recently crowned with the crown of righteousness—and we not only received it rejoicing, but also glorified God who has already caused the Gospel of His Christ to be observed among all the nations. Let us urge you to remember in your prayers us who love you, and to pray earnestly to the Lord for our souls in order that we, also, at some time may be considered worthy to begin to serve God according to the way of His commands which He has given to us for our salvation.

166. To Eusebius, Bishop of Samosata[1]

Although our most revered brother, Eupraxius,[2] is in every way dear to us and is among the truest of our friends, he has seemed dearer and truer because of his affection for you. Even now he has hastened to your Reverence like a hart (to use the words of David[3]) which quenches its great and

---
[1] The present letter seems correctly to be attributed to St. Gregory of Nazianzus by the Benedictine editors. The style is rather St. Gregory's than St. Basil's epistolary style. Moreover, Eusebius had written to St. Gregory at about this time, and, as Eupraxius was passing through Cappadocia on his way to Eusebius, it gave St. Gregory an opportunity to send an answer. Moreover, the letter is found in only four of the later group of MSS. of St. Basil's Letters and this is a very small number of the extant MSS. It was written in the late summer of 374. Cf. Loofs, *op. cit.* 46 n. 5.
[2] A disciple and intimate friend of Eusebius of Samosata.
[3] Cf. Ps. 41.2.

intolerable thirst at a clear fresh spring. Happy is he who has been considered worthy to be associated with you, but more happy is he who has so crowned his sufferings for the sake of Christ and his toils for the sake of truth as few of those who fear God have done. For, you did not exhibit a virtue untried, nor in the time of fair weather only did you sail in a straight course and guide the souls of others, but you displayed a light amid the difficulties of trials, and you became mightier than the persecutors by nobly departing from the land which bore you.

Others still possess their paternal land; but we, the city above. Others, perhaps, possess our throne; we possess Christ. Wonderful transaction! Despising what manner of things, what things we have acquired! We have passed through fire and water, but I trust that we shall also be led out to a place of rest. For, God will not abandon us in the end, nor will He suffer the persecution of sound doctrine, but, according to the number of our distresses will His consolation gladden us. For this, then, we trust and pray. But you, I beseech, pray for our Lowliness and, as often as an opportunity arises, do not hesitate to bless us through your letters and make us more cheerful by informing us of your own state of affairs, as you have now deigned to do.

167. To Eusebius, Bishop of Samosata[1]

You gladden us by writing as well as by being mindful of us, and, even more than this, by blessing us in your letters. But, if we had been deserving of your sufferings and of your combat for Christ, we would also have been considered worthy to visit you, to embrace your Reverence, and to take the example of your patient endurance in sufferings. Now, since we happen to be unworthy of this, being entangled in many afflictions and cares, we do what is second best—we salute your Perfection and we ask you not to grow weary of remembering us. For, to be esteemed worthy of your letters is not only an advantage to us, but it is likewise a boast and a source of pride among the many that some notice is taken of us by a man so great in virtue and enjoying such intimacy with God that he is able to make others, also, His friends both by word and by example.

168. To Antiochus the Presbyter, a Nephew of Eusebius, Who Was Living with His Uncle in Exile[1]

As much as I grieve that the Church has been deprived of so great a shepherd,[2] to that extent do I deem you happy

---

1 This letter, like the preceding one, seems to be correctly attributed to St. Gregory of Nazianzus in the Benedictine edition. Tillemont's objection that 'afflictions and cares' fits St. Basil rather than St. Gregory does not have much weight. St. Gregory also had much to occupy him at this time. Moreover, the fact that the letter is found among the MSS. of St. Gregory and is found in only four of the MSS. of St. Basil's letters would seem sufficient reason for assigning it to St. Gregory. It was written in the late summer of 374. Cf. Loofs, *op. cit.* 46 n. 5.

---

1 Theodoret (*Eccl. Hist.* 4.12-13) describes the scene of Eusebius' forced departure into exile at the command of Valens. This letter was written in the late summer of 374. Cf. Loofs, *op. cit.* 46 n. 5.

2 I.e., Eusebius.

who at such a time have been thought worthy of being with a man struggling desperately in the strenuous defense of religion. I am convinced that the Lord will consider you, who are nobly stimulating and supporting his zeal, also deserving of the same lot. And how great a gain it is to enjoy in profound tranquillity a man who has acquired so much from his education and from his experience in life! Therefore, I am persuaded that you now know the man, how great his intelligence is, because in the past not only did he have his mind spread over many subjects, but also you yourself did not enjoy leisure from the affairs of life so as to be wholly devoted to the spiritual stream pouring forth from the pure heart of the man. But, may the Lord grant not only that you be a comfort to him but also that you yourself may not need consolation from others. Of this, then, I am convinced as far as concerns your hearts, judging both from my own experience made when with you for a short while, and from the exalted doctrine of the good Teacher, whose companionship for one day is sufficient provision for the journey toward salvation.

169. Basil to Gregory[1]

You have undertaken a fitting, kindly, and humane act in bringing together the captive troop of the disdainful Glycerius (for, thus we must write for the present), and in having covered over our common disgrace as far as was possible.

---

[1] Letters 169, 170, and 171 treat of the strange actions of the deacon Glycerius. W. M. Ramsay, *The Church in the Roman Empire before A.D. 170* (2nd ed., London, 1893) 443-464, discusses this incident. His explanation is 'that Basil is giving us a picture, colored to his view, of a naive and quaint ceremony of early Cappadocian Christianity, which he regarded with horror and was resolved to stamp out.' This letter was written to Gregory (manuscript evidence favors Gregory of Nazianzus) in 374,

Nevertheless, there is need for your Reverence to learn the charges against him, and so to wipe out the dishonor.

For, this Glycerius, at present swaggering and proud in your opinion, was by us ordained deacon of the church at Venesa,[2] both to serve the presbyter and to care for the work of the church. The man is, even if intractable in other respects, at least not without natural talent in manual labor. But, since his appointment, he has neglected his work as if it had not existed at all. Yet, after having gathered together some wretched virgins by his own personal power and authority, some having joined him willingly (now, you know the readiness of the young for such things) and others unwillingly, he attempted to be leader of the company. Assuming for himself the name and dress of patriarch, he on a sudden began to give himself airs, not following this course through any idea of conformity or piety, but preferring this opportunity of livelihood as another would some other occupation. And he has almost caused the upset of the whole church, defying his presbyter, a man venerated for his manner of life and his age, showing disdain for his suffragan bishop and for us as if we were deserving of no attention, and filling the city and the whole clergy with uproars and disorders.

Finally, lest he be mildly rebuked by us and also by the suffragan bishop so that he would not continue his contemptuous conduct toward him (for he was also training the young people with him to the same spirit of rebellion), he is planning an affair exceedingly daring and flagrant. After having carried off from us as many of the virgins as he could, and having watched for a night, he departed in flight. These acts will appear exceedingly direful to you. Also, consider the time. The local festival was being held and an immense crowd was streaming in from all sides, as was natural. And

---
2 Other spellings are Veesa, Venata, Synnasa.

he, in turn, led out his chorus, following young men and dancing around them, and stirring up much sadness among the pious, and much laughter among the intemperate and more flippant. Even this is not enough, although it is of such enormity; but also, when the parents of the virgins, as I hear, not being able to endure the loss of their children, and desiring to lead back again the scattered group, embraced with tears their daughters, as is natural, this admirable young man with his piratical band wantonly insulted and dishonored them.

Let not these things appear tolerable to your Reverence, for the derision touches all of us in common, but, above all, order him to return with the virgins. In fact, he would meet with some kindness if he would come back with a letter from you, but, if he will not, at least send the virgins back to their mother, the Church. If you cannot do this, at all events do not permit those who wish to return to remain under his sway, but command that they return to us. Otherwise, we protest to you, and also to God and to man, that this is not rightly done nor is it according to the laws of the Church. Now, if Glycerius would return with understanding and with proper stability, that is best; if not, let him be deprived of his ministry.

170. To Glycerius[1]

To what extent do you abandon your common sense, and, while planning unwisely concerning your own actions, both disturb us and shame the whole order of monks? Return, then, trusting in God and in us who imitate His loving kindness. For, even though we have rebuked you like a father, we shall

---
[1] On the same subject and of the same date as the preceding letter.

also pardon you like a father. This is our attitude toward you, since many others are pleading for you, and above all, your presbyter, whose venerable hair and kindly heart we revere. But, if you prolong your separation from us, you have fallen altogether from your rank. Moreover, you will also separate yourself from God with your songs and your robes, by which you are leading young maidens, not to God, but to the pit.

171. To Gregory[1]

I wrote to you just lately concerning Glycerius and the virgins. They have not yet returned even to this day, but they are still delaying; for what reason and how they are doing so, I do not know. Now, I would not bring this as a charge against you, that you are doing this to discredit us either because you are somewhat ill-disposed toward us or wish to show favor to others. Therefore, let them come without fear; and you become surety for this. For, we suffer when our members are cut off, even if they have been rightly cut off. But, if they should resist, the burden falls upon others and we are acquitted.

172. To Bishop Sophronius[1]

How much joy your letter gave us, we need not write. For,

---
1 For explanation of content and for date, cf. Letter 169.

---
1 This Sophronius, otherwise unknown, is distinguished by the Benedictine editors from Sophronius, *magister officiorum*, to whom Letters 32, 76, 96, and others are addressed. This letter was written in 374.

you can assuredly surmise it from the nature of the news which you sent. In fact, in your letter you showed us the first fruit of the Spirit, which is charity. Now, what could be more precious to us than this in the present state of affairs, when 'because iniquity has abounded the charity of the many has grown cold'?[2] For, nothing is so rare now as a meeting with a spiritual brother, and peaceful conversation, and spiritual fellowship; since we have found this fellowship in your Perfection, we have given sincere thanks to the Lord, asking that we also may share the perfect happiness that is in you. For, if your letters are such, what will a meeting be? And, if you thus win me from afar, how estimable will you prove to be when you are near at hand? But, be well assured that, if a throng of innumerable cares as also the present inexorable necessities by which we are bound were not holding me fast, I myself would have hastened to your Perfection. Although the same old weakness of my body greatly hinders me in moving about, nevertheless, because of the profit which I expect, I would not have taken this obstacle into account. For, to have been considered worthy to be near a man who holds the same sentiments and maintains the faith of the Fathers, as is reported of you by our honored brothers and fellow presbyters, is truly to return to the pristine happiness of the churches, when sufferers from unsound argumentation were few and all were in tranquillity, fulfilling the commandments as workers that have no cause for shame,[3] serving the Lord through frank and simple confession and preserving inviolate and simple the faith in the Father and Son and Holy Spirit.

---
2 Cf. Matt. 24.12.
3 Cf. 2 Tim. 2.15.

173. To the Canoness Theodora[1]

The fact that we are not sure of our letters being placed in the hands of your Charity, but through the wickedness of those serving as carriers they may be read first by countless others, makes us hesitant about writing, especially now, when affairs everywhere are in such confusion. Therefore, I am waiting to be in some manner censured and to have the letters forcefully demanded, to be assured by this very fact of their delivery. At all events, whether we write or keep silence, we hold in our hearts one duty—to guard the memory of your Modesty and to pray the Lord to grant that you may complete the course of the good life you have chosen. Truly, there is no small struggle for him who makes profession to fulfill his promise. In fact, choosing the manner of life according to the Gospel is the privilege of everyone, but carrying the observance even to the smallest point and neglecting none of its written rules—this is successfully accomplished by very few of those who have come within our knowledge. It is to have the tongue guarded and an eye disciplined according to the intention of the Gospel, to work with our hands with the intention of pleasing God, to move our feet and to employ each of our members in the manner in which our Creator directed from the beginning. It is to observe modesty in dress, caution in our conversations with men, moderation in food, and frugality in the acquisition of the necessaries. All these things are small when thus simply mentioned, but they require a

---

[1] Canonesses were women who devoted themselves to education, district visiting, funerals, and various charitable works, and who lived in community apart from men. Cf. Socrates 1.17; Sozomen 8.23. Rules were laid down for their guidance, as St. Basil here sets forth, but St. Augustine in 423 drew up the first general rules for such communities of women. They are distinguished from nuns in not being bound by vows, and from deaconesses as not so distinctly discharging ministerial duties. This letter was written about the year 374.

great struggle for their successful accomplishment, as we have very truly found out. Furthermore, the perfection of humility, so as neither to be mindful of renowned ancestors, nor to exalt ourselves because of any natural excellence either of body or soul that really may exist in us, nor to make the opinion of others about us an occasion of elation and pride —these things belong to the evangelical life. So do strength in self-control, assiduity in prayer, sympathy in brotherly love, generosity toward those in need, subjection of pride, contrition of heart, soundness of faith, moderation in depression, an attitude of mind which never foregoes the memory of the fearful and inexorable judgment to which we are all hastening, although very few remember it and are solicitous about the issue.

174. To a Widow[1]

Although I desired very much to write regularly to your Nobility, I always restrained myself. I feared lest, perchance, I should seem to provoke trials for you because of those who are ill-disposed toward us, and, as I hear, are pushing their hatred to such a measure that they inquire impertinently if anyone by chance even receives a letter from us. But, since you yourself have happily begun the correspondence and have written, communicating with us, as was necessary, concerning the affairs of your soul, I am impelled to answer, thus correcting what I omitted in the past and at the same time replying to the message sent by your Nobility.

For, blessed is the soul which night and day reflects upon no other care than how, on the great day on which all creatures will stand around the Judge giving account of their

---

[1] Her identity is unknown. This letter was written about the year 374.

deeds, it also may be able to set forth with light heart the record of its actions during life. In fact, if anyone keeps that day and hour before his eyes and always meditates upon his defense before the tribunal which cannot be deceived, such a one will sin either not at all or very seldom, because sin is committed by us through absence of the fear of God. And, to such as have present to their minds a vivid expectation of what is impending, the fear associated with it will give no opportunity of falling into ill-advised acts or thoughts.

Accordingly, be mindful of God and have the fear of Him in your heart, and invite all to a union with you in your prayers. For, great is the assistance of those who are able to move God. And do not leave off doing these things. Indeed, while we are living in this flesh, prayer will be a goodly help for us, and, when we are departing hence, it will be sufficient provision for the future life. Moreover, just as solicitude is something good, so again despondency, despair, and loss of the hope of salvation are among the things which are injurious to the soul. Hope, then, in the goodness of God and await His support, knowing that, if we turn to Him rightly and sincerely, not only will He not cast us aside forever, but, while we are still uttering the words of our prayer, He will say: 'Behold, I am here.'

175. To Count Magnenianus[1]

Recently, your Dignity sent me a letter about certain other matters, and also expressly enjoined that we should write concerning the faith. I do admire your zeal in this affair and I pray to God that you may adhere unyieldingly to your choice

---
1 This Magnenianus may be the one mentioned in Letter 325, but he is otherwise unknown. This letter was written about the year 374.

of the good, and that, always advancing in knowledge and good works, you may attain perfection. But, because I do not wish to leave behind me a treatise on the faith nor to compose different creeds, I have refused to write what you requested.[2]

Only, you seem to me to be surrounded by the din of men there[3] engaged in no labor, who speak slanderously against us, as if by this means to brace their own position, telling most shameful lies against us. For, the past reveals them and the future will make them more obvious. Moreover, we urge those who have hoped in Christ to busy themselves about nothing except the faith of old; but, as we believe, so to be baptized; and as we are baptized, so to give glory.[4] And, as for names, it is enough for us to admit those which we have received from the Holy Scripture and to avoid innovations in these matters. For, not in the invention of names is our salvation, but in the sound confession of the Divinity in which we believe.

176. To Amphilochius, Bishop of Iconium[1]

May the holy God grant that this letter of ours come into your hands when you are in good health of body, free of all business, and faring in all things according to your will, in order that our invitation may not be unavailing. For, we are inviting you now to visit our city in order that the festival,

---

[2] A short time later, St. Basil did this very thing for Amphilochius of Iconium, and wrote the treatise *De Spiritu Sancto*.
[3] The Benedictine edition (*Vita Basilii* xxx) thinks the allusion is to Atarbius of Neo-Caesarea and some of his presbyters.
[4] Cf. St. Basil, *De Spiritu Sancto* 26.

---

[1] St. Basil invites Amphilochius to a festival in honor of St. Eupsychius. This letter was written in 374.

which it is a custom for our church to celebrate yearly in honor of the martyrs,[2] may be made more impressive. In fact, be convinced, my most honored and truly beloved friend, that, although our people have had experience of many, they care for no visit so much as for your presence, so keen a shaft of love you released at that short meeting. In order, therefore, that God may be glorified, the people delighted, the martyrs honored, and we old men may meet with the attention owed to us by a true son, deign unhesitatingly to come over to us and to anticipate the days of the synod. Thus we may converse with each other at our leisure and together console one another by the sharing of spiritual gifts. The fifth[3] of September is the day. Therefore, we urge you to be on hand three days in advance in order that you may also make the memorial chapel[4] of the almshouse great by your presence. By the grace of the Lord, may you be preserved for me and for the Church of God healthy and happy in the Lord and praying earnestly for me.

177. To the Master Sophronius[1]

To enumerate all those who have received benefits from

---

2 I.e., Damas and Eupsychius. For Eupsychius, cf. Letters 100, 152, and 252.
3 This date seems to be a mistake for the seventh, the feast day of St. Eupsychius in the Greek calendar.
4 By *mnēmē* the Benedictine editors understand the *memorial* church erected by St. Basil in his hospital at Caesarea, i. e., the church in the sense of a memorial. Cf. Letter 94. For the use of *mnēmē* in this sense, Du Cange cites *Act. Conc. Chalced.* 1.144.

---

1 Sophronius was a fellow student of St. Basil at Athens, and also a friend of St. Gregory of Nazianzus. Other letters addressed to this Sophronius are Letters 76, 96, 177, 180, 192, and 272. This letter was written in the year 374.

your Lordship through our mediation is not easy. We are indeed conscious of having aided many through your mighty hand, which the Lord has bestowed on us as an ally in the most critical times. However, most deserving of all, perchance, is the one who is now being introduced through our letter, our most revered brother, Eusebius,[2] who has fallen a prey to absurd calumny, which it is in the power of your Rectitude alone to dispel. Therefore, we urge that, complying with justice and taking thought of the lot of man and also bestowing on us the accustomed favors, you become all things to the man, defending him and the truth. For, he has no weak ally—righteousness—and, if the present critical moment should not damage this alliance, it will be very easy to give clear and incontrovertible proof.

178. To Aburgius[1]

I am aware that I have frequently recommended many persons to your Honor and have been quite serviceable at most critical times to those in affliction. Yet, I know that I have sent to your Modesty no one who is more honored in my sight or who is striving for anything of greater importance than our most beloved son, Eusebius, who is now placing in your hands this letter from us. And, should he meet with an opportunity, he will explain in detail to your Dignity in what sort of trouble he is involved. But, what we can fittingly say is this: the man must not be swept aside, nor, because there are many around who have been caught in most atrocious

---

2 Eusebius of Samosata.

1 Previous letters addressed to Aburgius are Letters 33, 75, and 147. The date of this letter is the same as that of the preceding.

acts, must he share at all in the suspicion against the many. On the contrary, he should obtain a trial, and his life should be submitted to an examination. In this way, both the calumny will very easily become evident, and the man, having met with most just protection, will be a perpetual herald of the benefits bestowed on him by your Clemency.[2]

179. To Arinthaeus[1]

Both the generosity of your nature and your affability toward all make sufficiently plain to us that you are a lover not only of freedom but also of man. We, therefore, serve confidently as an ambassador for a man illustrious through a long line of ancestors, but deserving of himself more honor and respect because of the gentleness of character inherent in him. As a consequence, we urge you to defend him in his struggle against a charge which is deserving of contempt, as far as regards the truth, but is especially difficult to meet on account of the severity of the calumny. In fact, it would be for him a decisive influence toward safety if you would condescend to speak a kindly word for him, complying in the first place with justice, and in the next bestowing on us, your chosen friends, in this instance, also, the customary honor and boon.

---

2 According to the Benedictine editors, St. Basil is referring to the terrible cruelties inflicted by Valens on those who were accused of inquiring by divination as to who were to succeed him on the throne. Cf. Amm. Marcell. 29.1.2.

1 Arinthaeus was an able general under Valens. He was a friend of St. Basil and a staunch defender of the Church, although, according to the custom of the times, he was not baptized until on his deathbed. Cf. Letter 269. He was consul in 372 and must have died before St. Basil (379). According to Theodoret (*Eccl. Hist.* 4.30), he seconded the general Trajan's rebuke of Valens in 378, so he must have died only a few months before St. Basil. Cf. Tillemont, *Empereurs* 5.100.

180. To the Master Sophronius, in Behalf of Eumathius[1]

I have suffered much in spirit on meeting with a worthy man who had been subjected to an unendurable situation. For, since I am a man, why should I not share the suffering of a free man who is involved in troubles beyond his desert? After deliberating how I might become useful to him, I found one solution for the difficulty which beset him—if I might make him known to your Modesty. The rest, then, is your duty—to exhibit for him the zeal which you have shown for many, as we have witnessed.

The petition presented by him to the emperors will make known the facts; let me urge you to take it into your hands and to co-operate with the man as far as possible, for you are showing a kindness to a Christian who is both a noble person and one who invites respect for his great learning. But, if we add that we also receive a great favor through your beneficence to him, certainly, although our affairs are otherwise insignificant, yet, since your Dignity is always willing to consider our interests of some account, the favor granted to us will not seem trifling.

181. To Otreius of Meletine[1]

I realize that the separation from Bishop Eusebius, dearly beloved of God, affects your Reverence as much even as ourselves. Since, then, we both need comfort, let us become a

---

[1] Nothing is known about this Eumathius except for this present letter written in 374.

[1] Otreius, one of the leading orthodox prelates of the fourth century, was at Tyana in 367, and at Constantinople in 381. Meletine, now Malatia, is in Armenia Minor. This letter was written in 374.

consolation to each other. You write to us the news from Samosata, and we shall report whatever we can learn from Thrace. For, to me it brings no little alleviation of the present distresses to know the constancy of the people, and to your Excellency to learn in what condition our common father is. Of course, at the present time we cannot explain by letter, but we have commended to you a man who knows exactly, and who will report in what a state he left him and how he was bearing his troubles. Pray, therefore, both for him and for us, in order that the Lord may bring a speedy release from these sufferings.

182. To the Presbyters of Samosata[1]

As much as we are grieved when we consider the desolation[2] of your church, to that extent do we congratulate you, who have already reached this point of the struggle. May the Lord grant that you pass through this with patient endurance, in order that you may receive the great reward for the faithful stewardship and the noble constancy which you have shown for the name of Christ.

183. To the Senate of Samosata[1]

Whenever I consider that our trial has already spread through the whole world, and that the greatest of the cities in Syria have experienced misfortunes equal to your own, and

---
1 This letter was written in 374.
2 The reference is chiefly to the exile of Eusebius.

---
1 This letter was written on the occasion of Eusebius' exile in 374.

that nowhere is there a Senate so esteemed and distinguished for good works as yours at present proclaimed for its zeal in good works, I almost feel grateful for what has been ordained. For, if this affliction had not occurred, your excellence would not have shone through. Therefore, it seems that, what the furnace is for gold,[2] this the affliction endured for our hope in God is for those who seek after some virtue. Come, then, admirable men, see that you bring forth subsequent labors worthy of those already accomplished, and that you show you are placing on a mighty foundation a more illustrious finishing touch. When the Lord grants that he appear on his own throne, stand about the shepherd of the Church, narrating the various achievements each of you has accomplished for the Church of God in proportion to your labors. But, by being mindful of us and writing as often as may be possible, you will not only act rightly in answering us, but at the same time you will give us not a little pleasure by sending us through your letters visible symbols of a voice most sweet to us.

184. To Eustathius, Bishop of Himmeria[1]

I know that orphanhood is a condition of sadness and much work because it entails the loss of those set over us. Therefore, I infer that your Reverence, too, being saddened by what has happened, does not write to us and is at the same time even more engaged now in visiting the flocks of Christ because the enemies are rising up from every side. But, since conversa-

---
2 Cf. Prov. 17.3 and 27.21.

1 Himmeria was in Osrhoene. This Eustathius is otherwise unknown. This letter was written in 374.

tion with those of like spirit is an assuagement of every sorrow, deign, as often as may be possible for you, to write to us and not only to rest yourself by addressing us but also to console us by sharing your words with us. And this we likewise shall be eager to do as often as our occupations may permit us. But, do you yourself pray and urge all the brethren earnestly to beseech the Lord, in order that He may some day offer us release from the gloom which is enveloping us.

185. To Theodotus, Bishop of Berrhoea[1]

I know that, even if you do not write to us, the memory of us is nevertheless present in your heart. And I take as an indication of this, not the fact that I myself am worthy of any kindly remembrance, but that your soul is rich in its superabundance of charity. However, as far as is possible for you, make use of the opportunities which occur to write to us in order that we may be of better courage on learning of your affairs and may ourselves seize the occasion to inform you of ours. For, this is the method of communication for those who are so far separated in body, namely, through letters; and let us not deprive each other of it in so far as circumstances may permit. May the Lord grant us a personal meeting in order that we may increase our love, and may abound in our gratitude to the Master because of the greater gifts received from Him.

---

[1] Theodotus was the orthodox Bishop of Berrhoea in Syria under Valens; nothing more is known about him. This letter was written in 374.

www.ingramcontent.com/pod-product-compliance
Lightning Source LLC
Chambersburg PA
CBHW032025290426
44110CB00012B/676